GOD, ETERNITY AND THE NATURE OF TIME

God, Eternity and the Nature of Time

Alan G. Padgett

Assistant Professor of Philosophy
Bethel College, St Paul, Minnesota

St. Martin's Press

First published in Great Britain 1992 by
THE MACMILLAN PRESS LTD
Houndmills, Basingstoke, Hampshire RG21 2XS
and London
Companies and representatives
throughout the world

This book is published in Macmillan's *Library
of Philosophy and Religion* series
General Editor: John Hick

A catalogue record for this book is available
from the British Library

ISBN 0–333–56319–0

Printed in Hong Kong

First published in the United States of America 1992 by
Scholarly and Reference Division,
ST. MARTIN'S PRESS, INC.,
175 Fifth Avenue,
New York, N.Y. 10010

ISBN 0–312–06813–1

Library of Congress Cataloging-in-Publication Data
Padgett, Alan G., 1955–
God, eternity and the nature of time/Alan G. Padgett.
p.   cm.
Includes bibliographical references and index.
ISBN 0–312–06813–1
1. Eternity.   2. God—Immutability.   3. Time—Religious aspects-
-Christianity.   I. Title.
BT912.P33   1992
231'.4—dc20   91–24451
                                                    CIP

To my beloved Sally

Contents

viii　　　　　　　　　　　　*Contents*

Preface

The book that lies before you began life as a doctoral dissertation at the University of Oxford (Oriel College). The authoring of such a monograph gives one the opportunity to express thanks to all who have helped and encouraged the author along the way. I would like to thank, first of all, my wife Sally and my son Luke. Words cannot express the love I hold for them both, and my gratitude to them for the many sacrifices they have made to enable my education. I am grateful, too, to my mother, Mary, and my father, Hank, who have always been of support and help to me throughout my life. They, too, have made my Oxford experience possible, not to mention my life, health and education.

Professor Richard Swinburne is a model philosopher and graduate supervisor. He always puts a great deal of energy into the task of supervision, and I appreciate his patient tuition. I have learned a great deal from him, and much of this book was hammered out in long discussions in his rooms in College. To him, too, I give heartfelt thanks.

Professor James Barr was my supervisor for the Biblical Studies section of my work, and I truly enjoyed my meetings with him, as well as learning a great deal. He and Jane have been very kind and friendly to me and my family. Thank you both.

I could never have hoped to come to Oxford without the support of the Ralph L. Smith Foundation, and I am very grateful to the Foundation and to Ralph Smith. My cousin Dr Len Abrams, and stepfather Dr Jack Kent, have also been of help and encouragement. Len read part of my thesis at an early stage, and I have benefited from his knowledge of physics. Equally important support has come from A Foundation for Theological Education, who honored me with a John Wesley Fellowship. Ed Robb, Jr., Ed Robb, III, and Ken Kinghorn have been very kind. I appreciate the trust they and AFTE have shown in me. The Laguna Hills United Methodist Church has also honored me with a scholarship from their congregation, and I thank the church and the Scholarship Committee for their friendship and support.

Many people have helped me with their friendship, support and general good will. I wish I could thank them all in person. In particular, though, Rev Dr Richard Sturch, Rev Martyn and Heather

Skinner, and Dr Nigel and Ginny Biggar have been most kind to me; even letting me intrude upon their homes and I am very grateful for their hospitality and Christian fellowship. Richard also read my thesis as a whole, and his comments were very helpful, and saved me from some mistakes. Dr Jonathan Lowe was also kind enough to comment on the chapters on the philosophy of time, and I found his general support while I stayed in Durham most encouraging. Errors that remain in this work are my own, and should not be attributed to those who have been kind enough to comment upon it.

One of my first classes in philosophy was from Professor Steve Davis, and I first became interested in divine eternity through discussion and correspondence with him concerning God's foreknowledge. I am grateful, too, for his friendship. Professor Doug Parrott urged me while I was a pastor to return to graduate school. His support gave me courage to think that I could succeed.

Finally, but not least by any means, I am grateful to the Creator who not only is the subject of this thesis, but whose love and grace sustained me in my humble, feeble attempt to better understand his nature and being. I appreciate his sense of humor, too, in allowing me to write this essay about him. *Soli gloria Deo.*

ALAN G. PADGETT

Abbreviations

BAGD W. Bauer, *Greek–English Lexicon*, trs. and eds., W. F. Arndt,
      F. W. Gingrich, and F. W. Danker.
BDB   F. Brown, S. R. Driver and C. A. Briggs, *Hebrew–English
      Lexicon.*
CD   K. Barth, *Church Dogmatics.*
LXX   Septuagint
NT   New Testament
OT   Old Testament
PR   A. N. Whitehead, *Process and Reality*, Corrected Edition.
SCG   Thomas Aquinas, *Summa contra Gentiles.*
ST   *idem, Summa Theologiae.*
STR   Special Theory of Relativity

Note: Full details of all works cited in this essay are given in the
Bibliography.

The transliteration of Greek and Hebrew words follows the scheme
used in the *Journal of Biblical Literature.*

1 Establishing the Parameters

INTRODUCTION

The problems of time, eternity, and the relationship between them have fascinated people for millennia. This book is written in the context of the ongoing dialogue on these topics, with a focus on one particular problem area: the doctrine of God's eternal existence.

The doctrine of divine eternity interacts with a number of other important Christian teachings on God, and raises questions regarding their compatibility with timelessness. For example, is it possible for a personal God to be timeless? A theologian's understanding of the simplicity and immutability of God depends upon the model of divine eternity she adopts. Divine agency, creation and providence, too, turn on the relationship between God's eternity and human time. Thus, "the position that a theologian takes on the topic of divine eternity has a kind of controlling effect on the general shape and texture of his broad theological view about the nature of God."[1] John O'Donnell has also pointed out the importance of the relationship between time and eternity for modern revisionist theologians:

> If we think of God not in terms of Aristotle's Unmoved Mover, but in terms of the God of Israel and Jesus Christ, then we must think of a God who goes out of himself, who acts in history, who is involved in the affairs of his people and even enters into contention with them. If then we are to revolutionize our concept of God, the critical question appears to be the relation of God to history and temporality (*Trinity and Temporality*, 24).

In this work I will propose an understanding of God as a "relatively" timeless being, a view which differs from the traditional one of absolute divine timelessness.

No doubt a short survey of the territory will be helpful before we begin detailed exploration. After some working definitions in chapter one, I look at the Bible to see what it has to say about this subject. I argue that Scripture knows nothing of a timeless God, as this doctrine is found in Christian tradition (chapter two). This leads to a look at the history of the doctrine of divine timelessness (chapter three). We discover there an idea of timelessness different from the traditional one, namely, that Being is timeless because it is immutable and Measured Time Words do not apply to it. I then move on to develop the concept of divine timelessness as traditionally understood. This fourth chapter concludes that if God sustains the universe, then he is timeless as traditionally understood only if the stasis theory of time is true. The next chapter argues at some length that the stasis theory of time cannot be accepted, both on scientific and philosophical grounds (chapter five). I conclude, then, that the doctrine of divine timelessness as normally understood cannot be true, if indeed God sustains the universe. Since divine sustaining is so central to our doctrine of God, we should reject the traditional doctrine of divine timelessness, when what we strive for is true theology.

Yet arguments that God cannot be in our human time still hold force. We do seem to feel, in an intuitive way, that God is greater than anything merely temporal. Can the Infinite be limited by the finite? So in the final chapter (six) I develop a revised understanding of divine timelessness which separates it from strict immutability. A relatively timeless God can change in relationship to his creation. God is not in our Measured Time system, nor is he subject to time; but he is temporal, even though his time (eternity) is infinite and immeasurable. We are in God's time, which is eternity. Thus God is both temporal in some sense, and timeless in some sense, yet still able to sustain the universe of time and change.

DEFINITIONS

Before we begin studying the main problems of divine eternity in more detail, some preliminary definitions will be necessary. In particular, a good deal of time will be spent in this section defining time, Measured Time, their connection with change, the relationships that can hold between times, and between time and causation. Also of concern is the distinction between process and stasis theories of time, and the various possible definitions of eternity. These definitions will be important later in the argument.

The Nature of Time

Recent writers on the issue of divine eternity have not investigated the nature of time.[2] Yet the position one takes on the nature of time is important for a consideration of the relationship between God and time. As much as one would like to avoid them if possible, thorny issues in the philosophy of time press themselves upon the theologian interested in eternity.

Such difficult issues begin with the definition of the word "time." Time is notoriously difficult to define. Augustine's well known lament is usually cited: "What, then, is time? If no one asks me, I know; but if I wish to explain it to one who asks, I know not" (*Confessions*, 11.14). Richard Gale may well be correct, that time cannot really be adequately defined (*The Language of Time*, 5). In a very general way, I will think in this essay of time as a series of durations. A duration is a period of time, bounded by instants. Instants, in turn, are durationless "points" of time. Of course these moves do not define time so much as plot out the inter-relationships between the different words I will use for it. As for the many problems associated with time and with our experience of it: I cannot, alas, enter into all the fascinating areas of the philosophy of time. Only those topics which bear upon divine eternity can be considered at this juncture. The issue between the process and the stasis theories, and also the relationship between time and change, does impact one's theory of divine eternity. These topics, then, I will consider in more detail.

The difference between the stasis and process theories of time can best be understood by first making a few definitions. Time is such a difficult philosophical problem that one must be careful about the words one uses, and clear about their meaning. Many writers casually refer to different theories of time, for example, with unhelpful metaphors like "block Universe" or "the flow of time." To avoid such metaphors, which only confuse the issue, I will make a few distinctions in the way we will refer to the history of objects. The word *object* will signify a particular continuant, such as a cabbage, a car, or a King, but not a prime number or an event. An object, then, will be something like a "substance" in traditional philosophy. Any physical enduring object in this world has a history over time. Various changes in the object will take place (this is not the place to consider the problem of identity over time). Let us call a *state* of the object a set of true statements about the object at a particular time.[3] A state will refer to a particular instant or duration in the life of some object. On the other hand, if we think from a concrete perspective of the actual, physical object (rather than statements about it) it passes through various "phases" as it changes over time. Let us call the actual, physical phases of an object *episodes*. How short or how long an episode lasts will depend in part upon the sorts of changes and properties one is focusing on. No episode can last longer than the history of the object it is an episode of. Further, no episode can be instantaneous, since any object which exists at a time takes a certain amount of time to exist.[4] However, one can always think of any episode as divided up into smaller episodes. Finally, the term *event* will be understood in two ways, depending upon whether the event includes a single object alone, or a number of objects. An event will be used to refer to either (*a*) some process or change which a particular object undergoes alone, or (*b*) a complex set of inter-related episodes of different objects: a mereological sum of different episodes. An example should help us to flesh out these distinctions.

To give these definitions of the terms object, state, event and episode some flesh, take the example of the event of a wedding. This event is made up of the concrete episodes of many different objects, such as the two rings, the clothes the bride and groom wear, the bride and groom themselves, the minister, and so forth. Each concrete object can be given a definite description which is the state of the object. Thus the bride may be in a state of being nervous, being over five feet tall, being pretty, being 22 years old, etc. at some particular instant of the wedding. As the bride and groom, the minister, the witnesses, and other objects involved go through changes over time, they go through various concrete episodes of their histories. The wedding is an event. These definitions of state, episode and event will help us to understand the two theories of time.

The stasis theory of time (also called the B-theory, or the tenseless theory) holds that there is some sense in which all episodes of all existing objects exist (in a tenseless sense of the word "exist") no matter what time human beings identify as "now." This does not deny the reality of change – changes occur because objects do have histories, and different episodes of any object exist at different times. While it is true that only the present episode of an object presently exists (using "exits" in the present tense), this fact does not imply that other episodes do not exist at all. Of course those episodes do not exist now, for only the present episode of any object exists now (i.e. in the present!) D. H. Mellor, in his recent and clear defense of the stasis view, *Real Time*, writes that according to this theory:

What exists cannot be restricted to what is present, or present or past, because the restriction has no basis in reality. The world can neither grow by the accretion of things, events or facts as they become present, nor can increasing pastness remove them (p. 103).

In the stasis theory, the universe is seen as a four-dimensional space-time manifold in which events simply "occur" at various points – they do not come into being nor pass out of being simply because observers identify different times as "now." In order to distinguish time as duration from the movement from past, to present and then to future, let us call this latter aspect of time "process." The stasis theory of time denies the reality of process, but not of different events occuring at different dates. According to the stasis theory of time, the ontological status of episodes and events is unchanging, when the world is seen in its true four-dimensional nature. In this it differs fundamentally from the process theory of time.

The process theory of time (also called the A-theory or the tensed view) is contrary to the stasis theory. For the process theory, the fundamental nature of things is dynamic, and undergoes changes in ontological status. The world is made up of three-dimensional objects which constantly change, come into being, and go out of being. Only the present episode of an object exists, period. There is no sense in which past or future episodes exist "tenselessly." One can, of course, refer to future events or episodes – we do it all the time. But it is only by *using tenses* that, according to a process theory, we can refer to past or future episodes of an object. It is true that past episodes used to exist, and future episodes will exist: but here we are using tenses. "[T]he present simply *is* the real considered in relation to two particular species of unreality; namely the past and the future" (Prior, "The Notion of the Present," 245, his italics). Hegel wrote, in a similar vein:

> In the positive meaning of time, it can be said only that the Present *is*, that Before and After are not. But the concrete Present is the result of the Past, and is pregnant with the Future (*Philosophy of Nature*, p. 39, original italics).

For the process theorist, the world in its totality is an ever-changing reality. The present episode of any object is that unique episode which is real.

This may be the best place to put to rest the idea that on the stasis theory of time, things "always" exist and do not change. An object exists (tenselessly) at the time at which it exists. Say a hot poker near the fireplace in the Senior Common Room existed yesterday, and call the poker *H* and yesterday *T*. The stasis theory asserts that *H*-exists-at-*T*, regardless of what point in time humans call "now." Since *H*-exists-*at*-*T* it is wrong to say that *H* "always" or "everlastingly" exists, since such statements imply that *H* exists at every time; which clearly it does not on the stasis theory. Instead of such misleading expressions, we should speak of *H*'s "tenseless" existence. This means that *H*-exists-at-*T* no matter what tense humans would give the word "exists" here. For the tense of the word "exists" in the sentence "*H* exists at *T*" depends upon the human experience of past, present and future. Since *T* is past, we would say that "*H* existed at *T*." If *T* were future, we would say "*H* will exist at *T*." Since the tense of words depends upon the experience of process, the stasis theory asserts that things and events *exist tenselessly*, that is, they deny that existence itself is "tensed." This is not the same as saying that a tenselessly existing object "always" exists, for that would be to hold that the object exists at every date.

As for the problem of whether or not there is change in the world, this question depends upon what one means by "change in the world." If we define change as "something having incompatible properties at different dates" (Mellor, 89) then the stasis theory does allow for change. The hot poker which exists (tenselessly) yesterday has today the incompatible property of being cold. Thus the poker undergoes a change in temperature. But if by "change in the world" one means that the world in its totality undergoes some fundamental alteration, the answer must be "no." The world in its totality exists (tenselessly) apart from and without any regard to process. "The world in its totality" already includes all episodes of all objects that ever exist (tenselessly) and their dates. If the poker is hot-at-*T*, then the poker is (tenselessly) hot-at-*T*. This fact does not undergo any change or alteration. And so it is with any object, event and property: "the world in its totality" does not change, because all changes are already found in the spread of episodes at different dates across the fourth dimension. This then, in outline, sets out the difference between the two theories of time that will interest us. However, the distinction drawn here does not exhaust the problem of the definition of time; we have yet to consider the relationship between time and change, and the nature of Measured Time.

Measured Time

Having looked at the ontological status of the difference between past, present and future, our next topic concerns the actual measurement of time. Measured Time is a temporal system which can be given a distinct metrication. In order for such metrication to be possible, certain conditions must be fulfilled. Rudolf Carnap gave three rules for the metrication of time: (*a*) additivity, (*b*) equality or congruence, and (*c*) the unit rule (*Philosophical Foundations of Physics*, 71–73).

Additivity insists that two intervals of a periodic process, when summed, will equal the extent of the combined intervals. In other words, when two measured durations are added together, the sum of their given units will equal the length of time which the two durations would take up if next to each other. Therefore, a four minute duration, added to a six minute duration, will yield a ten minute duration. When the four minute duration immediately follows the six minute one, the rule of additivity insists that they both together take up ten minutes. But this rule itself depends upon the equality or congruence of the temporal intervals (such as minutes) measured by the periodic process, that is, on the second rule.Only if the durations measured by our standard clock are isochronous, viz. equal to each other, will it yield a metrication properly applicable to all of space-time.Finally, the unit rule states that some natural process is chosen as a standard of temporal measure, and the temporal unit is defined in terms of it. This definition often makes the temporal unit some function of the process, under particular conditions. For example, a second might be defined in terms of a certain number of vibrations of an atom under particular conditions, or a function of this and some other processes. In any case, the main point is that one process is chosen as a "standard clock," and this process defines by its regular changes under the prescribed conditions the standard temporal unit of a Measured Time.

As implied in the unit rule, the durations referred to by Measured Time Words are related to one another by a constant ratio (e.g. 60 seconds in 1 minute; 60 minutes in 1 hour; etc.) There is thus, in a sense, only one basic unit of time in any system of Measured Time. These three rules for metrication are fundamental for the measurement of time, i.e. for Measured Time. Where they cannot be applied, it will not be possible to develop any Measured Time. An interesting fact about Carnap's three rules for temporal metrication is the necessity of laws of nature for their application to any given space-time. And this will be true whether one is a Conventionalist or a Realist with respect to temporal congruence.

The dispute between the Realists and the Conventionalists is about the rule of congruence. How can we be sure that the standard clock is uniform or isochronous, i.e. yields equal durations? We know from time to time some clocks must be adjusted, and further that transportation through space can affect the uniformity of clocks. How do we know our standard clocks are isochronous in transport? The Conventionalist will insist that questions about temporal interval, and about simultaneity, can only be settled by reference to the choice of a standard clock and accompanying frame of reference. Choice of a standard clock is "conventional," in that apart from reference to this measuring device, statements about the equality of temporal intervals, or of simultaneity at a distance, do not have a definite truth value (i.e. are not objectively true or false, apart from the choice of some particular metric). The Realist, on the other hand, does assert that there is an objective truth about the simultaneity or not of two events, or whether or not two different durations are equal. Measuring devices only grant us epistemic access to the truth of these matters, for the Realist. One can, then, be a Realist about either congruence (i.e. the equality or not of temporal intervals) or about simultaneity.[5] One must be careful not to confuse Realism with the view of "absolute time" one associates with Isaac Newton. Absolute time signifies a duration that exists apart from any relation to physical objects or events, and whose metric is independent of any particular frame of reference. "Absolute, true and mathematical time," wrote Newton, "of itself, and from its own nature, flows equably without relation to anything external" (*Principia*, I, p. 6). The idea of an "absolute time" in this Newtonian sense can and should be rejected.[6] Yet such a rejection is not inconsistent with Realism with respect to, say, distant simultaneity. It would appear, though, that if one were a Realist with respect to both simultaneity and congruence, one would be committed to something like absolute time.

However one answers these difficult questions about Realism *vs.* Conventionalism will not effect the point I wish to make about Measured Time. The point I insist on is that the laws of nature, or better the law-like regularities of nature, are essential to the measurement of time. It is the laws of nature, among other things, that allow for the periodic processes that underlay isochronic clocks. Even if one is a Conventionalist there are still certain empirical preconditions for the existence of Measured Time, that allow for the choice of some clock as a reasonably periodic process. As Newton-Smith, himself a Conventionalist, points out:

> Suppose a number of clocks are assembled, synchronized, and then moved about to time various events. If they were found not to be synchronized when later brought together, we would have no basis for making judgments of the relative temporal duration of the events timed by these clocks. We require clocks which tend to keep in step, or as we shall say, tend to preserve *congruence* (*The Structure of Time*, 159, his italics).

In order to find physical systems that even *tend* to "keep in step," we require the law-like regularities of nature. Even if Conventionalism is correct, after we merely stipulate some system as our standard clock in order to create Measured Time, we assume the uniform character of the laws of nature when we apply a metric based on this system to times and places never reached by it. Scientists assume in the very act of assigning a particular physical process the role of "standard clock" the uniformity of this clock throughout time and space. As G. J. Whitrow has pointed out:

> Greater accuracy in the measurement of time can be obtained by means of atomic and molecular clocks. Implicit in these developments is the hypothesis that all atoms of a given element behave in exactly the same way, irrespective of place and epoch. *The ultimate scale of time is therefore a theoretical concomitant of our concept of universal laws of nature* (*The Natural Philosophy of Time*, 43, my italics).

Whitrow makes our point for us quite well. In the very act of assigning and developing a metric for our Measured Time, we assume the universal application of laws of nature. The law-like regularity of nature is essential to Measured Time. For Measured Time does not apply to one place only, but to all of a space- time; if we imagine our "clocks" spread throughout space-time, the law-like regularity is assumed between the processes that we have selected as a good "clock." In addition, we find that we can use our Measured Time system of "clocks" to derive simple and rather elegant laws of nature: and this further corroborates our choice of that process as a good "clock."

This can be further seen by imagining a possible world so chaotic that there is no type of periodic process that makes a good "clock," i.e. that keeps even rough congruence (Newton-Smith, 174). In such a world, Measured Time would not be possible. Even if on such a world one arbitrarily selected some process (chaotic by definition) as a standard clock, one would not find, as we do in our world, that other processes tend to roughly "keep the same time" as our pseudo-clock. This temporal chaos is a result of the complete lack of law-like regularities in that world. In our world, such regularities do hold, and we find that processes do "tend to keep in step" or tend to congruence (see Harper, "On the Nature of Time in Cosmological Perspective," for the experimental data). As Rudolf Carnap, another Conventionalist, correctly saw in this regard:

> It is a fact of nature that there is a very large class of periodic processes that are equivalent to each other in this sense [i.e. they roughly measure the same intervals with their different processes]. This is not something we would know a priori. We discover it by observing the world (*Philosophical Foundations of Physics*, 83).

Even for the Conventionalist, then, the law-like regularities of nature are essential to Measured Time. "Clocks" are not good clocks on their own. We think of them as keeping good time (this is why we pick the process concerned), and this enables us to derive simple and elegant laws of nature. This point will play an important part in our considerations of the relative timelessness of God.

Qualitative, Relative and Real Change

So far I have been writing about change, without any clear definitions of just what is meant by a change. I hope to redress this fault here, by making a distinction between real changes and merely relative changes.[7]

By a change I will understand a happening which makes a difference in an object. Two objects, or two states of the same object, are different if they do not have the same properties. Certain properties I will call "qualities" by which is meant a property which an object has at a time, and which, it is logically possible, it could have apart from its relation to any other object or event which is not a part of the object. The roundness of the ball, and the intelligence of the woman, are both qualities they possess. Properties which an object or event has at a time, which of logical necessity require a relation with something else (and which is not part(s) of the first object or event), I will call relative properties. Being an uncle is a relative property, as is having a particular weight (as opposed to having a certain mass). An object only has a particular weight in relation to the gravitational field of some mass.

Using the difference between a quality and a relative property, we can distinguish two sorts of change, i.e. qualitative and relative change. A change in object Q is qualitative if and only if a quality of Q is either gained or lost (or Q comes into existence or ceases to exist) in the change. A change in Q is relative if and only if a relative property of Q is either gained or lost in the change.

What, then, about "real" change? We have this intuitive feeling that, if Xanthippe becomes a widow because Socrates dies, then the "real" change is in Socrates, not Xanthippe. All qualitative changes I will treat as real changes.[8] But while all qualitative changes are real, some relative changes are real in an object while others are not. How, then, do we distinguish between real and merely relative changes? David-Hillel Ruben has recently argued that real change in an object has a basis in some qualitative change in that object, while a merely relative change in an object has no such basis in a qualitative change in that object ("A Puzzle About Posthumous Predication," 227).

Following his insight, a real change will take place in an object at a time if a qualitative change takes place in that object during that time, which is the basis for the relative change. A change is a merely relative one in an object if there is a possible world in which the change takes place in that object at a time and no qualitative change occurs in that object during that time (Ruben, 229). If God changes by being worshipped by Paul, this is a relative change in both God and Paul. But it is a real change in Paul, not in God, since it is grounded in a qualitative change in Paul. The change in question is something that happens in Paul which can be described whether God exists or not. On the other hand, it is a merely relative change in God, since it is possible for God to undergo it without any qualitative change taking place in God. So if my son grows taller than me, I change in that I go from being taller to being shorter than my son. This is a merely relative change in me, but a real change in my son. If Jim stops thinking about Sue, Sue changes in that she stops being thought of by Jim. This is a merely relative change in Sue, but a real change in Jim. And as previously noted, any qualitative change, such as a change in mass, will also be a real change.

However one qualification must be made at this point. As T.P. Smith has correctly noted ("Applicability," 331), we do not think of mere change in spatial or temporal location, apart from any other changes, as a real change for an object. If I move my pen from one side of the desk to another, this need not be or cause a real change in either the desk or the pen (even though it meets the criteria I have laid down so far for a real change). Likewise it is conceivable that a rock could be absolutely immutable , yet still grow older: mere change in temporal location, apart from any other change in the object, need not be or cause a real change in the object. So I will exclude mere changes in space or time, which occur apart from any other change, from the list of real changes.

This distinction between real and merely relative changes may suffer some future philosophical attack. But for our purposes, it will serve until others develop a fully satisfactory distinction. When and if such a better distinction is made, I believe that the main thesis of this work will still stand even when these new and better criteria are applied. The important thing is to note the importance of the distinction between a real and a merely relative change. In the rest of this work, by a "change" I will mean a *real* change, unless otherwise specified. Having examined both change and time separately, we are now ready to look at time and change together, that is, the relationship between them.

Time and Change

Consideration of the nature of time and change raises the question of the relationship between them. Again, by "change" I will always mean a real change, unless otherwise noted. Two inter-related topics are of interest in considering change and time. First, considering the words we use to refer to time, we will explore the relationship between temporal terms and change. Second, considering time as an aspect of the real world, we look at the relationship between durations and change.

Most philosophers would be willing to admit that Measured Time requires some change. For there must be some changing physical process to act as a standard clock. A Measured Time Word is any term in a natural language which designates some measure of duration. In English, Measured Time Words include terms like "year," "second," "day" and "millennium." All natural languages known to me include at least one Measured Time Word, like our "day" for instance; here we will stick to English, and assume the application to other languages.

Although one would think that Measured Time Words are fairly simple to define and understand, there can be problems even here. For example, what exactly is the relationship between the meaning of

Measured Time Words and physical change? I will argue that the denotation of Measured Time Words is learned through physical change, and further that meaningful use of Measured Time Words is impossible without change at some time or other. I am not arguing that talk of Measured Time can be reduced without remainder to talk of physical change. I agree with Newton-Smith that the "reductionism" he describes should be rejected (*The Structure of Time*, 6). I will insist, though, that learning and properly using Measured Time Words is impossible apart from some change. This point could lead to misunderstanding. This is particularly so, given the existence of "empty time" in models of the General Theory of Relativity. Michael Friedman is surely correct when he notes that (*Foundations of Space-Time Theories*, 338):

> The full space-time manifold – including, if need be, unoccupied space-time points – plays an essential role in the process of theoretical unification. One simply cannot drop the unoccupied events from the domain of our spacio-temporal representations without a genuine loss of inferential power.

Once again, I am not adopting a "reductionist" theory of time, which Friedman refutes so well. I am arguing that if in our models of space-time, we say that the metric of space-time would indicate that there is a year, or a century, or a second of empty space-time between two points, this implies that if the standard clock existed between those two points, it would measure the amount of time in question. It is not necessary that such a clock, or indeed any material object, exist between these two points. All talk of time cannot be reduced to talk of change. However, words like "second" and "year" having the meaning they do depends upon the logical possibility of physical verification, not every time they are used, but at least at some time or other. The public definition of such terms will refer to some physical process, and therefore such words would be meaningless if all physical processes never occurred. This still allows for empty space-time, or the "empty universe" solutions in the General Theory of Relativity. This relationship which I am urging between Measured Time Words and change goes back, in a slightly different form, to Aristotle.

Aristotle defined time as "the numbering of change (*kinēseos*) according to before and after" (*Physics*, book 4, 220A). I will grant that Aristotle thought he was defining time itself, whereas our concern is with a basic understanding of Measured Time Words. But Aristotle's definition is helpful, nevertheless, for our purpose. For Aristotle, time is not identical with change but is contingent upon it (*op. cit.*, 218B): an important point against "reductionism." Aristotle did not hold that time is the same thing as change, or that talk of Measured Time can be reduced to talk of change. Aristotle's definition, when applied to a modern interpretation of Measured Time Words, implies that our epistemic access to the public meaning of such words takes place in the context of physical changes. Let us agree for the moment that the period of time known as a "day" might go by without any change taking place during this period. Nevertheless, we learn the proper meaning of the term "day" in the context of the sun moving across our sky. "Day" refers to a unit of time measured by the "movement" of the sun from the perspective of the earth. Someone who lived underground might, indeed, learn the meaning of "day" by learning that it is a temporal period of 24 hours – but this simply moves the problem back to the meaning of "hour." Learning the meaning of some Measured Time Words, then, can only take place in the context of physical change. Furthermore, the public meaning of a system of Measured Time Words will be given by reference to some physical process. In a world where such physical processes were impossible, it would not be possible to give public definition to a system of Measured Time Words.

We are now in a better position to understand the relationship between change and a system of Measured Time Words. Measured Time Words are given a precise, public meaning with reference to some physical processes, in other words to some temporal measurement. Thus units of time are publicly defined by reference to some process which acts as a standard clock. Physical processes are sorts of physical change. Therefore, any meaningful use of Measured Time Words implies a prior measurement which gives public definition to that word. So it is impossible to have and to understand a system of meaningful Measured Time Words without change. For it is impossible to have and to understand meaningful use of Measured Time Words without measurement. And it is impossible to have measurement of time without change. The public meaning of Measured Time Words, therefore, entails in this way some measurement, and therefore some change.

We have shown that learning of, and meaningful use of, a system of Measured Time Words will involve some measurement, and therefore some change. Now an important point to note is: normal, ordinary language about time uses Measured Time Words. When we speak of our **own** past, or of the present, or of the future – when we talk about time at all in ordinary conversation – we often use Measured Time Words. Ordinary talk about time, then, is talk about Measured Time, at least for the most part.

Those who hold that there can be time without change need not deny the conclusions we have reached so far. They might agree that meaningful use of Measured Time Words involves some change at some time in the way just outlined.The point they are concerned with is a different one. In a well known article about time without change, for example, Sydney Shoemaker's issue is whether "during every interval of time, no matter how short, something or other must change" ("Time without Change," 364). This is clearly a different point from the issue we have just been considering. What is the relationship between time and change, as Shoemaker understands this issue? What is the logical relationship between time and change, if any? I will argue that, if time goes by, then it is logically possible that a change occurs during that time. Finding out exactly what this means will take some development.

I begin with a truth which is generally acceptable: necessarily, if time does not go by, then a change cannot occur.[9]

If the universe were timeless, then it would not include any changes. If we imagine a world without time, then evidently no changes occur in it. Equally, if one were to take an instantaneous time-slice out of the history of our world, no changes would occur during that durationless instant. Reflection brings us the the general truth that if time does not go by, no change can occur. Here "time goes by" should be replaced by something less metaphorical, so let us substitute the word duration. My obvious truth, then, is:

(D1)   Necessarily, if no duration occurs then no change occurs.

A "change" in the terms of (D1) must be understood as a real change. It follows by a simple transformation of (D1) that:

(D2)   Necessarily, if a change occurs then a duration occurs.

Now (D2) is verified all the time in our world, in fact every time a duration is measured by a changing thing (clock). Some philosophers have in fact defined change in terms of difference over a duration, and thus assumed the truth of (D2). This is further confirmation of the obvious truth of (D1) and (D2).

Since (D1) is true, it is false that, if a duration occurs, then a change cannot occur at that time. To see why this is so, let us assume the following (false) proposition (D3):

(D3) If a duration occurred, then it would have to be the case that a change did not occur during that time.

It is clear that (D2) and (D3) cannot both be true, when we assume that some change or other occurs. To see why, suppose a particular change takes place. According to (D2) a duration must occur; but according to (D3), by *modus tollens*, a duration does not occur. Both cannot be true. If the conditional of (D2) is true, then the conditional of (D3) must be false. Since (D1) and (D2) are true, (D3) must be false. To spell things out:

(D4) It is false that (if a duration occurred, then it would have to be the case that a change did not occur during that time).

Now (D4) can be stated in a more positive form, without using two negatives. From (D4) it follows, according to the definition of an "if . . . then it might be . . ." conditional sentence, that:

(D5) If a duration occurred, then it might be the case that a change occurred during that time.

We have finally arrived at the conclusion we were looking for in the beginning. (D5) states that if "time goes by," then it is logically possible for a change to take place during that time. This, then, is the logical relationship between time and change. If there is a change, then some duration must occur (D2). If some duration occurs, then change might occur at that time (i.e. it is logically possible).

Despite all that is said above, we do seem to be able to imagine a world in which no change ever happens, but still the world "grows older." Does not time go by in this possible world? Three responses can be made to this question. First, any notion of how old such a world would be (1,000 years, or one second) smuggles Measured Time Words from our world of change into that changeless world. Second, whatever "time" is on the unchanging possible world, it is nothing like time in the actual world. Ordinary language includes a great deal of meaningful talk about Measured Time, which needs to be cashed out in terms of some change. Thus we can learn little about our normal talk and thought about time, from a changeless world. Further, we can learn little about time in the actual world from this hypothetical situation. For in the actual world, change does occur. We have set forth, then, the logical relationships between change, our talk of time, and actual time. This will help us to understand better the relationship between God and time. I would now like to consider the relationships that can hold between different times.

Temporal Relations and Temporal Metrication

To consider the question of God's relationship with our time, and with any Measured Time, one ought to examine temporal relations and temporal metrication as topics in their own right. In this essay, I will understand "a time" as a set of inter-related durations. Temporal relations are the relations that can hold between instants or durations: simultaneity, before or after (later I will add the Zero Time Relation). Two different durations which do not overlap are in the same time if and only if one is before another. "Our time" will thus be any set of durations related to our "now." With respect to being in a time, Holt has correctly pointed out ("Timelessness and the Metaphysics of Temporal Existence") that in ordinary language temporal terms do not refer to people but rather to their acts, states and lives. We normally say, "John Wesley lived in the 18th century," not simply that he was in the 18th century. In the light of this, some person being "in a time" will imply that his temporally located properties (his thoughts, acts, episodes) are wholly locateable at some instants of some temporal system. It follows from these definitions that two objects are in the same time, if the times they exist at are part of the same time.

If this is what it means to be in the same time *tout court*, what about being in the same Measured Time?[10] If two Measured Times are temporally related, are they necessarily the same Measured Time? To answer this question, consider the following story. Imagine two separate time streams, in two separate spaces, which we will label *A* and *B*.[11] Both *A* and *B* are in Measured Time. The scientists of *A* and *B* are also magicians, and they find that they can transport objects from one space to another by their magical arts. Alas, such objects soon disintegrate, but the people in *A* and *B* soon find that they can communicate by sending messages back and forth, by a similar process, and they learn to read each other's languages and mathematics. By a series of careful experiments, quickly transporting clocks from one world to the other using precisely timed spells, the magicians infer that there is something wrong with time in the other world, but they cannot agree as to which world this is.

A strange phenomenon becomes apparent over a long period of inter-communication between the two groups of scientists. Time in *B* is erratic as measured by scientists in A, while time in *A* is erratic as measured by scientists in *B*. This comes about by comparing the temporal intervals each measures between two given magical transportations. It is decided to make one transportation every 100 hours, in each space. *A*-scientists send their clocks to *B* at exactly the same time as measured in *A*, with exactly the same temporal interval between sendings. But the magician–scientists in *B* receive these clocks, which do not work well at all in *B*, at erratic intervals. The same thing happens in the other world, only it is *B*-scientists who are sure they are sending clocks to *A* with the same temporal interval between sendings, but the people in *A* receive these badly-working clocks at different temporal intervals. After a great deal of thought, the scientist–magicians in *A* decide that there is something wrong with the laws of nature in *B*. This is what causes time to be measured in an erratic way in *B*. The *B* scientists come to the same conclusion, only they assume that there is something wrong with the laws of nature in *A*! Who is right? I am not sure myself – perhaps both are correct.

In such a situation, one would conclude that *A* and *B* are in the same time, but they are not the same Measured Time. Our story, then, yields an important result: two objects can be in the same time, without being in the same Measured Time.

Clearly more is needed than simple temporal relations to establish that two Measured Times are the same. Two such metrics would be the same Measured Time, if they gave the same temporal measure to the interval between two given events. If, then, in one Measured Time five units were measured between two events, and in the other Measured Time five units were measured between the same events, then they would be the same Measured Time. But since the choice of temporal unit is fairly arbitrary, we will also say that two Measured Times are the same if they give linearly related measures to isochronic intervals. By "linear relation" we mean that one can multiply the results of the measurement of some process according to one Measured Time by a constant, and accurately obtain the results of measuring the same process according to the other Measured Time. In other words, the ratios of intervals between events are the same, independent of our choice of temporal unit. If this had taken place in the story about the magicians in worlds *A* and *B*, they could correctly have concluded that they were in the same Measured Time.

Such are the relationships that can occur between times, and between Measured Times. With these in mind, we are in a better position to examine the different definitions of "eternity."

Time and Eternity

In order to decide whether or not God is eternal, or in what sense he is eternal, we will need to grasp the different notions of eternity. It has become commonplace, since Boethius, to distinguish between eternal as timeless, and eternal as everlasting. Both definitions are possible for the word "eternal." An eternal being is "everlasting" if it has beginningless and endless existence in a time. An eternal being is "timeless" if it has a mode of existence that is somehow non-temporal.

I distinguish two senses of "timeless." When "time" means duration in the abstract, "timeless" will mean that no duration ever occurs in the life of that which is timeless. Something "timeless" in this sense would lack any extension or location in *any* time whatsoever (Pike, *Timelessness*, 7). On the other hand, by a "time" one may mean a system of Measured Time. In this case, something will be "timeless" if it does not exist within any Measured Time. Measured Time Words, then, would not truly apply to that which is timeless. The former sense is a non-durational timelessness, while the later sense is a durational timelessness. We can distinguish between these two senses by calling the former an "absolute" timelessness, and the latter a "relative" timelessness. I will argue that God is timeless in a relative sense, and not in an absolute sense. The concept of God's being in time and yet timeless obviously needs fuller development, but there remains one more preliminary topic to discuss: the relationship between time, causation, and God sustaining the world.

Time, Causality, and Divine Sustaining

Of central importance to our investigation of time and eternity is the theological doctrine that God sustains the existence of the world at every moment it exists. Some philosophical analysis of this relation is important to any discussion of time and eternity. In particular, I will argue that God's sustaining act is a direct act which is "Zero Time Related" to its effect.

My own view of divine sustaining is basically Thomistic, with a change from Aristotelian to modern science as a working assumption. Thomas argued that God is the cause of everything that exists in the universe. We would say today, I think, that God is the cause (among other things) of the basic matter/energy of the universe and of any natural laws. A consequence of this, in Thomistic terms, was the point Aquinas emphasized that God is the cause of the distinct being (*esse*) which is the essence of each particular thing, at each moment of its existence (ST, Ia, q. 104, a.1). We would say today, I think, that God is the cause of the essential properties of an object "hanging together" over time (if I may use this metaphor). Or, what amounts to the same thing, God is the cause of whatever it is that itself holds these properties together. This does not make God the cause of every effect. Rather, God is the cause of the essential properties any object has at every episode of its existence, including its causal properties (i.e. its ability to bring about some effect). God is also the cause of the continuing in existence of any object. Thus if I strike a match, it is true that I cause the match to light. God is the cause of my continued existence, and that of the match; also of my and the match's essential properties, including my property of being able to strike a match. Therefore without God's continued effort to sustain me and the match, I could not light the match. The sustaining power of God, then, is a necessary but not sufficient cause of every effect in space-time. No physical object can continue to exist apart from the exertion of some power from God. For no physical object can continue to exist apart from its essential properties. As Aquinas wrote, "Were God to annihilate, it would not be through some action (*per aliquam actionem*) but through the cessation from action" (ST, Ia, q. 104, a. 3, ad 3um.) The universe cannot exist on its own right, but must at all times be dependent upon its Creator. I take this point as an axiom of Christian theology. But to prove that this is so, from scientific and philosophical considerations alone, is a difficult undertaking at best. So we will here assume this as a basic principle, without extra-theological proof.

The act by which God sustains each moment of creation is a direct act. By a direct act I mean an act whose immediate effect is brought about without the intervention of any other causal sequence. An indirect act causes an effect which involves some causal sequence additional to the sequence of direct act – immediate effect. In the philosophy of action, scholars have come to talk about "basic acts."[12] Because of difficulty with the slippery and polysemous term "basic," as well as the fact that this vocabulary has been developed with regard to embodied agents (whereas God is an unembodied agent), I shall use the terms "direct" and "indirect." What I am calling a "direct" act would be known in the literature as a causally basic act (see for example, McCann, "Volition and Basic Action"). For God, a direct act is one that excludes any created causal chain between the divine cause and its effect.

Humans can directly cause certain brain states, which then cause through their bodies certain bodily actions (McCann). The indirect act of my typing this sentence is cause by the direct act of my causing certain brain states, which in turn cause my fingers to type the letters. Now God's sustaining creation is a direct act. Here I have in mind particularly God's sustaining the basic matter/energy of the universe, any natural laws, and the *esse* of each object. The sustaining of these creatures by the Creator is a direct act, for elements of any causal sequence by which God might indirectly act will *themselves* have to be created and sustained. These more fundamental elements will then have to be sustained by a direct act of God. So God cannot sustain the created universe through indirect means alone. God brings about each object, and its causal powers, as well as the natural laws upon which any causal sequence in our universe depends. So the power of God is directly involved in any causal sequence in our universe. Furthermore, the direct act by which God sustains the created universe is what I shall call "Zero Time Related" to its effect. Two events are Zero Time Related if and only if no duration occurs between them. God's direct acts, in other words, take no time to be accomplished. This is as it should be, since God is omnipotent and omnipresent, and is not limited in causal powers in the same way that physical things are. Any theist ought to agree with this, regardless of one's theory of time. But further argument can be made for this point.

Any direct act must be Zero Time Related to its immediate effect. Now one might think that objects in the distant future might also be directly acted upon. But remember, we are talking here of a direct act, so any causal chain is ruled out. We can only act on future episodes not Zero Time Related to our present one through causal chains. This is because the mere passage of time, of itself, does not have causal efficacy. I can think of no argument for this plausible doctrine that does not already assume it. Yet few philosophers will deny it. D. Ehring, writing in favor of the logical possibility of temporal gaps in causation, still admits that "the option of attributing causal efficacy to the passage of time *as such* is an unwelcome and unacceptable prospect" ("Non-simultaneous Causation," p. 30, his italics). The passage of time is only causally relevant when all of the sufficient causes are not present, and one or more such causes must be waited upon, before the effect in question can occur.[13] To cite Ehring again, "*e* [the effect] occurs precisely when the final member of the set of sufficient conditions occurs" (p. 31). Even if it takes time for all the sufficient causes to accumulate, what makes an effect happen at a particular temporal distance from some cause is the fact that not all the sufficient causes for the effect are present. Such temporal gaps do not occur on the basis of a need for some amount of time to pass, considered apart from any other thing. In cases of direct causation, once all the sufficient conditions are present, there will be a Zero Time Relation between the complete set of causes and the effect. Consider also that a cause is, in part, a reason why some event happened (Lucas, *Space, Time and Causality*, 40– 42). If all the causes are present at time T1, except for the mere passage of time, the effect should take place at (or Zero Time Related to) T1. The fact that, say, two hours passed between cause and effect does not *explain* anything. We want to know "what went on," what caused the effect to wait for two hours before taking place. The mere passage of time does not bring anything about. The present episode of the agent, then, will be Zero Time Related with the episode of the object immediately affected. The mere passage of time, then, has no causal efficacy. It follows from these principles that God's direct act of sustaining creation must be Zero Time Related to its immediate effect in our universe. This rules out the possibility of causation at a temporal distance, for cases of divine sustaining.

Having defined some key terms, and considered the relationships between time, change, and causation, we are now in a better position to examine in detail the nature and character of divine eternity. I will begin with an historical sketch, which itself starts with the view of divine eternity in the Bible.

2 The Witness of Scripture

There are good reasons for beginning any Christian theological inquiry with an examination of the Bible. Scripture is the wellspring of theology in the Christian tradition, as even a cursory reading of the Fathers demonstrates. No Christian theologian can or should ignore the witness of the Bible. Scripture remains the source of, and norm for, theology. This is implied in the very concept of a canon. Thus before beginning philosophical or abstract theological discussion, we do well to examine the Biblical view of divine eternity.

As the Bible is not meant to be a book of philosophy or dogmatics, our philosophical and dogmatic questions (like the nature of eternity) will not be directly answered. Rather, such concepts are often behind the text, assumed or undefined. The more abstract, philosophical doctrines which interest modern theologians are usually not the concern of the text. What the text says is important for these doctrines, as it supplies data for the proper answer to our questions. But answers to abstract questions of dogmatics and philosophical theology often have to be coaxed from the text. The philosophical theologian discovers that the Bible alludes, assumes, and implies more often than it actually teaches. I will use the verb "imply", therefore, when speaking of the Biblical views on the issues of concern to us in this section.

My concern with the Scriptural text is very limited. We will look specifically and carefully at the concept of God's eternity. My goal is not a full and adequate discussion of the texts in question, but rather to determine what help the Bible offers us in deciding between different understandings of eternity (viz. everlastingness or the two senses of timelessness). This narrow concern must be kept in mind throughout the chapter.

The Bible speaks in many places of the "eternal" things, both in the Old and New Testaments. Is there a definite meaning to such words as they are found in Scripture? Can the passages which speak of God's eternity allow for an absolutely timeless interpretation? Does the Bible imply a definite view of divine eternity? As we turn our attention to such questions, the discussion will be much clearer if the reader will open the Bible to the passage under discussion and read the verses in context. I begin in the first part of the canon, the Old Testament.

OLD TESTAMENT

By far the most common word used to describe the divine eternity in the OT is ^côlām. Other words are, from time to time, used to describe God's eternal existence (e.g. ^cad, "until, ever": Is. 57:15) but the overwhelming majority of the time ^côlām is used. An understanding of the meaning(s) of this word is thus important for our topic. The meaning of the word is indicated by BDB (p. 761) as "long duration, antiquity, futurity." This is in accord with the best study to date of the word, the published dissertation of Ernst Jenni, who gives it a basic meaning of "remote time."[1] Following the substantial work of Jenni modern commentators have rejected the idea of "eternity", in the sense of a timeless realm, as a possible meaning for this word. Jenni correctly noted that: "*Andere wieder, die ^côlām nich mit so viel philosophischem und theologischem Schwergewicht belasten wollen.*"[2] The word can be used of remote time in the past (Deut. 32:7), or in the future (Ps. 78:66). It also speaks of things which last a long time, or are perpetual, for example: the temple (1 Kng. 9:3), the earth (Eccl. 1:4), the king (Neh. 2:3), even singing (Ps. 89:2) or slavery (Deut. 15:17) which are clearly perpetual, not eternal. The definition given by BDB, then, is generally acceptable. When this word is applied to God, the meaning is clearly not an absolute timeless eternity. Most scholars agree that a philosophical conception of timeless eternity cannot be borne by the word as it is used in the Bible. For example, Schoonhoven ("Eternity," 162) writes:

> we should be wary of construing God's eternity as some sort of metaphysical timelessness . . . In the understanding of the writers of the OT and NT, eternity is not timelessness but endless time.

Not every scholar would agree with Schoonhoven. The longest and most thorough book on the concept of eternity in the OT comes to different conclusions: J. Schmidt, *Der Ewigkeitsbegriff im alten Testament*. Schmidt's methodology is outdated and dominated by Roman Catholic dogmatic concerns, yet his is still the most thorough discussion of our theme. Criticism of his thesis will form the basis of my investigation of divine eternity in the OT.

Despite its shortcomings, this work is a solid exegetical discussion. After a survey of the literature, Schmidt reviews the various words for eternity or "a long time" in the Bible. He then discusses topics relating to eternity, following a format one would expect in a traditional systematic theology. God is discussed first, of course, in chapter two.

Chapter three is devoted to mankind and eternity, and finally in chapter four eschatology and eternity are surveyed. In the process, Schmidt touches on such subjects as the eternal covenant; the eternal king/throne; eternity in the prophets; death, eternal life, the under-world and resurrection. Chapter two, which specifically focuses on the doctrine of God, includes a section on "God's eternal being" (pp. 28–35), which is one of the few exegetical discussions of our theme in recent years. Moreover, Schmidt is almost the only modern exegete to argue that at least in some ways the OT implies an absolute timeless notion of divine eternity (e.g. p. 175).

Schmidt begins his book with a definition of eternity from Boethius, and generally assumes that the Thomistic notion of timeless eternity is the full and complete religious meaning of the word. It is clear that the book as a whole is written within the confines of pre-Vatican II Roman Catholic dogmatism. On page one of the book, after citing Boethius, he writes: "*Den Begriff der Ewigkeit gewinnen wir nicht aus dem der Zeit, sondern nur im Gegensatz zu dem Zeit. . . Alles, was zum Begriff der Zeit gehört ist beim Begriff der Ewigkeit auszuschliessen.*"[3] At no point in his book does Schmidt deviate from traditional Catholic teachings.

A second criticism of this book is that Schmidt bases his interpreta-tion of texts and words on the old, etymological method of semantics. This means that, for example, he sees the word (rather than the sentence) as the basic unit of meaning, and he thinks that etymology reveals the basic or root meaning of a word. This is clear from his review of Hebrew words in chapter one (pp. 3–23). Schmidt wrote before the book which called Biblical scholars' attention to modern linguistics, James Barr's *The Semantics of Biblical Language* (1961). One would hardly expect him to adopt modern methods in his semantics – but this is still a weakness in the book, from our point of view. These two general criticisms, however, fail to grasp the true strength of this book, which is exegetical. We now turn, therefore, to a consideration of the texts that Schmidt discusses.

Schmidt believes that texts about the creation of the world, especially Gen. 1:1 and Prov. 8:22f., imply a notion of divine time-lessness (p. 31). But this reads too much into these texts. Whether time exists apart from physical objects is a philosophical question, and Schmidt simply begs the question here. Neither of these texts teaches or implies that time began with creation, or indeed say anything about time or eternity. Schmidt simply reads his view into the text at this point.

Schmidt is a better guide when he leads us to the two most exalted views of God's eternal nature in the OT, in Ps. 90 and Second Isaiah. If a timeless definition of eternity is found in the OT at all, it will be in these texts. Schmidt (p. 34) correctly notes of Ps. 90, that "*Eine Synthese all dieser alt. Gedanken uber die Anfangs- und Endlosigkeit Gottes findet sich in Ps 90,2.*"[4] This psalm begins by calling on the Lord, who has been the refuge of His people from generation to generation. Already the author begins in a definite temporal mode, reflecting on God's duration in time. The important second verse reads, "Before the mountains were born, and You gave birth to the earth and world, from eternity (*mēᶜôlām*) to eternity (*ᶜad ᶜôlām*) You are God." Here the implied view of eternity is clearly everlastingness in time. From before creation, from remote time past to remote time future, God always exists (Kraus, *Psalmen*, II, 630). Briggs correctly wrote that this verse is "asserting the divine existence and activity during all this interval, from an everlasting time prior to the creation of the world on until an everlasting time in antithesis thereto" (*Book of Psalms*, II, 273.) So far we can agree with Schmidt, that this verse implies an everlasting divine life.

On the other section of Scripture which has an exalted view of Divine eternity, Second Isaiah, Schmidt's interpretation may not fare so well. He recognizes that this section of the Bible, like Ps. 90, begins with a view of eternity as "*Anfangs- und Endlosigkeit.*" But he goes on to say that, of verses 40:28, 41:4, 43:10, 44:6 and 48:3 in particular: "*Was Is[aias] durch seine Texte betonen will, ist: 1. Jahwes absolute Zeitlosigkeit.*"[5] Does Isaiah indeed emphasize Yahweh's absolute timelessness? An examination of the important texts cited by Schmidt will tell.

Isaiah 40:28. The first verse cited by Schmidt occurs in the context of the famous first chapter of Second Isaiah, praising God who is above all his works in heaven and earth. God's power, majesty and transcendence are emphasized in vv. 21–26, but this is clearly prologue to answering the lament in v. 27, that Yahweh has not heard the cries of his people. To this the prophet responds in v. 28, "Don't you know? Haven't you heard? The eternal God (*'ĕlōhê ᶜôlām*), Yahweh, creator of the ends of the earth, does not grow weary or tired. His understanding is unsearchable." The prophet is exalting the majesty and power of God, who of course knows the problems of his people. There is a connection here between the ends of time and the ends of the earth: God is greater than both. "One of the creator's properties is his limitless extension in time (everlasting) and in space (ends of the earth). The creator's vastness is set over against the narrow lot of Israel and the challenges which faced her" (Westermann, *Isaiah 40–66*, 60.) The idea of a timeless eternity in the traditional sense is foreign to this verse.

Isaiah 41:4. The next verse supposedly supporting the timelessness of God occurs in a pericope (41:1–5) which begins the series of Yahweh-speeches where the nations and coastlands are called into court as witnesses. In this case, the nations are witness that Yahweh has called up from the east (v. 2) the Babylonians. He is greater even than that mighty empire: indeed, in our verse, he has "called the generations from the beginning: I, Yahweh – the first and with the last – I am he!" The idea of living from the beginning to the end (of time), and of God's action "from the beginning," make impossible an absolute timeless interpretation of this passage.

Isaiah 43:10. In another "witness" pericope (43:8–13), this time calling Israel herself as witness (v. 8, 10), Yahweh declares that he is the only savior (v. 11) and the only God: "before me was no god made, and after me there will be none." While denying that there were any gods before or after Yahweh, this verse does not imply an absolute timelessness. It is ambiguous, and does not give any weight to either understanding of eternity. The real emphasis is on the uniqueness of Yahweh as the one and only true God.

Isaiah 44:6. Once again in a "trial speech" of Yahweh, we find his incomparable nature emphasized by the prophet. This verse combines two elements from the verses just examined. God is both the first and the last, as well as being uniquely God: "apart from me there is no god." The remarks made about the previous verses apply here, too. Once again, we can find no implication of an absolutely timeless Yahweh.

Isaiah 48:3. The next section to be considered is a harsh criticism of Israel's idolatry. In contrast to idols, Yahweh foreknew the future and declared it to his people long ago (v. 3, 5). One supposes Schmidt believed that foreknowledge implies a timeless God, but one need not follow this line of reasoning. God can still have foreknowledge, whether his eternity is everlasting or timeless. To argue simply from the foreknowledge of God to divine timelessness is a *non sequitur*.

Our brief survey of the verses cited by Schmidt has lead to the conclusion that his interpretation of *"Zeitlosigkeit"* cannot be sustained. Might there not be other verses which could lead to this conclusion? The only one mentioned by exegetes not covered by Schmidt is Eccl. 3:11. Though this verse does not speak specifically of divine eternity, some scholars have argued that it does speak of some sort of timeless reality.

A verse of particular difficulty, 3:11 occurs at the end of the famous pericope about times and seasons (Eccl. 3:1–15). The text of 3:11 reads: "He [God] has made everything beautiful in its [or His] time, and He has put $h^c lm$ in their hearts, yet so that humankind cannot discover the work which God has done from beginning to end." Amongst older commentators there was a tendency to interpret the word $h^c lm$ in 3:11 as "eternity", in the sense of another world, in contrast to this world of time. E. W. Hengstenberg wrote of this verse, "It is man's highest privilege to discern something eternal behind the transitory objects of the present world" (*Commentary on Ecclesiastes*, 107). One assumes this means a "timeless" eternal reality, but of course this line of thought is undeveloped by commentators who are rightly interested in exegesis rather than philosophical theology. A meaning of timeless eternity at Eccl. 3:11 is based upon vocalizing the text as $ha^c \bar{o}l\bar{a}m$. But is this the correct pointing?

The word $^c \bar{o}l\bar{a}m$ almost always occurs in a prepositional expression or its grammatical equivalent in the Hebrew Bible (Jenni, 222). Eccl. 3:11 is an exception, yet the word is used almost 500 times in the OT. Perhaps this "exception" is not an exception at all, but a different word. Various alternative meanings have been suggested based on different vocalizations, perhaps the most common one being "mystery, enigma."[6] If these alternative interpretations are followed, then 3:11 obviously does not refer to any sort of "eternity".

If we do follow the traditional pointing, what does Eccl. 3:11 say about eternity? First, we should focus on the verb "give," *nāthan*, which is always used in a positive sense in Eccl.[7] This forbids the negative meaning "mystery" or "confusion" described above, since "eternity" is given (*nāthan*) by Yahweh. Also, whatever "eternity" means, it is given by God to the "mind" (lit. "heart," the seat of reason and emotion). God has given humanity, then, a capacity to seek what is perpetual, or what is non-transitory, so that we can gain wisdom about what endures, and what happens perpetually (namely, 3:2–8). Even though we can grasp the perpetual structures and cycles of human existence, we still cannot understand what *God* is about "from beginning to end". This at least is my suggestion concerning the meaning of this difficult verse. Even if this view of the verse is rejected, no basis remains for the older view, which saw the verse as referring to some timeless reality.

Even after a quick look at some of the important texts in the OT about Yahweh's eternity, we can see the weakness of Schmidt's thesis. The everlasting (or at best relatively timeless) nature of God's eternity has been clearly implied in Ps. 90:2, Isa. 40:28, 41:4, 43:10, and 44:6; while Isa. 48:3 allows any view. Eccl. 3:11, too, will not support an absolute timelessness. Thus Schmidt's thesis that the OT supports a Boethian understanding of non-durational timeless eternity cannot be maintained. We can conclude with the vast majority of scholars that Yahweh is understood by OT writers to be everlasting, or at best "timeless" in a relative sense.

Both Ps. 90 and Second Isaiah form the most exalted notions of God's eternity in the OT, and are the texts usually referred to in the secondary literature when looking at the OT view of divine eternity. For example, Jenni writes ("Time," 647): "The transcendence of God over all time was probably first fully recognized and expressed by Deutero-Isaiah" (cf. Sasse, "*aiōn*," 201). Since timelessness is not found here, it is clear that the OT knows nothing of a timeless God. As Bultmann once wrote ("*ginōskō*," 697): "the OT reality is not constituted by the *aei on*, by the timeless and permanent forms and principles which give shape to things, but by that which constantly takes place in time. . . . God is not regarded as that which always is" [here "always is" stands for *aei on*]. The OT knows nothing of a timeless God in the Boethian sense. But what about the New Testament? Will this more Hellenistic document support the theory of absolute timeless divine eternity?

NEW TESTAMENT

In the NT, passages which discuss God's eternity use the noun *aiōn* or one of this word's other grammatical forms. The sole exception to this is Rom. 1:20, which uses the term *aidios*. The use of *aiōn* is determined to no little extent by the LXX, and is thus very close to the Hebrew ^c*ôlām* in meaning.[8] BAGD (p. 27) gives the basic meaning, "time, age", and further defines it in use as:

   1. very long time, eternity . . . 2. segment of time, age . . . 3. this world . . . 4. the Aeon as a person.

The latter meaning (No.4) does not occur in the NT. So compared to ^c*ôlām* as used in the OT, *aiōn* in the NT takes on an additional meaning of "world" (No. 3) similar in semantic range to *kosmos*. Other than this addition, the meaning(s) stay the same.

With respect to the significance of eternity in the NT, scholars generally agree that the idea of an absolute timeless eternity is absent from the NT, as it is from the Old (see for example Sasse, 200–202). This conclusion has been forcefully presented by Oscar Cullmann in *Christ and Time*, arguably the single most important book on the subject of time and eternity in the Bible. Cullmann has been rightly criticized by Barr (Time, 50–85) for over-emphasizing the difference between *kairos* and *chronos*. Yet the force of Cullmann's argument, that the NT knows nothing of a non-durational timeless eternity, is exegetically sound.

Since Cullmann's widely read book was published, the majority of scholars have followed his conclusions regarding the everlasting nature of God in the NT. Yet in the article on "Time" in the *New International Dictionary of New Testament Theology*, Cullmann's conclusion is called into question. In one section of the article, H. C. Hahn writes (p. 844): "at the consummation of the divine mysteries time will cease to exist (Rev. 10:6)." The verse he refers to occurs in a fantastic apocalyptic vision of an angel who stands on the earth and the sea, and swears that *chronos ouketi estai*, "time shall be no more." The next verse continues the statement by the angel, that this will take place "in the days of the voice of the seventh angel, when he is going to sound, and the mystery of God is fulfilled, as He preached to his servants the prophets." In the context of the angel's speech, the meaning of "time" is that of time in the sense of delay, as modern English translations have it (Schoonhoven, "Eternity," 163). Jenni correctly interprets this verse:

> Nowhere [in the NT] is time interpreted abstractly as temporality, not even in Rev. 10:6, where the statement "that there should be time no longer" (KJV) is not announcing a future suspension of time. The word *chronos* means "delay" here, as in Rev. 2:21 ("Time," 645).

More precisely, the word means "time," but the sense of the phrase is that there will be no more delay (Barr, 80). An examination of Rev. 10:6 in context leads one to view with some skepticism the statement by Hahn, above.

In a later section of the "Time" article, Guhrt also calls Cullmann's view into question. He states (p. 830):

> It is further clear that passages such as Matt. 21:19 . . . are speaking
> of a future within time . . . On the other hand, the statements of the
> Johannine writings, which cannot always be pinned down with
> absolute certainty of meaning . . ., Heb., where the meaning is
> quite clear . . ., and naturally those cases where *aion* is used in the
> plural, all reveal a strong inclination to conceive of a timeless,
> because post-temporal, eternity.

Guhrt argues, here, that in three places in particular, the NT could
imply a timeless eternity, because this eternity is "post-temporal."
Guhrt simply adopts here the questionable assumption that future
eternity will be timeless. If divine eternity is not timeless, why will
future eternity be so, either for God or for the next age? In fact since
the eternity of the next age *has a beginning*, it cannot possibly be
timeless in the traditional sense! But perhaps the Bible is not so precise
in its thinking here; Guhrt cites many passages (omitted in the
quotation above) from doxologies, from John and from Hebrews to
support his conclusion. Since our concern here is specifically with
divine eternity, notions like "eternal life" in John need not detain us.
In any case, eternal life cannot be absolutely timeless since it has a
beginning. So I will focus on each of Guhrt's categories concerning
divine eternity: doxologies, John and Hebrews.

Doxologies. That the doxologies of the NT speak of praising or
blessing God "for ever and ever" (*eis tous aiōnas tōn aiōnōn*) might
lead one to suppose that an "intensified" eternity is meant. Even so,
the idea of timelessness is foreign, and not implied here. The LXX at
Ps. 83:5, for example, contains just this formula; since the LXX is a
translation of the Hebrew text, and the meaning of the original is
surely not that of a "timeless" eternity, it seems unlikely that this is the
meaning in the NT. Furthermore, at Eph. 3:21 Paul can speak of
giving glory to God, "to all generations for ever and ever". The terms
"forever and ever" are the same, yet his use of the term "generations"
(*geneas*) excludes an absolute timelessness. Of the use of the plural in
these doxologies, Jenni ("Time," 645) correctly states that:

> nowhere is a clear distinction made between limited and unlimited
> duration of time . . . The intensifying plural occurs frequently in the
> NT, especially in the doxologies . . . but it adds no new meaning.

If the doxologies are of little support for a traditional interpretation of
eternity, perhaps John will be of more help.

John. Guhrt cites, among other verses, John 12:34 and 14:16. Most of the other verses cited deal with eternal life. John 12:34 occurs in the context of Jesus' foretelling that he will be "lifted up" (12:27–36). The multitude then asks (v. 34): "We have heard from the Law that the Messiah will remain forever" (*eis ton aiōna*). The OT background to this statement (Ps. 110:4?), combined with the fact that the Messiah arrives at a point in time, forbids a traditional timeless interpretation for this usage.

John 14:16 is a promise from Jesus that, when he departs, he will send the Spirit of Truth (14:17), who will "be with you forever" (v. 16). This is the same formula as John 12:34, and since the giving is at a point of (future) time, the same conclusion is in order. The other Johannine texts cited by Guhrt do not deal with God, and in any case a timeless interpretation of those verses is dubious as well. No verse in John, therefore, leads to an absolutely timeless eternity.

Hebrews. Of the verses Guhrt cites from Hebrews, most are quotations from the Psalms which, because of their OT basis, are very unlikely to imply a timeless eternity (e.g. Heb. 6:20, 7:17, 21, 24, 28.) If Guhrt were to argue that, for the author of Hebrews, these Psalms could very well imply a timeless divine eternity, he will have to argue this on the basis of the text. But a glance at each verse indicates that there simply is no such indication given by the author of Hebrews.

Guhrt also refers to Heb. 9:26 and 13:8. He is right that in Heb., "the meaning is quite clear" as these two verses illustrate. But the clear meaning is not that of an absolute timeless eternity, but of an everlasting or perhaps relative timeless eternity. Heb. 9:26 occurs in a context of the OT sacrifices being a "copy" (9:23) of the heavenly ones which are superior. Jesus Christ only died once, the author points out (v. 25). Otherwise (v. 26): "it would be necessary for him to suffer many times, since the beginning of the world; but now [only] once at the fulfilment of the ages" (*aiōnōn*) did Christ have to offer himself. The notion of having to make sacrifice over time, since the beginning, clearly implies a view other than absolute timeless eternity in this sentence.

Heb. 13:8 is equally clear in meaning. That famous verse, saying that Jesus Christ is the same "yesterday, and today, and forever" (*eis tous aiōnas*) is obviously implying an everlasting sameness: the presence of "yesterday and today" assures this fact.

In the three sections just covered, my concern has not been full-fledged exegesis. We are only concerned to see what weight (if any) these verses lend to Guhrt's conclusion. The answer is: very light weight indeed. Having looked at the three categories cited by Guhrt one is very hard pressed to see how he can conclude that these passages "all reveal a strong inclination to conceive of a timeless . . . eternity" (*ibid.*) Cullmann's conclusion stands: the NT, like the Old, knows nothing of a timeless eternity, at least in a traditional sense.

Having looked at certain texts brought forward by Biblical scholars who think the Scriptures teach or imply a timeless divine eternity, it would be fitting to examine some of the proof-texts which philosophers have referred to. In their article on "Eternity", Eleonore Stump and Norman Kretzmann write: "passages that have been or might be offered in evidence of a Biblical conception of divine [timeless] eternality include Malachi 3:6; John 8:58; James 1:17" (p. 429) I will examine each proof-text in turn, to see if there is any basis for their claim.

Malachi 3:6 states that "I, Yahweh, do not change." The context of divine judgment makes it clear that a moral changelessness, not a philosophical and ontological one, is what the prophet has in mind in this verse. Exactly the same can be said of James 1:17, where it is said that the Father does not change like shifting shadows. But the context indicates, again, that a moral change is in view here. James' point is that God does not tempt people to do evil: only good comes from him (1:13, 17).

In John 8:58 Jesus declares that "before Abraham was, I AM." There is a reference to some notion of eternity here, but the philosophical distinction between everlastingness and timelessness is not resolved by this verse. Any concept of divine eternity will do, since John is at most suggesting that Jesus is eternal in that he existed even before Abraham. There is also an oblique reference to the divine name, YHWH, which was thought to mean something like "I am that I am" (cf. Exodus 3:14 LXX), but this tells us nothing of God's eternal being other than his everliving nature. None of these proof-texts, therefore, is of any weight. I conclude, then, that the Bible knows nothing of a timeless divine eternity in the traditional sense.

What response might defenders of divine timelessness make to these conclusions? In a recent book (*Thinking About God*, ch. 6), Brian Davies considers the kind of exegetical arguments presented above. He argues for a doctrine of absolute divine timelessness on philosophical grounds. While he admits that his view of a timeless, non-personal God is not Biblical, he believes that there is some textual support for the doctrine of divine immutability (p. 159f.) This is true, but not for the sense of "changeless" necessary to Davies, namely absolute immutability. As we have just seen the verses which speak of a "changeless God," when taken in context, teach that God is morally changeless: that his character is reliable and the same from age to age.

Davies has a second argument against the conclusion that God is temporal. He holds that anyone in Biblical times would have lacked the concepts necessary for expressing timelessness. When speaking of God they would have to use temporal language. The language and world-view of Biblical times were bound by temporal thinking.

Davies' second argument is exploded by the evidence of 2 Enoch. The author of this apocalyptic work conveys the idea of a timeless eternity, without going outside the lexical stock of the Biblical languages:[9]

> And then the whole creation, visible and invisible, which the Lord has created, shall come to an end, then each person will go to the Lord's great judgment. And then all time will perish, and afterward there will be neither years nor months nor days nor hours. They will
> , be dissipated, and after that they will not be reckoned.

The original version of 2 Enoch is culturally, geographically and temporally close to the NT documents. Had the NT writers wished, they could have expressed themselves in a manner similar to 2 Enoch, in order to convey some notion of timeless eternity.

Finally, Davies argues that those who reject divine timelessness on the basis of Scripture are inconsistent. If they were consistent, they would interpret as literal other metaphorical expressions for God (e.g., Rock, or Fire). But this simply will not do as exegesis, or as a theory of metaphor. Metaphor is a linguistic device. Careful attention to the genre and nature of the text will help us to decide when Biblical language is metaphorical, when symbolic, when historical, and so on. And the various literary devices are used by Biblical authors to convey ideas. Ideas are not "metaphorical," but philosophers can and do argue that ideas or thoughts about God are inadequate because they are anthropomorphic. Davies' basic problem is that he confuses linguistic metaphor with "metaphorical" (i.e. anthropomorphic) ideas about God. Metaphor can convey non-anthropomorphic ideas. For example, to speak of God as a Rock is to convey (among other things) the idea or thought that God is reliable. And this idea, conveyed by metaphor, is not anthropomorphic, and certainly not "metaphorical." Biblical metaphors can be used to convey non-anthropomorphic ideas.[10]

What Davies has failed to do is demonstrate that when the Bible speaks of divine eternity using metaphor, the ideas it conveys about God and time are *themselves* not to be taken at face value. He fails to argue that metaphors must convey anthropomorphic ideas about their subjects. To return to Ps. 90:4, for example, the author clearly used simile here, but it does not follow that the idea of divine eternity which is expressed by this simile is anthropomorphic. Davies fails to demonstrate that the ideas about God conveyed by Biblical metaphors are themselves, as ideas, "metaphorical." In each of his arguments, then, Davies has failed to demonstrate that a Biblical theology can affirm the absolute timelessness of God.

A BIBLICAL VIEW OF ETERNITY?

If the OT and NT nowhere teach nor imply an absolute timeless divine eternity, how did exegetes and theologians so deceive themselves? Cullmann is surely right to point to the influence of Platonism on the Christian tradition (*Christ and Time*, 69–80). A beautiful example of this, unfortunately unknown to Cullmann, is found in the article "Eternity" in the old ISBE. Lindsay begins (p. 1011):

> Eternity is best conceived, not in merely negative form of the non-temporal, or immeasurable time, but positively, as the mode of the timeless self-existence of the Absolute Ground of the universe . . . Timeless existence – being or entity without change – is what we here mean by eternity, and not mere everlastingness or permanence through time.

He then goes on to note sadly that, "In the OT, God's eternity is only negatively expressed, as implying merely indefinitely extended time," and that "even in the NT, the negative form of expression prevails." However, Plato's definition of time and eternity is declared to be "a type o[f] revelation" (*ibid.*) We thus have the ludicrous situation of a Bible dictionary article defining a term in knowing contradiction to the actual usage of the Bible, and preferring instead the meaning supposedly found in the "revelation" given to Plato! The confusion noted by Pascal between the god of the philosophers and the God of Abraham, Isaac and Jacob is most evident.

I have so far established the negative thesis, that the Bible knows nothing of an absolute timeless divine eternity. But does the Bible imply its own, positive understanding of eternity? Scripture at most gives a brief indication of what divine eternity might be like, which can be developed by philosophical theology. Barr correctly points out that there is a "very serious shortage within the Bible of the kind of actual statement about 'time' or 'eternity' which could form a sufficient basis for a Christian philosophical–theological view of time" (*Biblical Words for Time*, 138). The Bible alone may not help us decide between the two definitions of divine eternity. After all, one might be able to argue that the Biblical statements, while not teaching or implying a timeless eternity, are compatible with it. Perhaps Boethius was right; if so, the Bible does not *contradict* this correct philosophical perspective.

The Biblical literature could well be compatible with the absolute sense of "timeless," if one were to have independent reasons for affirming the absolute timelessness of God. This is because, as Paul Helm correctly writes,

> perhaps the very idea of a 'doctrinal formulation' and the question of whether some document such as the New Testament teaches a particular doctrinal formulation is not a matter of what the words and sentences of the document imply as of there being an appropriate intellectual context in which these matters are considered (*Eternal God*, 9f.)

Helm's point is well taken. The Biblical authors were not interested in philosophical speculation about eternity, and thus the intellectual context for discussing this matter may simply not have existed at that time.

On the other hand, given the complete lack of absolute divine timelessness in Scripture, such a view is tenuous at best. In two places in particular, Ps. 90:4 and 2 Pet. 3:8, we are given ideas that could lead to a quite different understanding of divine eternity. In these two verses, the Bible does give us some "raw data" upon which one could develop a theological understanding of divine eternity. But what we do with this raw data will depend a good deal on philosophical, not Biblical, considerations. Still, these texts merit futher study.

Ps. 90, as we have seen, is one of two places in the OT where an exalted view of divine eternity is found. The fourth verse of this great poem reads, "for a thousand years in Your eyes are like yesterday when it passes, or a watch of the night." This verse implies a radical distinction between human time and divine time or eternity. Kraus rightly says of this verse, "*Gottes Ewigkeit ([v.] 2) und menschliche*

Zeit sind letztlich inkommensurabel – das is die Intention der gradiosen Aussage."[11] The psalm is indicating here that God's eternity is a (very different) kind of time. Kraus notes that one of the answers to the question "*Wer ist Gott?*" in this psalm is, "*Er is der Ewige, dessen Zeit eine andere ist als die des Menschen.*"[12]

This verse became something of a favorite in rabbinic and apocalyptic literature. The rabbis took the verse literally, as though God's "day" really was a thousand earth years. They used this idea, for example, to calculate from Prov. 8:30 that the Torah was given two thousand years before the earth was created.[13] Apocalyptic literature also found Ps. 90:4 to be a favorite verse.[14] In this literature, too, the meaning of the verse is understood to be that "God's time is not measured like man's time."[15] In other literature it was not taken literally, but rather understood to mean that for God 1,000 years is not very long. In God's eternal perspective it is a short time. For example, God says to Moses in Pseudo-Philo: "But this age will be before me like a fleeting cloud, and passing like yesterday" (19:13, see also 2 Baruch 48:12f.)

This verse in Ps. 90 is also picked up in an apocalyptic section of 2 Peter.[16] The problem in this pericope (3:3–9) is the mockers, who come in the "last days" (v. 3) and question the coming of the Lord. The Lord is not slow about keeping his promises, the author says (v. 9) but is patient, waiting for more to repent rather than perish. It is in this context that he says, "with the Lord one day is like a thousand years, and a thousand years like one day" (v. 8). The fact that the author says that a day for the Lord is "like" a thousand years, may only be taken over from his source (Ps. 89:4 LXX); or it may indicate that he does not want his readers to take him literally, as in Pseudo-Philo above. Bauckham (p. 310) correctly concludes concerning this verse:

> The intended contrast between man's perception of time and God's is not a reference to God's eternity in the sense of atemporality . . . The point is rather that God's perspective on time is not limited by a human life span. He surveys the whole of history and sets the times of events in accordance with his agelong purpose.

It just might be possible, then, to develop a "Biblical" view of divine eternity. But the verses I have examined will only hint at a particular direction. Exactly which notion of eternity one develops from Scripture will depend as much on our philosophical theology as on our exegesis. Nevertheless, Scripture does seem to this exegete to point in the direction of relative timelessness.

3 The Doctrine of Divine Timelessness: An Historical Sketch

Any new understanding of divine timelessness will obviously be indebted to previous theologians and philosophers who have wrestled with this difficult doctrine. The focus of this work is not historical, but a brief survey of the history of the idea of divine timeless eternity may help set the stage for further reflection. Christian thinkers from Origen to Karl Barth have spent time pondering the nature of time and eternity. The history of the idea of eternity in Western thought shows that the originators of the concept of timeless eternity were Greek philosophers.[1] The Semitic peoples, who with the Greeks form the root of Western culture, did not have a notion of timeless eternity. For the ancient Egyptians, for example, the gods lived in another kind of time, a "mythic Time" (Assmann, *Zeit und Ewigkeit im Alten Ägypten*, 10). The same could be said of the Hebrews, as we have already seen. Thus the first section of our historical survey will examine the thought of major Greek philosophers on this issue. Then our survey will follow the stream of Christian thought up to the modern period. We reserve two contemporary thinkers, Karl Barth and A. N. Whitehead, for fuller discussion in chapter six.

There is some debate about whom to credit, among the ancient Greeks, with making the philosophical distinction between a timeless and an everlasting eternity. We are probably safe to attribute this distinction to Parmenides (ca. 510–450 BC).[2] His poem on Being itself, "The Way of Truth" was apparently well known and admired in the ancient world. Unfortunately, we only know of it through quotations in other authors. The section that deals most clearly with the issue of time and Being is known to us as Fragment 8. Lines 1–9 read as follows (citing Coxon's translation):

> Only one story of the Way is left: that a thing is. On this way there are many signs: that Being is ungenerated and imperishable, entire, unique, unmoved and perfect; it never was nor will it be, since it is now all together, one, indivisible.

"The Way of Truth" is about the Way of Being Itself (*to eon*). Parmenides never identifies Being with God or the gods, but he did influence others who used his predicates of God. For example, this is an early philosophical occurrence of the predicate "ungenerated" (*ageneton*) which looms large in Patristic writings. He does tell us that on this Way there are many signs, meaning that Being has several predicates. What Parmenides thought about Being and time is debated among scholars. Did Parmenides deny any temporal duration to Being in these lines? If Parmenides does teach that Being is timeless, then these lines represent the earliest occurrence of this idea in history.

None will doubt that Parmenides means to teach that Being is unchanging. This much, at least, is clear. So with respect to the relationship between Being and time, Parmenides could be teaching one of three opinions, similar to our three definitions for "eternal."

(01) Being is unchanging and exists in time, forever.
(02) Being is unchanging and timeless, having its own unchanging duration.
(03) Being is unchanging and timeless and non-durational.

These correspond to our three definitions of "eternal." Now the kind of "time" which Being does have in (02) must be understood as Measured Time. (02) states that Measured Time Words cannot truly apply to Being Itself, but that nevertheless Being is understood to have some sort of duration; or at least that non-durational eternity is not explicitly attributed to Being. (03) is thus a stronger opinion that (02), because (03) denies any sort of duration to Being.

The two scholars who have presented the best case for denying that Parmenides held to a timeless eternity are Malcom Schofield and John Whittaker. The debate centers on the meaning of 8.5 and 6a:

oude pot ēn oud' estai epei nun estin homou pan, hen, suneches.
It never was nor will be, since it is now all together, one, indivisible.

Schofield notes that in Fragment 8 as a whole, Parmenides argues for each of the characteristics or "signs" that he assigns Being Itself. The signs of "ungenerated" and "imperishable" are argued for in 8.6–21 on a variety of grounds. Parmenides specifically denies that Being can have any growth, beginning or end. But if Parmenides meant to teach that Being was timeless, thinks Schofield, then he ought to have argued for it in the Fragment as a whole.

Against Schofield we can note that arguments from silence are usually very weak. Parmenides may have meant to say that time in the sense of passage does not apply to Being, and thought that his poetic metaphors did indeed give this impressions. Further, Parmenides does specifically tell us that time cannot apply to Being in Fragment 8.36–37:

> And time [*chronos*] is not nor will be another thing alongside Being, since this was bound fast by fate to be entire and changeless (Coxon, 71f.)

Unfortunately, these lines are corrupt. As Barnes notes: "I am strongly inclined to think that we do not even know what words Parmenides used at this critical point in his argument" (*Presocratic Philosophers*, 206). If we follow Coxon's reading, though, how can these two lines be interpreted in anything except a timeless way? And another point to consider against (01) is the very wording of Fr. 8.5. It would be very odd to say that something exists forever by denying that it ever was or will be! So I find the everlasting interpretation (01) unlikely.

This leaves us with the other two opinions. Whittaker has argued at length that Parmenides did not know of a non-durational eternity (*God, Being, Time*, 16–32). We can safely conclude with him that "Parmenides could not possibly have propounded the doctrine of non-durational eternity" (p. 17). But we cannot conclude from the fact that (03) was not taught by Parmenides, that he did not teach that Being was timeless in the sense of (02). Fragment 8.36–37 leads us to this conclusion rather well, if we interpret this difficult and corrupt text as Coxon does. The word for time in these lines, *chronos*, indicated Measured Time to the Greeks, as Whittaker himself points out (p. 25 n.5). This makes (02) the most likely candidate.

Parmenides, then, was teaching that Being Itself is timeless (in the sense of being beyond Measured Time) yet still did not press on to the non-durational, "instantaneous" notion of eternity. This allows for the duration-like language of the poem in other places. For example, he says that "Therefore it is all united, for Being is adjacent to Being" (Fr. 8.13); and "it lies by itself, and remains thus where it is perpetually" (Fr. 8.29f.) A non-durational interpretation would allow for such language, and still take the apparent "timelessness" of Being Itself seriously.

Our safest interpretation of "The Way of Being" concerning eternity, then, is (02). For Parmenides, Being could not become, nor did it ever come to be. "And how could what becomes have being, how come into being, seeing that, if it came to be, it is not, nor is it, if at some time it is going to be" (Fr. 8.19f). He also excluded any notion of division in Being, and insisted on its perfection. But none of this implies absolute timelessness. We feel that Parmenides taught, therefore, that Being Itself always IS. It never came to be, nor will it come to be. It is perpetual, whole and perfect. This would seem to lead to a relative notion of timelessness, in which Being is beyond any Measured Time which applies to this world of becoming. To Parmenides, then, we can attribute the "discovery" of a timeless notion of eternity.

Plato (ca. 427–348 BC) was influenced by Parmenides, as historians of this period of philosophy know well. Coxon writes that "the theory [of Forms] was a pluralistic development of Parmenides' monism" (p. 26). We shall hold, with Whittaker ("The 'Eternity' of the Platonic Forms"), that Plato in the famous section on the creation of time by the Demiurge in *Timaeus* (37C–39E), also taught a timeless but still durational notion of eternity. "These all [months, days, and years; past or future existence] apply to becoming in time, and have no meaning in relation to the eternal nature, which ever is and never was or will be" (*Timaeus*, 37E).

Whittaker argues that Plato in this section as a whole distinguished between eternity (*aiōn*) and Measured Time (*chronos*). This is why Plato can say that "time is the moving image of eternity" (37D). The Forms are timeless, but there is no indication in Plato that the Forms lack any duration whatsoever. Because the notion of a non-durational timelessness is a more difficult and strict notion, we should want some more positive evidence in favor of (03) in order to feel comfortable with attributing this view to Plato. Otherwise we will rightly feel that what Plato had in mind was something like (02). What the Forms lack is movement and change; these things only apply to our temporal world, and this is why Measured Time is a part of our world, and not of the Forms. For the view that eternity is non-durational we must turn to later philosophers, who used this section of the *Timaeus* as a starting point for their reflection concerning time and eternity.

Like Plato, Aristotle does not teach that timeless things are without any duration. We have already had opportunity to speak of Aristotle's theory of time (see chapter one). With respect to eternity in his thought, generally Aristotle speaks of "eternal" things in a way that implies their everlasting nature (see for example, *On the Heavens*, 1, 279A). He does write in one place of timeless things, which are "not contained by time, nor is their being measured by time. A proof of this is that none of them are affected by time, which indicates that they are not in time" (*Physics*, 4, 221B). A timeless thing, then, has no temporal measure ("not contained by time, nor measured by time"), nor does it change ("not affected by time"). This is all Aristotle seems to clearly say about timeless being; in many ways it is a prosaic restatement of the view I have attributed to Parmenides and Plato (see [02]). Aristotle is, however, much clearer about exactly what he understands "timeless" to mean. Perhaps, then, we should call the durational and unchanging understanding of "timeless" the Aristotelian view!

If Parmenides and Plato are difficult to interpret precisely on this point, the Middle Platonist Plutarch (ca. 45–125) is clearer. Plutarch importantly applies the idea of timelessness to God, and not simply to Being Itself (Parmenides) or to the Forms (Plato). Plutarch (*On the E at Delphi*, 393B) denies that words involving time can be applied to God, since God is in eternity (*aiōna*) which is changeless and timeless. Thus God exists at no time. These assertions have become familiar, as applied to Being or the Forms. But significantly, Plutarch goes on to say (393B):

> Single, he [God] has completed 'always' in a single now, and that which really is in this manner only 'is,' without having come into being, without being in the future, without having begun, and without being due to end.

This is the first instance known to me where a timeless eternity is directly associated with God. Furthermore, this is the first instance of an *absolute* concept of timeless eternity (see Whittaker, "Ammonius on the Delphic E.") In Platonism, then, we discover the origin of the subtle concept of a timeless and non-durational divine eternity (03).

Christian thought, influenced by Middle Platonism, also developed the idea of a timeless God. Alexandrian theology was a blend of Christian and Platonist thought. One of the greatest proponents of this type of theology was Origen (ca. 185–254). His book, *On First Principles*, is the earliest example of something like a "systematic theology" in Christian history. In it he taught that God is beyond our conception of time, and our temporal language. "[T]he statements we make about the Father and the Son and the Holy Spirit must be understood as transcending all time and all ages and all eternity" (*On First Principles*, 4.4.1). In his discussion of the "begetting" of the Son by the Father, Origen is careful to remove any idea of this act taking place at some time or other (*On First Principles*, 1.2.2). It is from the Platonism of Alexandrian theology, then, that the doctrine of divine timelessness first enters into Christian theology.

But it was Origen's contemporary, the philosopher Plotinus (ca. 205–270), who in his *Enneads* (3.7) most consistently and regularly insisted that the One was absolutely timeless (see Beierwaltes, *Plotin über Ewigkeit und Zeit*). Plotinus wrote the fullest and most influential philosophical discussion of absolute timelessness in his day. His discussion influenced both Augustine and Boethius, thereby influencing Anselm, Thomas, and the entire medieval tradition.

Plotinus begins with Plato's distinction between time and eternity from the *Timaeus*. For Plotinus, they are distinguished as the life of the Soul (time) and the life of the Mind (eternity). Time, then, is in the soul for Plotinus: "In the movement of the soul, time moves" (3.7.11). Eternity is identified as the life of Mind, that is of intelligible substance. This is the first place where eternity and life are united, in the history of thought. Eternity is the life of Mind, the ultimate unitary reality behind the various realities humans encounter. Thus eternity "is always the selfsame without extension or interval," that is, without time and without duration. Plotinus then goes on to write:

> seeing all this one sees eternity in seeing a life that abides in the same, and always has the all present to it, not now this, and then again that, but all things at once . . . it is something which abides in the same, in itself and does not change at all but is always in the present (3.7.3).

The eternal Reality is a life that is whole and complete, lacking in nothing. It is, thus, timeless and durationless, existing always in the present, which is something like a geometrical point, and to whom all of changing time is present at once (*ibid.*) For Plotinus, eternity is like this because eternal being cannot be added to nor taken away from. It is always perfect, always what it *is*, and therefore immutable and non-durational (3.7.4). "[I]t must have all of its wholeness in such a way that it is deficient in nothing . . . If, then, nothing could happen to it, there is no postponement of being, and it is not going to be, nor did it come to be." (*ibid.*) In Plotinus, then, we find the seed of the fully developed notion of an eternal Now coexisting will all earthly nows; an immutable, timeless, and non-durational life which is God.

The *Confessions* of Augustine (354–430) is probably the ancient work best known to modern thinkers on our subject. In this area, Augustine was clearly influenced by Plotinus. In fact, Augustine himself tells us that he was influenced by Neoplatonism (*Confessions*, 8.2; *City of God*, 8.5,12; 9.10). This is evident, indeed, from his doctrine of eternity; for there is little in it which cannot find a parallel in Plotinus.

Augustine distinguished between time and eternity on the basis of change and movement. "The distinguishing mark between time and eternity is that the former does not exist without some movement and change, while in the latter there is no change at all" (*City of God*, 11.6). For Augustine, God is the creator of time, which came into existence with the rest of creation; hence God himself is timeless (*Confessions*, 11.13). Furthermore, because God is unchanging, God cannot be temporal. "If something began to be in God's substance, something which had not existed beforehand, we could not rightly say that his substance was eternal" (*Confessions*, 11.10). Augustine insisted, then, on the immutability of God; this lead him to assert the eternity of God.

What Augustine wrote as quoted above could be compatible with either a relative or an absolute understanding of divine timeless eternity. Like Parmenides, Plato and Aristotle, perhaps Augustine held that God is eternal in that he is timeless and immutable, without also holding that God's life is durationless. However, there are some passages which lead one to believe that Augustine, like Plutarch and Plotinus, held to an absolutely timeless notion of eternity. For example, he writes in *Confessions* 11.7 that all things are created or uttered eternally by the Word of God. "In your Word all is uttered at one and the same time, yet eternally. If it were not so, your Word would be subject to time and change, and therefore would be neither truly eternal nor truly immortal." Note that all things are created by God both eternally, and at the same time or simultaneously in God's eternity. Further, the eternal Word is *not subject to time*. Likewise, when discussing the immutable and eternal will of God, Augustine writes (11.15): "It follows that he does not will first one thing and then another, but that he wills all that he wills simultaneously, in one act, and eternally." These passages, combined with the known Neoplatonic influence on Augustine, lead one to believe that for him God is timelessly eternal, living all of his life "at once," in a single, durationless moment. This fact is based, for him, upon the immutability of God. God cannot change, and therefore God is timeless. But Augustine is somewhat unclear on this point. What Augustine leaves undeveloped is fully exploited and developed by the last Roman philosopher, Ancius Manlius Severinus Boethius.

Boethius (ca. 480–525) gave classic expression to the idea of an absolutely timeless divine eternity. His definition of eternity is the one which is most often quoted in discussions of divine eternity: "Eternity, then, is the whole, simultaneous and perfect possession of boundless life" (*Aeternitas igitur est interminabilis vitae tota simul et perfecta possessio; Consolation of Philosophy*, 5.6). This classic discussion owes much to the tradition of Neoplatonism (see Kneale, "Time and Eternity in Theology"). Even the wording is quite similar to the definition of eternity given by Plotinus, in particular that eternity is a "life" which is "whole" or "complete" and "simultaneous" or "always present" (see Beierwaltes, *Plotin*, 198–200). This definition occurs in a longer passage, which deserves to be quoted in full:

> Since, then, as was shown a little while ago, everything which is known is known not according to its own nature but according to the nature of those comprehending it, let us now examine, so far as it allowable, what is the nature of the divine substance, so that we may be able to recognize what kind of knowledge this is. Now that God is eternal is the common judgment of all who live by reason. Therefore let us consider, what is eternity; for this makes plain to us both the divine nature and the divine knowledge. Eternity, then, is the whole, simultaneous and perfect possession of boundless life, which becomes clearer by comparison with temporal things. For whatever lives in time proceeds in the present from the past into the future, and there is nothing established in time which can embrace the whole space of its life equally, but tomorrow surely it does not yet grasp, while yesterday it has already lost . . . Whatever therefore comprehends and possesses at once the whole fullness of boundless life, and is such that neither is anything future lacking from it, nor has anything past flowed away, that is rightly held to be eternal.

Several things emerge from this famous passage. First of all, Boethius is clearly concerned about the nature of God's foreknowledge. It is this issue which raises his interest in eternity. Because God's knowledge is eternal, and thus timeless and embracing all times at once, God's knowledge of the future is not strictly speaking fore-knowledge. God's knowledge of the future is based on what he "sees" the future to be in his timeless present, as is his knowledge of the present and past. "[H]is knowledge too, surpassing all movement of time, is permanent in the simplicity of his present, and embracing all the infinite spaces of the future and the past, considers them in his simple act of knowledge as though they were now going on" (*ibid.*) My present knowledge of your present free choice does not conflict with your free will. Neither, Boethius holds, does God's knowledge of our future choices in his eternal "present" conflict with our free will.

Second, Boethius clearly distinguishes eternal life from "sempiternal" life. The latter word was given a special, philosophical meaning by him, to refer to everlasting life in time as distinct from timeless eternity (*On the Trinity*, ch. 4). However, what distinguishes eternity from sempiternity is not just that eternity is timeless, while sempiternity is everlasting and temporal. Eternal life is also lived "at once" (*simul*) as Boethius makes clear by comparing our now with the divine now.

> He is ever, because 'ever' is with him a term of present time, and there is this great difference between the present of our affairs, which is now, and the divine present: our 'now' connotes changing time and sempiternity; but God's 'now,' abiding, unmoved, and immovable, connotes eternity (*ibid.*)

The fact that eternity is a "present" moment, a life lived "at once," indicates that for Boethius eternity is non-durational as well as timeless. This does not mean that Boethius, or Plotinus for that matter, never uses words similar to "duration" when writing about eternity. Rather, we use the word "non-durational" in the sense of lacking any temporal extension. God is eternal, and this means for Boethius that God completely lacks temporal extension. This doctrine is clear from the above quotations (*pace* Stump and Kretzmann, "Eternity," 432f.) One can see, then, that the doctrine of divine timelessness reaches a high point in the thought of Boethius. While it was not original with him, the doctrine remained undeveloped and under-exploited. With Boethius we find a clear definition, an explicit distinction of terms, and the use of the doctrine to solve a perplexing theological problem. In addition to the immutability of God as a reason for affirming God's timelessness, Boethius adds the problem of divine knowledge and human freedom as a good reason to hold to this doctrine.

The consensus of Augustine and Boethius dominated the Latin theology of the Middle Ages. For example, even though Richard of St. Victor (d. 1173) defined eternity as being without beginning or end, and without any mutability (*De Trinitate*, II, 4) which would allow an everlasting notion of eternity, he clearly also believed that God was timeless in an absolute sense (II, 9; IV, 7). A high point in the development of the doctrine of divine timeless eternity during this period occurs in the theology of Anselm (1033–1109).

Anselm was influenced by the theology of Augustine, as well as the philosophical rigor of Aristotle and Boethius. He writes in the first chapter of the *Monologion* that he does not wish to hold any doctrine not in accord with the consensus of the Fathers, "and above all with the writings of St. Augustine." D. P. Henry has also shown that Anselm was influenced by Aristotle, as interpreted by Boethius ("The *Proslogion* Proofs," 150). One thus expects that, like Augustine and Boethius, Anselm would hold to an absolutely timeless divine eternity. But the reasons he gives for this doctrine are interesting.

In his *Monologion*, Anselm demonstrates the existence of God, based on his definition of God. In the *Proslogion*, Anselm discusses the attributes of God which can be derived from this same definition. This definition is "You are something than which nothing greater can be thought" (*Proslogion*, ch. 2). On this definition Anselm based his famous "ontological" argument for the existence of God. This argument will not concern us here. Our interest focuses more on how Anselm used this definition to derive the timeless eternity of God. It is to the *Proslogion*, then, rather than the *Monologion, that we first turn.*

From the fact that God is the greatest conceivable being it follows that he is spaceless and timeless (*Proslogion*, ch. 13*)*.

All that which is enclosed in any way by place or time is less than that which no law of place or time constrains. Since, then, nothing is greater than You, no place or time confines You but You exist everywhere and always.

But granted this point, why does it not lead to a relative, rather than an absolute, notion of timeless eternity? Anselm goes on to explain (ch. 18) that,

Life and wisdom and the other [attributes], then, are not part of You, but all are one and each one of them is wholly what You are and what all the others are. Since, then, neither You nor the eternity which You are have parts, no part of You or of Your eternity is anywhere or at any time, but You exist as a whole everywhere and Your eternity exists as a whole always.

God is identified by Anselm with his eternity, and with his other attributes. Anselm does this on the basis of the simplicity of God. Because God is simple, his attributes are not part of him, but he is his attributes:

For whatever is made up of parts is not absolutely one, but in a sense many and other that itself, and it can be broken up either actually or by the mind – all of which things are foreign to You, than whom nothing better can be thought (*ibid.*)

It is better to be one and simple than to be made up of parts, and divisible. Something made up of parts is a plurality, and thus in some way other than itself. Since God is the being than which nothing better or greater can be thought, it is better that God is absolutely one and simple than that he is made up of parts. And because anything that exists at one time, and then at another, must be made up of parts, God is timeless (similarly, see *Monologion*, 20–22). But how is it that, according to Anselm, God who is his eternity exists as a whole always? He explains,

> You exist neither yesterday nor today nor tomorrow but are absolutely outside all time . . . For nothing contains You, but You contain all things (ch. 19).

So far, one could interpret Anselm as holding to a relatively timeless eternity. However, the greatness of God means that God is greater even than other eternal beings (ch. 20):

> You surpass even all eternal things, since Your eternity and theirs is wholly present to You though they do not have the part of their eternity-to-come just as they do not have what is past . . . because You are always present at that point (or because it is always present to You) which they have not yet reached.

Because of the greatness of God, then, God is simple. This means that God is timeless, since temporal things have parts. Furthermore, because God is the greatest conceivable being, God is greater even than other eternal things. For God's eternity is whole and present all at once, while other (everlasting) eternal things must live their life in parts. The influence of and similarity to Boethius' definition of eternity is obvious. What Anselm adds to the doctrine are his unique reasons for holding to an absolute timeless eternity: the greatness of God, and the absolute simplicity of God.

The definition of God's eternity as a timeless, durationless life we will simply call the traditional doctrine of divine eternity. This is the view, first propounded by Plutarch, that God is both timeless and that he lives his life all at once. We have found this doctrine expressed also in Plotinus, Augustine, Boethius and Anselm. The traditional doctrine reaches its acme in the thought of the most influential medieval theologian: Thomas Aquinas.

Thomas Aquinas (1225–1274) begins his great *Summa Theologiae*, after some preliminary discussion of the science of theology, with the famous Five Ways (ST, Ia, q.2). Aquinas demonstrates by reason the existence of God: an Object already given in faith (Hankey, *God in Himself*, 67). The result of this argument is well known. God is shown to be the unmoved source of all motion, change, existence, goodness and perfection found in the world.

After demonstrating the existence of God, Aquinas turns to examine what, for him, was God's most important attribute: his simplicity. Simplicity for Aquinas was the property of not having any attributes separate from one's being; all of God's attributes are identical with the nature or essence of God. Because God is simple, he does not have any accidental properties. Whatever God is, is an essential aspect of God – love, justice, eternity, action, and so forth. These things do not exist in pure form apart from God: in fact, they are God. The absolute simplicity of God requires that his essence and existence be one (q.3, a.4). Indeed, for Aquinas, "this name, Being Itself (*Qui Est*) is the most proper name of God" (Ia, q.13, a.11). The entire discussion within this first large section of the *Summa* (q.3–11) – which includes the section on eternity (q.10) – arises out of a quest to understand God's unity and simplicity. As Hankey points out, this section begins and ends with the idea of the simplicity and unity of God (p. 57).

When we understand the unity and simplicity of God, then we understand why Aquinas taught that God was timeless (see also SCG, I.13 and 15). Thomas accepted the Boethian definition of eternity, and defended it against misunderstanding (ST, Ia, q.10). God is timeless because he is changeless, and time is the measure of change. In a thing without movement, which is always the same, there is no before and after for time to apply to. But when we ask why God is changeless, Aquinas refers us to the simplicity and immutability of the one infinite Being.

God is changeless because God is simple. Given God's simplicity as perfect Being unified with essence, eternity is nothing less than God Himself (ST, Ia, q.10, a.2). God is identical with his attributes, including eternity, so that God is eternity. Further, because God is simple he cannot move or change, and thus cannot be temporal. For Aquinas, anything which changes or moves acquires by its changing something it previously lacked: but God, being simple, infinite plenitude, cannot develop in any way. In addition, anything that changes must have parts: but God does not have any parts, being absolutely simple (Ia, q.9, a.1). Since God cannot change or move,

God cannot be in time. From the simplicity of God, therefore, flows the divine timeless eternity.

Though Aquinas does allow for some "change" in God, this "change" is the "movement" found in understanding, willing and loving (*ibid.*). These "movements" are not things that we would call "changes" in modern philosophy, as Aquinas himself noted.

Central to the Thomistic notion of the existence, simplicity and immutability of God is the idea that God is *actus purus*: pure act or sheer actuality (Ia, q.2, a.3; q.3, a.2; q.9, a.1). This means, in part, that there is no potentiality in God, there is no motion or change. All that God does is done at once, timelessly and changelessly (Ia, q.3, a.8; q.8, a.1; q.10). God comes first in the order of agents, for Aquinas (Ia, q.19, a.4). He is not the only agent, but the first and primal one in whom the perfections and being of all other things and acts find their source. God does not act from the necessity of his nature, but rather upon the basis of his will (Ia, q. 25, a.5). Yet the will of God is unchanging (Ia, q.19, a.7) and timeless (*ibid.*, a.3). By his will alone, God creates whatever is created (*ibid.*, a.4). The unchanging will of God determines not only the existence of his effect, but also the time of its existence (SCG, II.35).

Aquinas, then, combines the reasons for holding to the traditional doctrine of eternity which we found in Augustine, Boethius, and Anselm. God is timeless because God is immutable and simple (Ia, q.10). Further, Thomas understood this doctrine to include the idea that God knows and wills all things in a single, eternal "moment" in which he lives all of his life. Aquinas illustrates his concept of the relationship between time and eternity with the model of a circle. According to Thomas (SCG, I.66):

> The center, which is outside the circumference, is directly opposite any designated point on the circumference. In this way whatever is in any part of time co-exists with what is eternal as being present to it even though past or future with respect to another part of time (cited from Stump and Kretzmann, "Eternity," 441).

God's eternity is durationless and timeless. God nevertheless "co-exists" with anything that ever exists – past, present, or future. By his immutable and eternal will, God determines the temporal location of everything that exists (SCG, II.35). In Aquinas, as we can see, the traditional doctrine of divine eternity reached its greatest and most brilliant development. Thomas combines in his unique way the best insights of a millennium of thought on this subject.

It was not until the 13th century that the traditional doctrine of eternity was questioned. The Oxford scholar, John Duns Scotus (ca. 1265–1308) did not accept the theory of the "eternal now" and of divine timeless knowledge he found in Aquinas. Scotus did hold that God was timeless and immutable (*Ordinatio*, I, d.9; d.30, q.1,2). He accepted and clarified the Boethian definition of eternity, and felt that the definition of Richard of St. Victor must be corrected (*Quodlibeta*, q.6, par. 1.2). However, with respect to God's foreknowledge, Scotus argued that the Boethian notion of all of time being "present" to God in eternity is incoherent (*Lectura*, I, d.39, q.5; cf. *Ordinatio*, d.38,39).[3]

The future cannot be present to God, even in eternity, if the future is truly future. The Boethian–Thomistic doctrine of eternal presentness to God vitiates the genuine difference between past, present and future. Take the model, used by Aquinas, that time is like a circle and eternity is like the center of the circle (SCG, I.66). With respect to this idea, Scotus (or possibly his disciple) has us imagine a line with two end points, *A* and *B*, where *A* is fixed and *B* moves around *A* (*Ordinatio*, I, d. 39, q.5, sec. 35). The movement of *B* will produce a circumference; but it is a flowing circumference. In this model, *B* remains the only existing point on the circumference, just as the present is the only existing moment of time. Scotus then argued against Aquinas that:[4]

> Since time is not a standing circumference, but a flowing one, of which circumference there is nothing except the actual instant, neither will any of it be present to eternity (which is like the center) except that instant which is like the present; and if, however, *per impossibile* it were supposed that all of time is at once standing still, then all of it would be present at once to eternity as to the center.

In our terminology, Scotus argued that the traditional doctrine of eternity is incoherent given the process theory of time. In the *Lectura* (I, d.39, q.5), which we know came from Scotus, he made a further argument. Whatever is present is actual; if the future is actual in eternity, then things which are future are already actual, and it is impossible for God to act newly in order to create new things when the future arrives. In other words, some new future things are by definition new; they cannot, therefore, already exist in the divine present if they are new in the future.

In both of these arguments Scotus assumed the process theory of time. Given this view of time, he argued that since the distinction between past, present and future is a real one, then it is real for God.

All times cannot be present to God, if they are genuinely past and future. Instead of the Thomistic doctrine, Scotus argued that God' foreknowledge of contingent events is based upon the divine choice among all contingent possibilities (*Ordinatio*, I, d. 43). The fact that God might have chosen otherwise means that these contingent events remain contingent (*op. cit.*, d. 39). But while Scotus questioned the mainstream consensus on the issue of foreknowledge and the eternal "now," he never questioned the absolute timelessness and immutability of the divine Being (*pace* Lewis, "God and Time," 35–40).

While Duns Scotus was followed by some students of theology and philosophy, for the most part his criticisms represent backwaters in the river of ideas about God's eternity. The mainstream continued to hold to the traditional doctrine of divine eternity. William of Ockham (ca. 1285–1347), for example, had a great deal of interesting things to say about divine omniscience and omnipotence. But concerning the simpicity and eternity of God, he followed the tradition of Anselm, Aquinas and Scotus (see, for example, his *Scriptum in librum primum Sententiarum*, I, d.9, q.3). The Reformers were uninterested in philosophical issues like the nature of time and eternity. They affirm the eternity of God, but without making the kind of philosophical distinctions that interest us. The Counter-Reformation and Protestant Orthodoxy alike followed the traditional definition of eternity as a timeless life or "duration" (e.g. Heppe, *Reformed Dogmatics*, 65). Even the "Church Father of the 19th century," F. D. E. Schleiermacher (1768–1834) conceived of God as timeless in the traditional sense (*The Christian Faith*, par. 54).

The philosophers of this period advanced the discussion of eternity no more than did the theologians. The so-called "rationalist" philosophers, such as Descartes (1596–1650), Spinoza (1632–1677), Malebranche (1638–1715) and Leibniz (1646–1716) all accepted the traditional doctrine of divine eternity.[5] The so-called "empiricist" philosophers, on the other hand, such as Bacon (1561–1626), Gassendi (1592–1655), Hobbes (1588–1679), and Locke (1632–1704) uniformly adopt an everlasting definition of eternity.[6] It is interesting to note that, in the most important discussion of time during this period, the famous Leibniz-Clarke Correspondence (1717), both participants in the debate accept the timelessness of God.[7]

Immanuel Kant (1724–1804), who learned from both rationalism and empiricism, also discussed the doctrine of divine eternity in his *Lectures on Philosophical Theology*. He accepted the traditional doctrine, but criticized the idea of a "simultaneous" eternal duration or life as being self-contradictory (pp. 71, 76–78). One might expect the traditional view from Kant, since he did not think time was an objective determination of things in themselves (*Critique of Pure Reason*, B 48). Yet none of these philosophers genuinely advanced the discussion of divine timelessness.

It was the work of G. W. F. Hegel (1770–1831), Schleiermacher's colleague at Berlin, who more than anyone else set the stage for the modern discussion of divine eternity. Hegel was one of a handful of truly great philosophical geniuses in Western history. His system radically called into question the traditional doctrine of divine eternity. For Hegel, Absolute Spirit (God) is involved in a process of movement and becoming. Thus Hegel placed Becoming in the center of the Real, rather than Being. He wrote, for example, of Spirit that "This sacrifice [of self-negation] is the externalization in which Spirit displays the process of its becoming Spirit in the form of *free contingent happening*, intuiting its pure Self as Time outside of it" (*Phenomenology of Spirit*, 492, his italics). For Hegel, then, in the process of creation and history Spirit becomes time. This same point is made with explicit reference to God's eternity in Hegel's *Lectures on the Philosophy of Religion* (although these are only compiled from student notes and must be used with critical care).

> The absolute, eternal Idea is, in its essential existence, in and for itself, God in His eternity before the creation of the world, and outside of the world . . . What is thus created is therefore an Other, and is placed at first outside of God. It belongs to God's essential nature, however, to reconcile to Himself this something which is foreign to Him . . . Put more definitely, what is involved in this idea is that the universal Spirit, the Whole which this Spirit is, posits itself together with its three characteristics or determinations . . . The three forms indicated are: eternal Being in and with itself, the form of the Universality; the form of manifestation or appearance, that of Particularisation, Being of another; the form of the return from appearance into itself, absolute Singleness or individuality (vol. 3, pp. 1–2).

For Hegel, Spirit is eternal but not absolutely timeless – Spirit enters into the Other, and into Becoming. Hegel's emphasis on the metaphysical movement of Spirit in Being, Negation and Becoming (in which Spirit becomes concrete and then returns to itself, thus coming to know itself) shattered the static notion of Deity inherited from traditional theology. However unclear and difficult Hegel's doctrine of God or Spirit may be, no one could take his thought seriously and still hold to the traditional view of a changeless, absolutely timeless God. This can be seen in Hegel's influence on theology and philosophy after his day.

Hegel turned the interests of philosophers and theologians to the historical and the temporal. Karl Marx (1818–1883) is one very important example of this interest among the students of Hegel. *Being and Time* by Martin Heidegger (1889–1976), to take another example, stands as a brilliant monument to the interest in history and time which Hegel sparked among Continental philosophers. At the beginning of this century on the Continent the rise of dialectical theology made the issue of "Time and Eternity" an important one again (see Schmidt, *Zeit und Ewigkeit*.) Continental theologians who wrote on this issue were typically interested in human destiny, the "super-historical," or the goal and end of history, rather than divine eternity *per se*. Such topics would come under the rubric of "History and Eschatology" in English language theology. But this Continental interest in time and eternity found a flowering in the great *Church Dogmatics* of Karl Barth (1886–1968), which does discuss in great detail the issue of God's own time and eternity (e.g., CD, I/2, pp. 45–70, II/1, pp. 608–678). Barth's theory of eternity is an attempt to blend the timeless with the temporal. The similarities to Hegel are obvious.

Hegel not only greatly influenced Continental theology and philosophy down to the present day, he also influenced English speaking philosophy and theology through two movements, Idealism and "process philosophy." The latter is developed by philosophers like Samuel Alexander (1859–1938) and A. N. Whitehead (1861–1947). Process theology is based on Whitehead's thought, as well as such theologian–philosophers as Pierre Teilhard de Chardin (1881–1955) and Charles Hartshorne (b. 1897). Process theology has tended to replace liberal thought among Protestants and some Catholics. For process theologians, God is becoming and growing. They naturally tend to affirm the everlasting concept of eternity. As Lewis Ford, a Catholic process theologian, has written: "The divine simplicity includes all there is, but as Hartshorne and Whitehead have pointed out, the future does not yet exist as actual, and cannot therefore be included as actual within the divine experience" ("Boethius and Whitehead on Time and Eternity," 51). God grows over time, therefore, by accepting the future into his being.

In addition to process philosophy, the philosophy of Idealism was much in debt to Hegel, although unlike process thought it tended to stress Being over Becoming. A good example of idealism is found in the thought of J. M. E. McTaggart (1866–1925). McTaggart is well known for his paradox concerning temporal becoming, which will interest us later on. Because like Kant he did not think that temporal passage was ultimately real, he did hold to the traditional doctrine of eternity, although he felt that the idea of a timeless "present" is only a metaphor ("The Relation of Time and Eternity," 347).

Idealist philosophy gave way to philosophy in the analytic tradition in the early 20th century. With the rise of the Vienna Circle and "logical positivism," interest in divine eternity waned. Less concern was given to "metaphysics" and philosophy of religion. As logical positivism swept over Anglo-American departments of philosophy, philosophers became almost hostile to theological issues like eternity. Thus while F. H. Brabant in 1936 could deliver the Bampton Lectures on the topic of *Time and Eternity and Christian Thought* (which defends a traditional view) few other English speaking thinkers seemed interested. The question of the nature of divine eternity was only studied in larger theological works of a philosophical bent, which considered the divine attributes as a whole (e.g. Farnell, *The Attributes of God* [1925], 254–262, who argues that a timeless God cannot create or act.) Following the meteoric career of logical positivism, interest in divine eternity was sparked in the early 1960s by an article of William Kneale's ("Time and Eternity in Theology") and an article on omniscience by A. N. Prior ("The Formalities of Omniscience.") A few years later Nelson Pike wrote a book which remains an important work on the subject (*God and Timelessness* [1970]). The consensus among these philosophers of religion in the analytic tradition was that divine timelessness is incongruent with other, more important doctrines: but by no means all philosophers are agreed on this point. Eleonore Stump and Norman Kretzmann, in particular, published a well known article in 1981 defending the traditional doctrine of eternity ("Eternity"). The most recent book on divine eternity, Paul Helm's *Eternal God* (1988), likewise defends the traditional view.

Thus many modern philosophers and theologians, following Hegel, have brought into question the traditional doctrine of divine eternity which dominated Western theology for over 1,500 years. Nevertheless some theologians and philosophers continue to defend the doctrine in one form or another. What the contours and assumptions of this defense might be is the subject of the next chapter.

4 A Coherent Model of Absolute Timelessness

In the history of the idea of eternity, we have seen that the traditional doctrine of eternity has dominated the discussion. The question then naturally arises, is this view correct? Many modern thinkers have argued that it is. In this chapter we examine several attempts to develop and defend the traditional doctrine of eternity. According to this doctrine, God is absolutely timeless and absolutely immutable. Traditional theologians would affirm, nevertheless, that God acts in human history. The congruence of these two doctrines with one another depends, as we shall see, upon the stasis theory of time. In fact Paul Helm simply assumes the stasis theory in his defense of the traditional notion of eternity (*Eternal God*, 24–26, 77–80).

The first task of any critique is understanding. So I will do my best to make a case for absolute timelessness in this chapter. In doing so, I shall adopt views which will be abandoned later in the book. In particular, I assume for the moment, as Helm does, that the stasis theory of time is true.

One central tenet of theism which does impact upon the doctrine of eternity is the sustaining of creation by God. To say that he sustains the created universe is to say that no episode of the universe would exist if it were not for the power of God supporting that episode in being. By an episode of the universe we mean the mereological sum of all episodes of real objects at a given period of time in the history of the universe. This excludes the deistic notion that God sets up the universe and its laws and does not need to support each episode in existence by a direct act (see chapter one). I will also assume the truth of this doctrine, as almost every theist does. I consider this doctrine, in fact, far more central to theism than any particular notion of eternity, and therefore the doctrine of eternity we adopt should conform to the idea that God sustains the world.

THE POSSIBILITY OF TIMELESS CAUSATION

Nelson Pike has recently argued that the idea of God directly sustaining each episode in the history of the universe is inconsistent with the traditional doctrine of eternity. He holds that an absolutely timeless God could not create anything in time (*God and Timelessness*, 97–120). For "the production-verb carries clear implications regarding the temporal position of the product relative to the creative-activity" (p. 105). Pike's point may be true of humans, and human language, but must it always hold for a God? Merely because an effect is in time, does it necessarily follow that the agent who causes it is in time? Pike nowhere demonstrates that, *of logical necessity*, every datable effect implies an agent with location or extension in time. Granted, the effect itself will have a date, but does every datable effect logically imply an agent who exists at some time? Let's state this question as a positive principle:

(1)   The occurrence of any temporal effect brought about by an agent implies that the agent in question is temporal.

Our question, then, is whether (1) is true of logical necessity.

The only type of agency human beings regularly have acquaintance with is agency in time. While some imagination is needed to allow a timeless agent to have a datable effect, there seems nothing logically contradictory in the idea itself. Although Pike claims there is something essentially temporal in production-verbs (p. 107), could this not be true of *any* description of action in a natural language? Most languages have tenses or similar indications of temporality for action-verbs. Of course such languages will thus give a time-aspect to all verbs. Perhaps the temporal aspects of our language must be set aside for the purposes of metaphysical accuracy. Further, all humans are in time and act in time. In fact all agents on earth are in time. So naturally we assume that agency logically implies temporality. But human language must not be allowed to limit the reality of God.

One could give an argument for (1) as follows. Science has taught us that every temporal effect has a prior, temporal cause. The effects of God's acts are temporal, thus God must be temporal, if he really affects the physical world. But the premise of this argument simply begs the question against divine timeless agency. Whether or not every temporal effect has a temporal cause is the very issue at stake. Furthermore, this premise applies to things and events in this space-time universe. All such things and events already have a temporal location: but God need not have one.

Another argument for (1) could run as follows. In order to bring anything about, an agent must change. Anything that changes is in time in some way. Ergo, any agent must be in time. But is it true that an agent must, of logical necessity, change in order to bring anything about? If a huge unchanging mass replaced the sun in the center of our solar system, other things being basically equal, the planets would still orbit this huge mass because of its gravity. Thus the huge mass would be a necessary cause of the orbiting of its planets, but it would not have to change in order to do so. The problem with this response is, the huge mass *is not an agent*. Surely the agent must, in order to cause some intended new effect, act differently at different times. Acting differently is a real change, and whatever undergoes real change is in time. Therefore, (1) is true of logical necessity. I can find nothing wrong with this objection, granting the assumption that *God acts differently*. Yet perhaps God only seems to act differently. Perhaps God's timeless, eternal, unchanging act is always the same "in eternity." Such a view is at least worthy of exploration, and we shall do so in the rest of this chapter.

In the case of God, he could sustain the universe of matter-energy without himself being in time. Yet at each moment of time we would be tempted to say from our perspective, "now God is sustaining the universe." In other words, it would seem to us that "now" God affects the universe, when in fact this act might be timeless in the absolute sense. Only from a *prima facie* human point of view – that is, only from a point of view within the structures of time – does the date of the effect seem to give the cause a date. Humans are naturally inclined to infer temporal causes from temporal effects. From a non-human point of view outside of the structures of time, the cause of the universe need not have a date. This basically Augustinian point (*Confessions*, 11.31) is well expressed in our age by Robert Neville (*God the Creator*, 104):

> [The power of God's creative] activity can be said eternally to have a temporal structure or form. Hence, although its productive activity is not temporal, from a point within time the power's activity may be viewed as coming before and after, and in serial order. This follows from the fact that what is productive of the determinations of being cannot be temporal so long as time is a determination of being.

If time is created by God, how can God be limited to temporal existence? Since God creates time, his creative activity (the defender of the traditional argument will urge) gives reality its temporal structure, but without he himself necessarily being temporal.

Perhaps a picture or example of how this might be possible would be helpful. Unfortunately the example given by Pike of a baritone holding middle C for a full minute (p. 111) begs the question by involving a temporal agent. Thus a better example is called for. Imagine a timeless world, W^*. In this world the god Atlas supports the earth on his back. Now in W^* Atlas is absolutely immutable. If Atlas did not exist in W^*, then the earth would not have existed in W^*. Further, if Atlas exists, then necessarily Atlas supports the earth. The act of Atlas supporting the earth in W^* is a timeless act, since time does not exist in W^*. Here, then, is another picture of a timeless agent acting.

We can apply this picture to God's sustaining the actual temporal world. God can timelessly and changelessly exert exactly the same power, in exactly the same way, to affect the entire universe, with its internal temporal structure. By one, single, timeless act God could sustain the universe, even though from a human perspective this act would seem temporal. In Neville's words, this act will give time its structure, and thus will seem datable, based on the date of its effect, from a human point of view: but in fact it is an absolutely timeless act.

This conception of how God could be absolutely timeless and yet sustain the universe depends upon the idea of a timeless causal process. Such an idea is difficult to imagine. Stephen Davis writes that "we have on hand no acceptable concept of atemporal causation, i.e. of what it is for a timeless cause to produce a temporal effect" (*Logic and the Nature of God*, 13). Despite this problem, unless one is going to argue that time is not contingent, then a timeless world is possible. And on such a world, God might have created something. On such a timeless world, nothing would change, since change implies time (see chapter one). But even so, the existence of, say, a timeless angel would depend upon God. For God could have (timelessly) chosen not to create that one angel. God's choice to create the angel would be logically prior to the existence of the angel; but since time would not exist, the existence of the angel would not be temporally antecedent to the existence of God. Both the angel and God would alike be timelessly eternal, but God would still be the cause of the angel's existence. Despite the remarks of Davis, there is nothing logically contradictory about such an idea. In fact, Davis himself admits as much (p. 21).

One way to show that two internally coherent propositions are not in contradiction with each other is to come up with some other non-contradictory proposition(s), consistent with the first proposition, which together with the first entails the second. Consider the following three propositions.

(2)　Possibly, the world is timeless.[1]
(3)　Possibly, an angel exists in every timeless world.
(4)　All angels are sustained by God.

Now (2) – (4) entail (5):

(5)　Possibly, God timelessly sustains an angel.

It is possible, in other words, for God to sustain something timelessly. Granted, (3) may not be true, but the point is that there is nothing contradictory about it. Indeed, it may be that (3) represents the will of God – I do not claim to know one way or the other. Further, there is nothing incoherent about (5) in itself. We can thus conclude that (5) is logically possible. Since God may do whatever is logically possible, God could have chosen to do (5). But this means that God could timelessly sustain any object which is itself timeless (that is, which exists in a timeless way).

Here the objector may point out that the actual world is not timeless, but an ever changing reality. One can accept this point as true, without abandoning the position we are advocating here. The power of this point is best made in a revised version of (1):

(1′)　The occurrence of an effect (which is itself a change) implies a change in some cause of the effect.

Surely (1′) is true: if the light goes out on my desk, this change or effect is the result of some change in the causes of the light. For example, the electric current may have ceased, or the bulb may have broken. Because the effect happened, and so some change occurred, we rightly infer some change in the causes of the effect. This principle is sound. Some causes may be unchanging, but at least one cause must change, if an effect takes place. The application of (1′) to our problem is also clear. If God is the only ultimate cause of changing things (that is, if God sustains by a direct act the changing episodes of the universe) then God, too, must undergo some change. He undergoes a change, in that he does different things at different times, and acting differently entails a real change for the agent in question. If I am running, or thinking, or writing and then I stop, I have really changed: the same holds if I begin such activities.

I suggest that in any universe where God exists, things do not just happen without any reason. So in any universe where God exists, (1′) will be true. Thus God, too, must really change since he directly causes different effects, and so acts differently.

But this objection can be turned. Let us allow, at least at this point in the argument, that the stasis theory of time is true (I am, remember, doing my best to make a case for divine absolute timelessness). Further, let us allow that God's sustaining activity relates to the fundamental ontological status of things and events. Now on the stasis theory of time, no particular episode or event is timeless, because they will all have dates. But the totality of the world, considered from a four-dimensional perspective, is both timeless and changeless. If we include in "the totality of the world" all events, things, and happenings *and their dates* (i.e. the before-after relations they have with each other, and any system(s) of reference for dating events in such an order) then the world will be timeless. The world as a whole does not occur at any time, because all dates are internally defined. What is true of the parts is not true of the whole, for all possible changes and times are contained within the whole. All changes and times will occur within the world; outside or beyond the four-dimensional universe, there will not be any change or time. As Helm writes:

A timeless being may not act within the universe, yet it makes sense to say that such a being produces (tenseless) the universe. The production of the universe is thus not the production of some event or complex of events in time; it is the production of the whole material universe, time included (*Eternal God*, p. 69).

God could thus sustain the four-dimensional space-time universe, just like he sustained the angel in the above example. For the fundamental ontological status of things is eternally the same. Changes in the sense of things having incompatible properties at different dates will still occur. But things and events will not change in their fundamental ontological status. Things and events will exist at the time they exist, no matter when "now" is according to humans. It is this fundamental ontological change that is at issue when we consider the act of God sustaining the world. And it is this sort of fundamental ontological change of status that the stasis theory denies. Such as conception of how a timeless God can sustain the world including dates depends upon the stasis theory of time, which some theologians advocating the traditional doctrine of eternity have rejected. We will have to see whether they may have been inconsistent on this point.

Given this idea of God sustaining the world, *pace* Pike, God could act eternally without changing and without being temporal. The question is, can a timeless God sustain the world without changing, if the process theory of time is true? We put the question this way because of the close relationship between change and time. If God had to change in order to sustain each different episode in the history of our world, then even if he need not be "in our time," he will not be timeless in the absolute sense.

In Christian tradition immutability and timeless eternity are mutually entailing. Time was closely linked with change in the thought of the Fathers, and the medieval theologians. For example, in Aquinas' great *Summa Theologiae*, the topic of eternity is dealt with immediately after the topic of divine immutability, and both topics are introduced together (ST, Ia, q.9, intro.) To take another example, after demonstrating in his *Summa contra Gentiles* that God was immutable (I.13), Thomas argues that God is timeless because he is changeless, and time is the measure of change (I.15). A God who changed would be in time; a God who was absolutely timeless could not change.[2] As Augustine put this point (*Confessions*, 11.7):

> In your Word all is uttered at one and the same time, yet eternally. If it were not so, your Word would be subject to time and change and therefore would be neither truly eternal nor truly immortal.

Though this linking of immutability and eternity will be called into question, it is obvious that among traditional Christian theologians a God who is timeless will also be changeless. All those who argue for divine timelessness in Christian tradition also argue for divine immutability, and see a close connection between them. A traditional view of eternity will therefore include absolute divine immutability. But a reconciliation of divine sustaining with timelessness and immutability requires the stasis theory of time.

DIALOGUE WITH SELECT DEFENDERS OF DIVINE TIMELESSNESS

We now turn our attention to certain representative theologians who have argued for absolute timeless divine eternity. We will see that the views held by these theologians lead to the stasis theory of time. Thomas Aquinas will represent ancient theologians. Among modern thinkers Eleonore Stump and Norman Kretzmann have been selected for dialogue.

Of all those thinkers in Christian tradition who have defended the doctrine of divine timeless eternity, Thomas Aquinas is one of the great minds. His genius did not lie in originality so much as in the penetrating nature of his thought, the thoroughness of his investigation, and his pursuit of clear and coherent theology. Thomas culled from previous centuries the best arguments for the timelessness of God. Among his theological predecessors, Augustine argued that God was timeless because of God's immutability. Boethius emphasized the issue of divine foreknowledge and human freedom as an important point in favor of the timelessness of God. Anselm argued that God was timeless and spaceless on the basis of divine simplicity. Thomas Aquinas used and refined all of these arguments (see chapter three). What is more, the arguments of several modern philosophers on this issue are a re-presentation of the Thomistic view.[3] So it is that we turn first to the writings of Aquinas in considering the relationship between God and time.

Recall from previous discussion the fundamental Thomistic notion of divine timelessness. God is simple, and thus immutable and eternal. Since God does not change or move, God is not in time. Further, all of time is present to God "at once" in eternity. Here we may recall again the image of a circle evoked by Aquinas (SCG, I.66). The center of the circle is outside the circumference, but all of the circumference is present to the center. God's eternity is like the center of the circle: he is outside of time, yet all of time is present to him.

This view of God creates a problem if one holds to the process theory of time, a problem which Duns Scotus clearly saw. Assuming this theory of time, things and events do change their fundamental ontological status with the passage of time. Since God maintains the fundamental ontological status of things, God must change over time. On the process view, the future and its events and episodes are not real. Thus future effects of God's direct sustaining act would not be real. Would not God have to change in order to bring about such new effects of his direct actions? Aquinas considered this objection (SCG II.32), and his response was, "newness of the effect does not demonstrate newness of action in God, since His action is His essence" (SCG, II.35). In seeking to understand this response, we will need to distinguish between "will" as used by Aquinas and what modern philosophers call "intention."

By "intention" here we simply mean any conscious purposing to do or to be doing. When used of the divine Agent, this term will include what philosophers have called "trying," "intention," and "motive." Of course when God tries to do something, it always gets done! Distinctions drawn by philosophers between these terms are important for human agency, but less important when speaking of God. But we should draw a distinction between God's "intention," or trying, which coexists with the act intended, and God's "design." By "design" we mean an agent's plans or purposes. God's design can be unchanging from all eternity; he can decide to act at time X, and need never change his mind (see Creel, *Divine Impassibility*.) However, to accomplish anything, an agent must add to her actual ability to bring about the intended effect, the particular instance of intention. If I always have the power to raise my arm, and I design to do so at time X, I must also add the intention to raise my arm at time X, in order to raise my arm at time X. We shall call this ability to bring about an intended effect one's "power-to-act." In order to act any agent must use or put forth power-to-act, or cease to do so for those effects one wishes to stop.[4]

Since God acts in sustaining the universe, he must exert his sustaining power-to-act in accordance with changing circumstances in our time. But does this mean he would have to change from an eternal perspective? It does not follow that God would have to be in our time to so act, as previously argued. But some kind of change in accordance with the changing circumstances of human time seems to be called for on the basis of principle (1′). If a timeless God does not change in any way, how can he sustain the changing universe? Would he not have to change to do so (not, indeed, in his design, but in his intention and power-to-act)? Thus it seems *prima facie* that a timeless God could not have a temporal effect, or he would have to change over time (that is, he would have to do different things at different times). But why could God not act *timelessly* in such a way as to bring about a temporal effect? This, in essence, is the response of Aquinas.

The divine simplicity assures that the divine will is the divine existence: "as his intellect is his own existence, so is his will" (ST Ia, q.19, a.1). As Pure Act, God's activity and his existence are unified in the Being of God. For this reason, God timelessly and changelessly does the same thing, and anything that God wills gets done! God does not "will" (which for Aquinas includes design, intention and power-to-act) that when future time F is present, then God will cause A. Rather, he timelessly wills A-at-F (see also Sturch, "The Problem of Divine Eternity"). He timelessly wills that each effect take place, in its temporal relationships within the process of time. This is seen more clearly from Aquinas' view of divine foreknowledge.

For Aquinas, strictly speaking God does not have foreknowledge. God sees everything in his eternal, timeless "present" (understanding "present" here to be analogous to the temporal present). He uses the image of an observer in a high tower, who can see all the men passing along a road, while the travelers themselves can only see the men next to each other (*Aristotle: On Interpretation*, I.14, sec. 19). God is like the observer in the tower, watching the passage of time. "God is wholly outside the order of time, stationed as it were at the summit of eternity, which is wholly simultaneous, and to Him the whole course of time is subject to one simple intuition." (*op. cit.*, sec. 20). In the same way, God acts throughout time in one, single, simple and eternal act which has multiple temporal effects.

But a problem clearly arises with this view, from a process perspective. God's sustaining power-to-act need not be "in time" if God is timeless. And it does not automatically follow that because God's power-to-act brings about a temporal effect, his power-to-act must itself be temporal. Certainly God's power-to-act seems to occur at a certain date *from our point of view*. But it does not follow from this consideration alone that God's power-to-act is temporal itself, rather than being the timeless foundation of all temporal structure. Would it not be possible, then, for God to will timelessly a certain effect take place, at a certain time? If by "will" one means design, no problem arises. But the problem is this: if God's "will" includes intention and power-to-act, as it does for Aquinas, then God cannot timelessly "will" that a certain effect take place at some non-present time if the process view of time is correct.

To see why , say that God will sustain an episode of the universe, *E*, at a future time, *F*. Since *F* is future, all episodes of things and events at time *F* do not exist. It's not merely that they do not exist now – they do not exist in any sense. It is true that they *will exist*; but this is just a species of non-existence *tout court* (see further, chapter five). Can God "will" something that does not exist? If God is eternally, immutably "willing" *E*-at-*F*, can *E* not exist (tenselessly, perhaps) at *F*? Surely *E*-at-*F* must exist in some way, if God changelessly forever "wills" *E*-at-*F*! But since God's will is actively sustaining any episode whenever it exists, this model of divine timeless agency leads to the stasis theory of time, according to which all states of affairs are equally real, whether past, present or future. According to the process view of time, God cannot changelessly "will" *E*-at-*F*, because *E*-at-*F* does not change-lessly exist. Yet anything that God "wills" to exist does exist. Since God "wills" *E*-at-*F* to exist, and God's will does not change, *E* is existing in some sense at *F* (ST Ia, q.19, a.4 and 6). Since God is eternally and immutably "willing" *E*-at-*F*, then *E*-at-*F* must be existing in some way also eternally and immutably. Thus *E* exists (tenselessly?) at *F* no matter what time humans call "now."

According to Aquinas, all things ultimately find their cause in God: God is present by his activity in all things, and throughout time (ST Ia, q.8 and 10). All items at every time in the history of the universe are eternally willed by God. Thus all items at every time in the history of the universe exist (tenselessly). These ideas, taken together, lead to the stasis theory of time (see also Craig, "Was Thomas Aquinas a B-Theorist of Time?"). If God is pure act, and if God puts forth unchanging, simple, eternal power-to-act that *E* exist at *F*, then *E*-exists-at-*F* immutably and eternally. It is not merely that God intends to sustain *E*, when *F* is the present time. This would make God's pure act depend upon changing circumstances. Rather, God eternally puts forth power-to-act as well as intention (i.e., "Will") in the single, eternal act by which he sustains all things. And since God sustains all things and events at every time, all things that exist at some time, exist (tenselessly). Thus the stasis theory of time is correct. This, at least, seems to be the implication of Aquinas' answer to how God can sustain a•changing universe without himself changing: "newness of the effect does not demonstrate newness of action in God, since His action is His essence" (SCG, II.35, cf. I.79).

We have seen that Aquinas' view of God's simplicity, immutability and eternity lead to the stasis theory of time. Whether or not Aquinas himself actually held to this theory of time is another question, of course (see Quinn, "The Doctrine of Time in St. Thomas"). But perhaps more modern defenders of divine timelessness can and will avoid this implication. Among the defenders of divine timelessness in modern times, Stump and Kretzmann are increasingly becoming influential.

Like other defenders of the traditional doctrine of eternity, Stump and Kretzmann deny the *prima facie* incoherence of divine timelessness with temporal action on the part of God. They define timeless eternity as an unending and illimited life of timeless duration, which is "lived" completely, all at once ("Eternity", 430–433). Given such a view, they develop the idea of an "eternal–temporal simultaneity" based upon the relativity of all simultaneity. We shall first consider their definition of eternity, and then their concept of eternal-temporal simultaneity.

The value of the article by Stump and Kretzmann lies in no small measure in the way they set out the problems of their view. Their definitions, too, are admirably clear and forthright. Stump and Kretzmann begin by defining eternity in accordance with Boethius, as "The complete possession all at once of illimitable life." They further consider eternity to be an "atemporal duration."

Now the first thing to be said is that Stump and Kretzmann have chosen the wrong word. The word "duration" *means* an interval of time, namely that interval of time through which something endures. The notion of an atemporal duration is, therefore, a contradiction in terms. Stump and Kretzmann continue to use the words "atemporal duration," however, even in the face of criticism ("Atemporal Duration"). They defend their usage, on the grounds that an analysis of time shows "temporal duration is only apparent duration" ("Eternity," 444; "Atemporal Duration," 218). Because past and future states of an entity do not exist, but only the present state does, actual duration is only apparent.

However, this Platonic argument does not show that the phrase "atemporal duration" is a meaningful use of language. At best it demonstrates only that atemporal existence is the fundamental mode of existence. Arguments about which mode of existence is most fundamental will not solve the problem of incoherence in the phrase "atemporal duration." The latter phrase is incoherent because of the nature of the language used, not because of the nature of time. So when they write concerning atemporal duration that "such duration must be fully realized duration, none of which is already lost or not yet gained – an atemporal duration" ("Atemporal Duration," 218), they should replace the word "duration" with the word "existence" (or something like it). To argue that "the apparent incoherence in the concept is primarily a consequence of continuing to think of duration only as 'persistence *through time*'" ("Eternity," 446) is to miss completely the point being made. It is not that we stubbornly continue to think of duration as an interval of time, when we could in fact think of some other kind of duration. It is, rather, that "interval of time" is just what the word does in fact mean.

In another place, however, they use the phrase "atemporal extensive mode of existence" ("Atemporal Duration," 215). This is surely better. But what does this signify? Stump and Kretzmann draw a picture of atemporal extensive existence using two infinite parallel lines. Along one line, which represents our time, the present is a moving spot of light. Along the other line, which is eternity, there is a strip of light all along the line. The "light" indicates presentness. But what is this "line" of present eternity? It must be an extension of the timeless life of

God in eternity. Stump and Kretzmann hold that eternity includes all the acts of God in a limitless and therefore infinitely enduring present ("Atemporal Duration," 218f.) This special, infinite "present" is not instantaneous but atemporal. It is potentially divisible conceptually, but only conceptually, and in fact the pure actuality of God's being knows of no succession or division (p. 216). Can we make any sense out of this?

Consider the following possible way of understanding Stump and Kretzmann's position. Any extension is a "spread" of something. What is eternity a spread of? It is an atemporal extension of the being or life of God. Thus the being or life of God has succession, but it is an atemporal succession (see also Duns Scotus, *Ordinatio*, I, d.9 and d.43.) God's being has "succession" only in a conceptual sense, not in a temporal one. But if there were no succession, then there would be nothing to "spread out" as it were, and there can be no extension. An example may help here. Think of the English alphabet, extended in your imagination. This extension is an atemporal extension. But it still involves succession. For the letter A is before the letter B, and B is before C, etc. One can still talk of the whole alphabet, of course. But in order to "spread out" the alphabet, some kind of succession is necessary: some thing must come before another.

Thus if the life or being of God is "spread out," if it is an extensive mode of being, then the being or life of God must have succession of some kind. It need not be temporal succession, but it cannot be non-successive if it is to be extended (realizing, of course, that God has no spatial extension.) Stump and Kretzmann state that God must have duration, since "any model of existence that could be called a life must have duration" ("Eternity," 433). If we replace "duration" with "extensive mode of being" in the quotation just given, then some sense can be made of this idea (*contra* Fitzgerald, "Stump and Kretzmann on Time and Eternity"). God has an extensive mode of being, because God's life can be ordered in a non-temporal succession.

Stump and Kretzmann's definition of timeless eternity is an important clarification of the traditional doctrine of eternity. This definition is generally helpful and enlightening given certain refinements. However, Stump and Kretzmann not only define eternity, they describe its properties. At the center of their description of divine eternity is the concept of "ET-simultaneity," and to this concept we now turn.

Simultaneity between God's eternity and all of human time is central to Stump and Kretzmann's account of a timeless God. In order to describe how a timeless God could act in, and know of, the temporal world Stump and Kretzmann develop the idea of an "ET" (eternal–temporal) simultaneity ("Eternity," 434–440).[5] They define ET-simultaneous as (p. 439):

> For every x and for every y, x and y are ET-simultaneous if:
> (*i*)   either x is eternal [timeless] and y is temporal, or vice versa; and
> (*ii*) for some observer A, in the unique eternal reference frame, x and y are both present – i.e., either x is eternally present and y is observed as temporally present, or vice versa; and
> (*iii*) for some observer, B, in one of the infinitely many temporal reference frames, x and y are both present – i.e., either x is observed as eternally present and y is temporally present, or vice versa.

One problem with this definition is equivocation. The "present" of a timeless eternity cannot be the same as the temporal present. Stump and Kretzmann state that an eternal being "has present existence in some sense of the word 'present'" (p. 434). But "present" is a temporal term, and eternity is non-temporal according their definition. Yet one can see an analogy between the eternal "present" and the temporal present.

Let us allow that an eternal being has a "present-like" existence. While one could grant that a timeless being exists in a present-like, atemporally successive mode of being, Stump and Kretzmann glide all too easily over the distinction between a temporal present and a timeless present-like instant. They state that x is temporal and y is atemporal (or vice verse) *and* that x and y are both "present." But one is temporally present, and the other is atemporal, and not really a part of our temporal system. The fundamental problem then, of how a timeless present-like being could share a moment of time with some temporally present event, is inherent within this very definition.

What Stump and Kretzmann want to develop is a simultaneity between eternity and temporality. This is unfortunate, for Stump and Kretzmann have labored to make a broad and clear distinction between eternity and time. But if timeless eternity and human time can be simultaneous, the distinction they make between temporality and timelessness is lost. If there are timeless beings, one would think they could not, by definition, be "at the same time as" (simultaneous with) something in time. How can something timeless and something in time be at the *same* time? ET-simultaneity is, *ex hypothesi*, self-contradictory.

Stump and Kretzmann realize this contradiction. For in describing ET-simultaneity, they state (p. 436) that this requires:

> a single mode of existence in which the two *relata* exist or occur together . . . But on the view we are explaining and defending, it is theoretically impossible to specify a single mode of existence for two *relata* of which one is eternal and the other temporal.

Our concern in this essay is not so much with a "mode of existence" as with the ability of a timeless God to sustain a changing, dynamic universe. But the basic problem is the same.

The conception of how a timeless God sustains a temporal universe depends upon one's understanding of time. As noted before, if the stasis view of time is correct, then God need not change over time in order to sustain the world. The events and things which exist at particular times are all equally real. They do not pass out of being, but exist (tenselessly). Since they exist tenselessly, God's eternal sustaining act can also exist, without God having to change in accordance with process. Of course it would seem to us that God was changing, but this would only be because we experienced the subjective distinction between past, present and future. In reality, and for God, this distinction would be an illusion. This theory of time allows divine timelessness and divine agency to be reconciled.[6]

Stump and Kretzmann are not willing to travel this philosophical path. They insist on the genuine reality of process, and reject the stasis theory of time ("Eternity," 441–444). Instead they appeal to the idea of ET-simultaneity. But their definition of ET-simultaneity does not address the fundamental problem of the simultaneity of a timeless present-likeness and a temporal present. In order to deal with this problem, Stump and Kretzmann turn to the Special Theory of Relativity.

In defending their idea of ET-simultaneity, Stump and Kretzmann appeal to the Special Theory of Relativity. This brings us to the central error made by Stump and Kretzmann: their misunderstanding of this very theory. In order to give some plausibility to their claim that a timeless present-like instant could be simultaneous with the temporal present, Stump and Kretzmann point out the *relativity of simultaneity* in the Special Theory of Relativity (STR). Their defense of ET-simultaneity depends on the relativity of simultaneity in the STR (p. 437f.) Stump and Kretzmann claim that this discussion of relativity is merely a heuristic device (p. 440). But even so, surely this idea is necessary to the demonstration of the coherence of ET-simultaneity, given the dependence of their explanation of its coherence upon relativity. Given its *prima facie* incoherence, the plausibility of ET-simultaneity greatly depends upon their interpretation of relativity.

Stump and Kretzmann state that due to the STR "there is no absolute state of being temporally simultaneous with, any more than there is an absolute state of being to the left of" (p. 438). This is a popular, but false, opinion. There are a number of absolutes in relativity theory, when by "absolute" we mean "the same for all physically possible observers." One such absolute is the round-trip speed of light, which is the same in all frames. Another absolute is found in what A. A. Robb called "conical order" (*A Theory of Space and Time*, 15f.)

Conical order is the temporal order of absolute past, absolute simultaneity and absolute future, according to the STR. This particular absolute is quite important for our dialogue with Stump and Kretzmann. Two events are absolutely simultaneous, in our sense, if they occur at the same time in the same place. If one observer finds that two things occur at the same time and place, all observers will find that they are simultaneous. Two events are absolutely past if one is in the past "light-cone" of the other. An event is in your "light-cone" if it is physically possible for a photon to travel from you to the event. Since causation can at best spread at the speed of light, anything in the causal past or future of my here-now is in my light-cone. Further, two events are absolutely future if one is in the future light-cone of the other.

What about Zero Time Relationships between events? Like simultaneity, events will be Zero Time Related for all observers, if they are so related at the same place. Since this absolute Zero Time Relation is so close to absolute simultaneity, I will not distinguish the two; but please remember that the terms "absolute simultaneity" include both strict simultaneity, and also Zero Time Relationships, which occur at the same place. So there *are* absolute temporal relations in the STR. It is simply not the case that "being simultaneous" is as relative as "being to the left of." In fact, *no event in my causal future or past can be simultaneous with my here-now*. We shall see that the very witness that Stump and Kretzmann bring into court contradicts their case.

What follows, then, from this misunderstanding of the STR by Stump and Kretzmann? Two things: first, Stump and Kretzmann commit the fallacy of false analogy. They use the analogy of the relative simultaneity between two events outside of their light-cones to support some notion of God's timeless cause being simultaneous with its effect. But if two events are outside of each other's light-cones, then *they cannot be causally connected*. On the STR, only events inside of the light-cone can be causally connected. Since Stump and Kretzmann want some sort of causal connection between God and the world to hold, they should not have appealed to the relativity of simultaneity between events that – by the very nature of things – cannot be causally connected. Second, the attempt by Stump and Kretzmann to explain away the *prima facie* contradiction in ET-simultaneity fails. Because simultaneity is not as "relative" as they need it to be to make sense of ET-simultaneity, the full force of the contradiction stands. The very idea that a timeless present-like instant could share a moment of time with the temporal present is just as incoherent as it was when the argument began.

Given this critique of Stump and Kretzmann, we are now in a better position to consider whether God could act once, changelessly, "from eternity," and have all of the effects of this divine cause occur at different times. Just for the sake of argument, assume that the process theory of time is true. Say that God acts such that, at some time $T4$, some episode B of an object was sustained. Further, at the present time, $T5$, God acts so as to sustain a different object's episode, C, which is in the same place as B. Now $T4$ and $T5$ are some distance apart in time, and not Zero Time Related. Can the same divine, eternal, immutable act sustain both B and C? Since $T5$ is not, B no longer exists, and so is not being sustained, either in our time or in eternity, by any act of God. Since God's sustaining of C is direct, he cannot (logically cannot) sustain C by an act whose effect is dated at $T4$, and by some causal chain indirectly sustains C-at-$T5$. Furthermore, the present effect of God's eternal act at $T5$ is Zero Time Related with the eternal intention of God; but this same eternal intention and act cannot also be Zero Time Related to B, since B and C are not themselves Zero Time Related. By a single, timeless act God can sustain C and any episode Zero Time Related to C. But since the divine sustaining is a direct act which must be Zero Time Related to its effect, the same divine act cannot sustain both C and B. At the present time ($T5$) B is not real, and so a different act (different, that is, than the act which sustained B) is now called for if God is to sustain C. The particular intention plus power-to-act, such that B-at-$T4$ is sustained, can only sustain episodes Zero Time Related to $T4$. Possibly, this includes episodes of object at $T4$ and the immediate next episode. I don't in fact think that this is the case; rather, it makes more sense to me to say that God puts forth a different act to sustain each different episode of every object. But the point to be made is the same, since the entire past and future of all objects must be sustained by God, not just the immediate next episode. No other disjunct episode of an object can be sustained by that particular act, since no other disjunct episode of that object is Zero Time Related to it. These considerations show that the possibility of God acting once, timelessly and changelessly, yet still sustaining all of the episodes of all objects, is ruled out if the process theory of time is true.[7] Thus God's direct action upon the present time cannot sustain an episode at another past or future time, disjunct from the present. Thus God must change over time, and the traditional doctrine of eternity must be false.

But couldn't God *timelessly* will that a certain effect take place at a certain time ("Eternity," 449)? We considered this same question in the section of Aquinas. Again, if by "will" one means only design, this view is possible. But if God's "will" includes design, intention and power-to-act, and if the stasis theory of time is false, then God cannot timelessly "will" that a certain effect take place at some future time, since the effects of his "will" do not yet exist. So Stump and Kretzmann have missed the fact, due in part to their misunderstanding of the STR, that given their assumptions about time, God cannot both be timeless and sustain a changing temporal world.

What follows from our dialogue with Stump and Kretzmann? The central point made above is that their notion of eternity is incongruent with the truth universally affirmed by Christian theologians that God sustains the universe, unless the stasis theory of time is true. If Stump and Kretzmann wish to hold on to their concept of eternity, and yet reject the stasis theory of time, then they must reject the doctrine that God sustains everything in its being (*esse*). But surely the latter doctrine is far more central to theology than absolute timelessness. For Stump and Kretzmann, then, there remains a choice between the stasis theory of time or the doctrine that God sustains the world, if they are going to be consistent and hold to absolute divine timelessness.

Just because the stasis theory of time follows from the arguments of Aquinas, or Stump and Kretzmann, does not automatically mean it follows from all traditional theories of eternity. I have closely examined the thought of Aquinas, Stump and Kretzmann on the doctrine of divine timelessness. In each case, when the ability of God to sustain a changing, temporal world is insisted upon, these representatives have led us to the stasis theory of time. Yet it is also possible to reach this conclusion directly from the assumptions that defenders of absolute timelessness make.

AN ARGUMENT FROM ABSOLUTE DIVINE TIMELESSNESS TO THE STASIS THEORY OF TIME

Given certain assumptions, it is possible to argue from the traditional doctrine of eternity to the stasis theory of time without having to consider a particular exponent of divine timelessness. In order to do so it will be important to summarize what we have learned about absolutely timeless eternity from the representative defenders already examined.

In dialogue with them we have learned, first, that any discussion of absolutely timeless eternity must admit that talk of such a timeless being is talk of a durationless existence with no temporal location nor extension. Thus any succession or extension in the life of God is logical, not temporal. Second, divine timelessness understood in this way entails the absolute immutability of God. "Absolute immutability" means not only the Biblical doctrine that God is unchanging in his abilities and character, but also the Augustinian doctrine that God does not change in any way whatsoever, apart from merely relative changes (*City of God*, 22.2: "They find God changed because *they* have undergone a change.") With these common assumptions in mind, we now assume the process view of time, to discover what results will follow.

Take a particular example of a direct sustaining divine act: God sustains an episode of the universe, E, at a certain time, $T2$. At one time in the past, call it $T1$, no episode which is part of E existed in any way. At a subsequent time, $T2$, God directly puts forth sustaining power-to-act so as to hold in being all the episodes of things and events in E. Finally, at a later time $T3$ no episode of E exists in any way. Assume that God immutably and eternally designed so to act at time $T2$, and only at $T2$. If it is not $T2$, then God is not sustaining E: he is not putting forth this specific power-to-act. Nor can God do so. For if he did so (immutably and eternally) then E would have to exist (or E-at-$T2$ would tenselessly exist, perhaps; see next paragraph). Even God, therefore, must wait until time $T2$ to act in the specified manner. At time $T2$, and at no other time, can he so act. God's sustaining power must change between $T1$ and $T2$, or either (a) E-at-$T2$ would already exist, and hence the stasis theory of time would be true; or (b) E would not come into existence at $T2$. The argument based on this example can be applied equally well to any sustaining act of God. If God sustains the episodes of a changing, temporal universe, then God changes over time with respect to his power-to-act, and cannot be timeless in the traditional sense. This argument assumes that the process theory is true.

On the other hand, if the stasis theory of time is correct, God does not have to change to act in the specified way at $T2$. He can timelessly act so as to sustain E (or any other episode) and it will be sustained at $T2$ and only at $T2$, since E tenselessly exists-at-$T2$ in order to be effected by the power of God. This could equally well be put the other way around: E exists (tenselessly) at $T2$, because God is eternally putting forth power-to-act so as to sustain E-at-$T2$. Thus a model of God's timeless, changeless activity, which sustains the universe at every moment of time, leads to the stasis theory of time. Assuming that God sustains the universe, the traditional doctrine of eternity is true if and only if the stasis theory of time is true.

What responses might be made to this argument? One might question whether design, intention and power-to-act can be separated in God. The one "will" of God includes them all, one might argue; whatever God wills is done. But if we do not make this distinction, then it will follow that God must change his "will" in order to act in the way specified in the above example.

Another objection might be that if the above argument is correct, God must wait until a certain time is present in order to sustain events at that that time. But (*a*) all times are equally present to an absolutely timeless God, and (*b*) such a notion does not suit the dignity and power of God.

All times may indeed be present to God, if God is absolutely timeless and the stasis theory of time is correct. However, on the process view there is one and only one present for any agent. For "present" simply selects those possible objects which really exist (this is discussed further in chapter five). And even God cannot act upon a non-existent object. Therefore, on process assumptions, even God cannot sustain a non-present, non-existing episode.

But another aspect of this conclusion, that God must wait for circumstances in order to act, seems odd or inappropriate. God, after all, is the source of all being, the source of the existence of all that exists. God does not have to wait until a particular time in order to act, it might be objected. He can act anywhere, at any time, since he already acts everywhere at all times. He can cause whatever he wants to exist, whenever he wants, in order to sustain it.

But returning to the above example, if God in eternity creates E in time (assuming, say, that $T2$ is future) then E will not exist at $T2$ and only at $T2$. And God cannot act in eternity in such a way as to bring about E-at-$T2$, since $T2$ is not yet (we assume, remember, that the process theory of time is true). It is logically impossible for some time to both be present and future. So it is logically impossible for God to act in eternity in such a way as to bring about E-at-$T2$, as long as $T2$ is not the present time. Only if $T2$ is the present time, then, will E exist at $T2$ and only at $T2$. Since God sustains E at $T2$, even he must wait until $T2$ if in his eternal design he wishes to sustain E at $T2$ and at no other time. So the fact remains that God would have to change to act in this way, if the process theory is correct.

This section has led us in one direction. Any model of absolute divine timelessness that wishes to retain the important notion of God sustaining the world should also affirm the stasis theory of time. The stasis theory of time helps to overcome the problems expressed by Pike about God's everlasting, timeless sustaining of the universe. God timelessly sustains every moment of time, and gives the universe its temporal structure. But this does not mean that God *changes*, since none of the things, circumstances nor events in past or future times ever change in their fundamental ontological status. Only from a mere human perspective do things come into being or pass out of being with process.

PRELIMINARY OBJECTIONS REFUTED

Why have certain advocates of the absolute definition of timeless eternity rejected the stasis theory of time? Mainly, these rejections have been based upon misunderstandings of the stasis view. William Hasker rejects that idea that events really are as God timelessly perceives them, because in that case time is an illusion, and God necessarily fails to grasp the temporally sequential nature of events ("Concerning the Intelligibility of 'God is Timeless'," 190f.) But the stasis view of time does not hold *time* to be illusion, only that process (the past-present-future distinction) is mind-dependent or subjective. Are colors an illusion, because they are likewise mind-dependent? Further, the stasis theory does accept the temporally sequential nature of events. What McTaggart called the B-series, the spread of events in their various temporal orders, is the very basis of the stasis view. If God is absolutely timeless what God does not experience is process. And this seems to be what traditional Christian theologians have affirmed when they spoke of all times being "present" to God. He does know the times that all events occur in, but not which moment out of the whole space-time universe humans call "now."[8]

Hebblethwaite, to take another example, rejects the stasis view because, as he says,

> on such a view time as we experience it is, ultimately speaking, unreal, and our freedom doubly illusory; for not only is the future not really open; there is no such thing as a real future . . . This would, of course, be a thoroughly predestinarian view ("Some Reflections," 436)

While a determinist can be a stasis theorist, it does not follow that the stasis theory of time leads to determinism.[9] The problem here lies not in the stasis theory of time, but in the assumption of the truth of the process view of time in most definitions of the freedom of the will in a libertarian sense (e.g. Pike, 57). What is needed is a definition of human free will that applies just as much to past free actions as it does to future free actions. For on the stasis view, the future is just as free, and just as necessary, as the past. To the extent, then, that past actions are (tenselessly) free, so future actions are (tenselessly) free.

In defending free will in his Gifford Lectures, Richard Swinburne gives the following definition: "humans have free will, in the sense that they are not causally necessitated to do the actions which they do by brain-events or any other events" (*Evolution of the Soul*, 231). This is one definition which will apply just as much to past free choices as to future. Take a future event in my life: whether I eat a cheese omelet on January 1, 2001. Call this time $T21$. Assuming I am alive and I have the choice, say that I am not causally determined as to whether I eat a cheese omelet or not at $T21$. According to the stasis view, my decision is made at the time in question: my decision is real, and so is my eating of the omelet at $T21$. God knows for certain that at $T21$ Alan eats a cheese omelet. But it does not follow that I am causally determined to eat the omelet at $T21$ from the fact that I actually do eat an omelet at $T21$ or that God knows this fact.

To see why this is so, consider the same act only in the past. Last Saturday, I ate a cheese omelet. God and I both know that I ate a cheese omelet last Saturday, and it is necessary in some sense that I ate a cheese omelet last Saturday, since in fact I did eat it. But it does not follow from any of these truths that I was *causally necessitated* to eat an omelet last Saturday. The same argument is valid with respect to eating an omelet at $T21$. We humans do not yet know if indeed I will eat a cheese omelet on January 1, 2001, as we do in the case of last Saturday. One is ignorant at a time of the outcome of later free or random events. But this epistemic point has no effect on the argument about causal determination. Assuming that I will eat the omelet, on the stasis theory of time I am (tenselessly) eating the omelet at $T21$, and this is the basis of Gods knowledge of that fact (even as my eating the omelet last Saturday is also the basis of God's knowledge of that fact). Still, just as it was in my power last Saturday not to eat a cheese omelet then, so it will be in my power at $T21$ to refrain from eating an omelet at $T21$. This does not contradict the fact that I actually did and will eat a cheese omelet at these times. As this example shows, Hebblethwaite's worries about the stasis view of time are premature: it need not lead to a fully predetermined universe.

Finally, Delmas Lewis has argued that the traditional view of divine timelessness leads to the stasis theory of time in a recent article ("Timelessness and Divine Agency.") He then argues that the stasis theory of time is inconsistent with the belief that God sustains and creates the universe of physical objects.

Lewis asserts that "it follows directly from the concept of [timeless] eternity that an eternal God cannot bring it about that a temporal object comes into existence" (p. 150). By an object X coming into existence, Lewis means that "reality is such that *first*, X does not exist and *next*, X does exist." Now Lewis seems to be using the terms "exist" in this quote in a tenseless sense, for he follows it with the assertion that "if time is tenseless, then the only available sense of 'exists' is the *tenseless* one" (p. 152, his italics.) Lewis seems to think that if the stasis theory of time is right, and if we use words in their normal sense, then if X comes into existence, first X does not exist (tenselessly), and then X exists (tenselessly). This notion of "comes into existence" surely is incorrect on the stasis theory. What Lewis has failed to take into consideration in his analysis of "comes into existence" is, every physical event only *exists (tenselessly) at some time*. An example may help here.

Consider my birth on 23 September 1955. This event exists (tenselessly). But it does not always exist (tenselessly); otherwise my mother would be very busy! My birth only exists-at-23-September-1955. How, then, can I "come into existence" in Lewis' sense? Clearly, I come into existence because at any time before 23 September 1955 I did not exist-at-that-time, and for some times during and after 23 September 1955 I do exist-at-that-time. Let us generalize from this into a definition of "comes into existence."

(D6)   For any object X, and for some time $T(n)$: X comes into existence at $T(y)$ if for any time $T(y-1)$, X does not exist-at-$T(y-1)$ and at $T(y)$, X does exist-at-$T(y)$.

This definition should not be read so as to exclude the possibility that X may also exist for some set of times $T(y+n)$. (D6) does preserve the first-next sequence mentioned by Lewis, without importing process into the definition. And this is where Lewis seems to have gone wrong.

Lewis allows the normal, process-laden speech about God to govern his understanding of such sentences as "God creates a mountain" (pp. 149–151). To allow the "normal sense" of words to govern our understanding of God begs the question with respect to the stasis theory of time. For it is part of the program of the stasis theorist that normal speech must be made more precise so as to exclude process, or at least that sentences in normal speech can be given precise truth conditions that are process-free (see chapter five). What (D6) amounts to, then, is a process-free or "tenseless" truth condition for tokens of the sentence-type "X comes into existence." Given this truth condition, it is coherent to assert:

(6)   God is absolutely timeless and immutable.
(7)   The stasis theory of time is true.
(8)   God causes X to exist and X comes into existence.

(6) and (7) are our basic assumptions. (8) is the point under discussion. Lewis seems to think that (8) and (7) cannot both be true. But this ignores that fact that tensed sentences can be given process-free truth conditions, according to stasis theorists. In fact, if the stasis theory of time is true, then there must be some sense in which (8) is true, since we know that what (8) reports happens all the time. If we reject Mellor's program of giving tensed sentences process-free truth-conditions, some other similar program must be followed by stasis theorists.

Exactly the same problem arises with Lewis' argument that divine timelessness is incoherent with the normal notion of God sustaining the universe (pp. 156–159). The important words in the previous sentence are "normal notion." The normal notion of many doctrines is based on common sense, process-laden language. In the case of God sustaining the universe, if one accepts the stasis theory then what is needed is a process-free concept of God's sustaining power. Now Lewis writes that,

> an essential part of the concept of one thing, *A*, sustaining the existence of another thing, *B*, is the idea that *B* would cease to exist but for the sustaining activity of *A*. However, if the tenseless view of time is correct, then it is necessarily true that no physical object or temporal stage thereof can cease to exist (p. 158).

Here Lewis plainly misunderstands the stasis theory. For if Lewis' view of the stasis theory were correct, then it would imply that every existing object is a necessary object. Clearly, however, most physical objects are contingent. What the stasis theory does hold is that: if an object *X* exists-at-*T*, then *X* exists-at-*T* regardless of temporal process. Obviously, Lewis' idea of "cease to exist" is process-laden. Something ceases to exist, for him, if it does not exist in the present moment. It is this process-laden notion that is in conflict with the stasis theory, not the idea of God's sustaining power itself.

The stasis theory does not hold that every existing object is logically necessary. Now God is a necessary cause of the tenseless existence of any object, no matter what time the object in question exists at. And the timeless, immutable power of God tenselessly sustains every object at the time when it exists (tenselessly). Thus if God's timeless, sustaining power were different (i.e., in another possible world) some objects that exist (tenselessly) would not so exist (see Scotus, *Ordinatio*, I, d.39 and d.43). Let us take an example.

Abraham Lincoln was sustained by the power of God. Both process and stasis theorists agree that, if Abraham Lincoln existed, there is a sense in which he cannot *not* have existed. However, Abraham Lincoln is a contingent object, in that it is logically possible that he did not exist (tenselessly) at all. Since he does exist (tenselessly), he is tenselessly sustained by the power of God; but God need not have chosen to so sustain Honest Abe's existence. This model of God sustaining an object is compatible with the stasis theory of time. Thus the idea of God sustaining the universe is not incoherent with the stasis theory of time. Only because Lewis has a process-laden notion of "cease to exist" does he find a conflict between the stasis theory of time and God's sustaining power.

Christian doctrine has been developed within languages that are process-laden. If theologians only half-heartedly adopt the stasis theory of time, then of course such language will be in conflict with the stasis theory. However, if a thoroughgoing stasis theory of both reality *and human language* is adopted, no incoherence results.

The point of this section has been to argue that the doctrine that God sustains the universe is coherent with the doctrine of absolute divine timelessness if and only if the stasis theory of time is true. Are there, then, good reasons to hold to the stasis theory of time other than the fact that it allows a timeless God to so act? This is the question which will be examined in the next chapter.

5 The Stasis Theory of Time: A Critique

In the previous chapter, a model of absolute divine timeless eternity was developed, which was true and coherent with the doctrine that God sustains the universe, on the assumption that the stasis theory of time is true. We now turn our attention to this theory of time for a closer examination. In this chapter I explore the arguments, philosophical and scientific, which have been given in its favor. The conclusion I reach is that we have no good reason to believe in the stasis theory.

One of the more compelling arguments for the stasis view of time is the argument from science. Indeed, many physicists and philosophers of science who have written on the subject hold to the stasis view of time specifically because of the argument from science. The Special Theory of Relativity in particular is thought to lead to the stasis theory of time. Most of the books and articles advocating a stasis theory of time mention this argument. They often assume that the stasis view has no rival, given the Special Theory of Relativity.[1]

There are two movements in the argument from science. The first movement contends that scientific disciplines take no notice of becoming or temporal process. Since science explores the nature of the physical world and does not recognize becoming or process, then what possible basis can one have in asserting that these things are real? The second movement in the argument from science holds that the Special Theory of Relativity, especially as interpreted geometrically by Minkowski, leads to the stasis view of time. We will explore each movement in turn.

THE ARGUMENT FROM SCIENCE

"It seems to me of decisive significance that no cognizance is taken of nowness (in the sense associated with becoming) in any of the extant theories of physics" (Grünbaum, "The Status of Temporal Becoming," 337). Grünbaum is not alone in arguing that the "ignorance" of process in "basic physics" is of material importance.[2] As Stein wrote, "the contrast between the deep role of the distinction [between past, present and future] in experience and the apparent irrelevance to the basic principles of the physical world is very puzzling, and constitutes one of the major philosophical problems about time" ("On Einstein–Minkowski Space-Time," 8). The central thrust in this line of argument is clear: if temporal becoming has physical reality, science should know of it.

We can respond to Grünbaum's challenge as follows. First of all, some sciences do seem to take cognizance of "becoming," or process, even if other branches of science do not. Any science which extrapolates from the present, existing state of some object to either the future state (as in meteorology) or the past state (as in geology) must of necessity take cognizance of the difference between past, present and future. And such extrapolation does take place, even in certain branches of modern physics. In quantum mechanics for instance, future states of particles are only probabilistically known, and this distinguishes past from future. Yet another example is found in thermodynamics, where entropy distinguishes past from future states (for these examples see Prigigone, *From Being to Becoming*). So the argument that physics or science takes no notice of the difference between past, present and future does not seem obviously true.

Grünbaum has a good response to this objection, however ("Are Physical Events Themselves Transiently Past, Present and Future?"). He distinguishes between the anisotropy of time, and "becoming," or what we have called process (see Grünbaum, "Status of Becoming," 324–332). The anisotropy of time implies that time "moves" in only one direction: if *A* is before *B*, then *B* cannot be before *A*. Certain physical processes change in one direction, and this change can be predicted. He insists that prediction and retrodiction are based only on the anisotropy of time. Any particular time could be chosen as the starting point for physical extrapolation. The point is that physics takes cognizance of earlier states or later states, rather than past or future. Just exactly what time human beings identify as "now" has nothing to do with prediction or retrodiction from a particular point in space-time (Grünbaum, "Physical Events," 148f.)

If we allow Grünbaum this rebuttal, and it seems a sound one, a further argument arises in response. Imagine a possible world "*U*" which was exactly the same as the actual world as Grünbaum understands it, except that process was a real part of the physical universe. Human experience of time in *U* would be exactly the same as in the actual world. How would human beings know that process was a part of the physical universe? To meet his standards, as exemplified in the above quotation, they would have to know it through physics. Further – and most importantly – they would need to know of process in some way which would not be interpreted as merely giving support to the anisotropy of time. This would mean that there was some measurable, mathematical aspect of the present time in U that distinguished it from all other times. Perhaps, in U, present objects give off a special kind of radiation which human cannot detect with their five senses. But scientists in U are eventually able to build machines which detect it for them. Would this satisfy Grünbaum?

One fallacious way of "proving" that something does not exist is to set criteria for knowing it which make it impossible for any particular case to quality as an experience of that thing. I claim that Grünbaum has made such a mistake. If it is possible for humans to know something at all, then the criteria for recognizing a thing must not be so rigorous as to exclude the possibility of humans detecting that thing under normal circumstances, or of humans building machines that will detect it for them.

Even though U may be radically different from our world, even on U process would not be detectable according to Grünbaum's criterion. For he would just insist that the radiation discovered by the machines points to that fact that all real objects give off this radiation. In the past, objects gave off this radiation, and in the present they do, and in the future they will, too. Since they all give off this radiation, no difference can be found between past, and present, and future events on the basis of the fact that "present" things give off this strange radiation. He would insist that all real things give off this radiation – but this does not allow us to assert that only present things do. And thus this radiation forms no basis for believing in process. But we must recall at this point that we already stipulated that on U, process was a real aspect of the physical world. But even on U, there is no way to detect this fact given Grünbaum's criterion. Thus, if process is a real part of the actual physical world, this fact cannot be detected by humans on Grünbaum's criterion. In the actual world humans can only know that process is a genuine part of the physical universe *through human experience and awareness*. Yet it is exactly human experience and awareness that Grünbaum excludes from consideration! Even when process is a real part of the physical universe, there is no way this can be demonstrated on Grünbaum's criterion. By excluding human experience of time from consideration, Grünbaum excludes the only possible basis for the knowledge of process in the actual world. Either Grünbaum must admit that knowledge is limited to what the natural sciences can demonstrate, or he must develop more appropriate criteria.[3]

Still, Grünbaum's defective criterion calls an important question to our attention: why should it be that science takes little or no notice of process? This question has a two part answer. First, while dates are a quantifiable property of things or events, being past, present or future is not. Physics is interested in quantifiable data concerning things. Since process facts are not properties like mass, velocity or spin, they do not add anything to the mathematical description of an object. For physics, whether an object still exists or not is of no importance in its mathematical description. In subatomic physics, for example, a past or future neutrino can have exactly the same properties as an existing neutrino. Thus physics can ignore the difference between past, present, and future in most cases.

Another fundamental reason why physics, and mechanics in particular, is often perceived as taking no notice of temporal process is, these branches of science are not meant to take notice of process (Meyerson, *Identity and Reality*, 215–233). Many of the basic laws of physics strive to be abstract and universal. Date and place are irrelevant. Take as an example Newton's third law of motion (viz., on action and reaction):

$$M \frac{\delta^2 x_1}{\delta^2 t} = -M \frac{\delta^2 x_1}{\delta^2 t}$$

This formula takes note of time (the "t" in the equation), but it is abstract and universal in that there is no reference to when this law applies. It is supposed to apply to all times and places equally. Of course, then, it takes no notice of the distinction between past, present and future.

Not only the laws, but the experiments which test the laws and theories of science are generally intended to be universal and repeatable. What date or time an experiment is performed is generally irrelevant. The same experiment should be performable in any laboratory at any time, given the same set of conditions. Thus, both scientific theories and their tests tend to be as universal and as abstract as possible. Philosophers, therefore, should not be quick to place weight on the fact that science tends to ignore the "passage" of episodes from past, to present, to future. For these reasons, the first movement of the argument from science cannot be accepted. Grünbaum and others like him expect something from science that it cannot provide, namely, the sole basis for all knowledge about time.

The second part of the argument from science, concerning the Special Theory of Relativity and its implications, is a much more persuasive one. Several philosophers have referred to it as the reason to reject a process view of time (e.g. Sellars, Reitdijk, and Fitzgerald). That the Special Theory of Relativity leads to a stasis view of time is clearly laid out in two articles in particular: Putnam, "Time and Physical Geometry," and Weingard, "Relativity and the Reality of Past and Future Events." Arguments from the Special Theory of Relativity to the stasis view made by other philosophers are quite similar to these two. Weingard is dependent on Putnam, so I shall focus first on Putnam.

Putnam's argument is a *reductio ad absurdum* based on two important assumptions (p. 240f.):

(9)   "All (and only) things that exist *now* are real."

(10)   "The principle that There Are No Privileged Observers: If it is the case that all and only the things that stand in a certain relation R to me-now are real, and you-now are also real, then it is also the case that all and only the things that stand in the relation R to you-now are real."

What is important about Putnam's article, compared to the others, is that he *begins* with a definition of "real" based on the process theory of time. He then argues that this definition, combined with the Special Theory of Relativity, leads to the stasis theory of time. Putnam begins with principle (9), but then finds reasons to reject it.

For Putnam, it is clear, relation R in (10) will be simultaneity with me-now (p. 241), as indeed principle (9) demands. But Putnam then points out that simultaneity is relative in the Special Theory of Relativity. The question then becomes, what things are genuinely simultaneous with me-now?

Realizing, further, that "is real" is transitive but "is simultaneous with me–now" is not (p. 242f.), Putnam defines "simultaneous-in-the-*observer's*-coordinate-system" as his relation R. By X "being real to" Y, one supposes that Putnam means a speaker at Y can truly assert that X is real. Furthermore, "is real" does not appear to be any kind of relation at all. Something either is real, or it is not, but this is not any kind of relation. But in this dialogue with Putnam, we will continue to use his phrases. These initial moves by Putnam set up the argument. The following diagram will illustrate the rest of it.

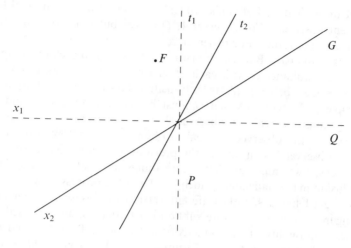

Figure 5.1

Imagine two observers at point *P*, each with her own reference frame, and associated coordinate system, which we will call S_1 and S_2. S_1 and S_2 are in relative linear motion. Now any observer in a inertial reference frame at *P* will note that causally connectable events in the light cone have the same before–after order, as long as said observer moves at a speed less than the speed of light (*c*) relative to *P*. In other words, if *A* and *B* are in the same light cone, and *A* is before *B* in time, (in other words, it is possible for a photon to pass between *A* and *B*) then *A* will be before *B* for all observers. There is, therefore, an absolute future, an absolute past and an absolute simultaneity in the Special Theory of Relativity. "Absolute" here means, the same for all observers or frames of reference. Robb (*A Theory of Space and Time*, 15f.) called the before-after order within the light-cone the "conical order" of events. Since no moving frame can have a relative speed greater than *c*, all observers recognize the absolute conical order of a particular series in such an order. Simultaneity is absolute for events at the same place. However, simultaneity is relative between here-now and points outside of my light-cone.

Putnam's argument is that two observers, one in S_1 and one in S_2 at *P*, will calculate different events outside the light-cone of *P* to be simultaneous with them at *P*. Say that observer 1 will calculate that *Q* is simultaneous with *P*, while for observer 2, *G* is simultaneous with *P*. Further, say that *G* is in the absolute future of *Q*, in *Q*'s light-cone.

One can see that on Putnam's principles, different objects are real for different observers. For observer 1, Q is real but G is not, since the latter is in the future. For observer 2, G is real but Q is not, since the latter is in the past. But the observers at P are real to each other since they are simultaneous with each other (in fact, absolutely simultaneous). Since "being real" is a transitive relation, given Putnam's principle (10), it follows that G must be real for observer 1 and in turn Q must be real for observer 2. In other words, G is real to observer 2, and observer 2 is real to observer 1, therefore G must be real to observer 1, contrary to the previous assertion. Hence Putnam concludes, "we must say that future things are real" (p. 246). This conclusion makes fallacious principle (9) and the process view of time.

Weingard has a slightly different version of this same argument. Weingard's argument is more subtle than Putnam's, and is based on the conventionality of simultaneity at a distance ("Relativity and the Reality of Past and Future Events," 120). He argues that since simultaneity outside of the here-now is a convention, any value for ε is equally valid (where $0 > ε < 1$; $ε = 1/2$ being standard simultaneity). This means that any event outside of my light-cone could be simultaneous with my here-now. He then argues (p. 121) that given Putnam's (9) and the transitivity of "is real to", events in P's absolute future must be real. Weingard correctly realizes that according to the Special Theory of Relativity, events in a given frame's forward light cone are absolutely future: "events in the upper lobe of P's light-cone are in P's (or events at P) absolute future" (*ibid.*) He continues:

> for any point F we can chose in the upper lobe of P's light-cone, we can find a point G outside P's light-cone such that F is outside G's light-cone. Since events at G are outside of P's light-cone, these events are real since me-now at P is real. But events at F are outside G's light-cone, and since events at G are real, so are the events at F.

The basic argument Weingard makes can be outlined this way (cf. the diagram above):

(11) Things at my here-now are real.
(12) All events outside one's light-cone are simultaneous with one's here-now.
(13) Things simultaneous to X are real to X.
(14) "is real to" is a transitive relation.
(15) G is simultaneous with here-now at P (from diagram).

(16)   *F* is simultaneous with *G*'s here-now (since *F* is outside of *G*'s light-cone).

(17)   *G* is real to here-now at *P* (from [15] and [13]).

(18)   *F* is real to *G* (from [16] and [13]).

(19)   *F* is real to here-now at *P* (from [14], [17] and [18]).

Both Weingard and Putnam, then, give a *reductio* to (9). For clearly, if future things are real, (9) cannot be correct.

Given the structure of any *reductio*, it is necessary to doubt one of the assumptions that the argument begins with. Both Putnam and Weingard want us to doubt (9). But they give no real reasons for this conclusion. Why should we doubt (9), instead of some other, perhaps less obvious and intuitively strong step in the argument? In fact, most people intuitively hold to (9), and I frankly see no reason to abandon it. As Mellor, a stasis theorist, correctly noted: "Tense [i.e. process] is so striking an aspect of reality that only the most compelling argument justifies denying it" (*Real Time*, 5). But this means that some other step in the *reductio* argument must be rejected. And the move that one ought to reject involves the simultaneity relation. Just what is it that satisfies Putnam's relation *R* in (10)? Since the relativity of simultaneity is based upon epistemology, not ontology, this is the step in the arguments of Putnam and Weingard that should be carefully examined. In other words, the relativity of simultaneity is based upon a limitation in human knowing, and it is only with the greatest care that we can make conclusions about reality on this basis.

When I say that the relativity of simultaneity is based upon epistemology, not ontology, I mean that because the speed of light is finite, and it is the fastest signal known to us, humans cannot know what is genuinely simultaneous in distant regions. But it does not follow from this epistemic limitation that there is no ontologically genuine simultaneity. Is there, in fact, a definite answer to what "now" is at distant regions? Against those who might say there simply is no discernible "now" in distant regions, or that it is a vacuous question to ask what moment is "now" in a distant region, consider the following. If we possessed an arbitrarily fast signal, we would know what moment was "now" in distant regions. We do not as a matter of fact have such a signal: but there is nothing illogical or impossible about such a signal from a philosophical point of view. The signal need not be composed of matter or energy as we know it: it is a purely logical point that is being made.[4] Unless one is willing to argue that reality must be limited to what humans can know, it follows from the fact that an arbitrarily fast signal could tell humans what time was now in distant regions, that there is such a thing as a time in distant regions genuinely simultaneous with my here-now.

Given the above argument, we need to take a very careful look at the role of simultaneity at a distance in the arguments of Putnam and Weingard. Both men assume only one view of simultaneity in the arguments, and this is where they are quite weak. There are, in fact, four different opinions in this matter, all based on results from Special Relativity. Let us refer to ontologically real simultaneity as "genuine" simultaneity. The first view is, then, that the only genuine simultaneity is simultaneity in the same place. There is thus no genuine simultaneity at a distance. Second, one can argue that there is one particular way of calculating simultaneity that is to be preferred in each frame, known as "standard simultaneity." The third view is that simultaneity is a convention. Fourth, one can develop a "cosmic time," in which there is a truly basic or proper frame in which events are genuinely simultaneous. Let us consider each option, in the context of the arguments made by Putnam and Weingard.

The first opinion was developed by Robb (*op. cit.*). There is a very important distinction between simultaneity at a distance (viz., relative simultaneity) and simultaneity at the same place (viz. absolute simultaneity). Robb argues that "the only events that are really simultaneous are events which occur in the same place" (p. 9). Sklar has recently argued that if we follow Robb's definition of simultaneity, we should arrive at the conclusion that all of reality is restricted to a single point ("Time, Reality and Relativity," 139f.)

> If the past and the future are to be declared unreal due to their 'epistemic distance' from us, what attitude are we to take toward events at spacelike separation from us? The answer is clear . . . everything outside the light-cone is unreal as well (p. 140).

Now the unreality of the past and future are not based on their "epistemic distance" from the present. Rather, the epistemic distance of past episodes is a result or symptom of the fact that past episodes do not exist. But Sklar's general point is well taken. If we follow Robb completely and fully – if we adopt absolute simultaneity as relation R – only what exists here-now is real. No distant event exists, therefore. But this result is unacceptable, to say the least.

The second view is based upon the assumption that light in a vacuum travels at the same speed in any direction. Granting this assumption, we then have a particular method of calculating distant simultaneity (i.e., in Reichenbach's terms, $\varepsilon = 1/2$). Adopting standard simultaneity yields the benefit of much simpler calculations. Malament has recently argued that, in addition to simplicity, standard simultaneity is the only simultaneity relation that can be defined on the basis of symmetric causal connectability ("Causal Theories of Time and the Conventionality of Simultaneity"). If these two arguments are followed, then distant simultaneity would not be a mere convention. Thus, standard simultaneity would yield the true, genuinely real events that are simultaneous with us in distant regions. And then, following Putnam's argument, we would conclude that "future things are real."

Adopting the thesis that light in a vacuum travels at the same speed in any direction is certainly the simplest theory. But simple theories that ignore facts, or lead to incoherent results, must be abandoned. If we adopt standard simultaneity with the observer as the ontological basis for deciding what is real in distant regions, this will lead us to reject a basic, fundamental intuition, namely the reality of process. It is better to adopt a different interpretation of the STR, which does not conflict with this fundamental intuition, if possible.

Another point against adopting standard simultaneity for ontological purposes is that in the real world, light does not travel in a vacuum. The Special Theory of Relativity must take into account the existence of matter, and this makes standard simultaneity not so obviously correct. It is more convenient to calculate on the basis that $\varepsilon = 1/2$, but we have little reason to assume that ontologically this is the way things are in themselves. In other words, granting the mathematical simplicity of standard simultaneity, this simplicity is gained only at the price of ignoring the world as it really is, that is, containing matter. Of course this still leaves the arguments of Malament. But Allen Janis has recently shown that Malament's arguments really have no greater force than the argument from simplicity ("Simultaneity and Conventionality"). And simplicity alone will not satisfy us, in the face of incoherence with fundamental beliefs about the world in which we act (viz. that process is real).

Weingard's argument assumes the truth of the third view of simultaneity, viz. that simultaneity is a convention.[5] By "convention" we mean that, since humans cannot discover exactly what distant event is simultaneous with our here-now, within certain limits any consistent answer is as good as another. This does not mean that there is no correct answer, as we have already argued. But if it is only a convention that an event at P is simultaneous with a distant event, then it follows that there is no absolute basis for saying that the distant event is real. Weingard's argument turns on the reality of distant events conventionally simultaneous with me-now. No argument is given for moving from a mere convention to true reality. As far as mathematical physics is concerned, one can treat simultaneity in the manner Weingard suggests. But this cannot satisfy the philosophical quest for a satisfactory ontology, not only of things in my light-cone, but of distant regions as well.

What has gone wrong with the three views already outlined? The basic mistake is made in assuming the *sufficiency of the Special Theory of Relativity for ontology*, in particular for the theory of time. How do we determine what is real in distant regions? Simply because all events are treated alike in space-time geometry does not mean that the concrete physical episodes which these "events" represent are all equally real (*pace* Yourgrau, "On Time and Actuality," and many others). In space-time geometry, it is necessary to treat events at all points in space and time equally. From a mathematical point of view, all events in space-time are equally real, in that all events in space-time are treated alike. Whether the point under consideration is past, present or future does not enter into the formulae. However, to move from this perspective to the perspective of concrete, physical reality is a matter of some delicacy. It does not follow that, because all points in a Minkowski diagram are mathematically alike, all events at those points are equally real from a concrete, physical perspective. The gravamen of this chapter is, a simple move from the mathematical perspective to the material perspective will lead to incoherence with our fundamental intuitions about the world in which we act and live.

Yourgrau and those making similar arguments have committed the fallacy of confusing the logical with the physical. They have taken a picture or truth from a logical, symbolic or mathematical realm and applied it with unfortunate results to the material realm of physical objects. The fallacy of confusing the logical with the physical is committed whenever one takes a truth from a logical or mathematical realm and applies it to the realm of physical reality with confusing or false results. For example, a philosopher would commit this fallacy if she were to define physical existence as "being the subject of a logical function." For such a definition confuses logical "existence" with concrete, physical existence. While all things that exist can be the subject of a logical function, not all things that are the subject of a certain logical function really exist. Some versions of the Ontological Argument also commit this fallacy. Further examples of the fallacy will be given later on in the chapter. David Pears warned us against this fallacy some years ago ("Time, Truth and Inference," 17f.):

> The timeless heaven of logicians has been lifted above the world of temporal happening. But this elevation is merely the work of thought . . . It is dangerous when people descend again from the logicians' heaven to the world of temporal happening without making it clear that they are descending.

Pears makes this warning to logicians, but it is equally important for mathematicians, scientists and philosophers of science to remember when considering the nature of time. The fallacy of confusing the logical with the physical is easy to make.

The STR teaches us a good deal about the world, but not all there is to know, even about time. For one thing, the STR is relativized by the *General* Theory of Relativity (Einstein, *Relativity*, appendix 5). The Special Theory of Relativity teaches us that there is an absolute conical order to time in our here, but that our knowledge of distant simultaneity is relative to the velocity of one's frame. The Special Theory of Relativity, therefore, does not really answer the question of which events in distant regions are real apart from human knowledge and experience. Some objects in distant regions, I have argued, are genuinely simultaneous. If one stays only within the realm of the Special Theory of Relativity, however, it appears that all events outside of my light-cone are equally real. But this mathematical viewpoint should not be imported into one's philosophical ontology.

The STR alone cannot help me discover just what distant events were genuinely simultaneous with some point in my past or present, at least for the purposes of ontology. There is no problem with saying that two distant events are relatively simultaneous, as long as we recognize the conventionality of our calculations. We must not assume, in an absolute and ontological way, that two distant events both existed at the same (relative) time we calculate them to have been at, based on the assumption that, e.g., $\varepsilon = 1/2$.

There does exist a theory which can answer our question as to the genuine simultaneity of distant events, and which does not lead to incoherence with (9). This is the fourth view of simultaneity, mentioned earlier. But this answer is theoretical only; one cannot use it to calculate distant simultaneity accurately, given the current state of science. With a cosmology based upon the General Theory, we can derive a simultaneity for distant events based on a cosmic time.[6] One first argues that there is a unique, local, basic frame of reference in which simultaneous events are genuinely simultaneous. We will associate this frame with a "fundamental particle" (for a definition, see Whitrow, 290.) To define this basic frame, think of the definite mean motion of matter in a region of the universe (say, a galactic cluster). The actual motion of large bodies (e.g. stars, galaxies) relative to this mean motion would be small compared to the speed of light. A "fundamental particle" is defined as a particle having this mean motion, and a mass equivalent to all the matter in that region. The frame of reference associated with this fundamental particle is then regarded as the basic frame for that region. In other words, $\varepsilon = 1/2$ for the basic frame, but not for other frames in relative motion to their fundamental particle (Whitrow, 293).

If we adopt Swinburne's "principle of equivalent clocks," viz. that "each process of the same kind occurs at the same rate on each equibasic frame" (*Space and Time*, 192), we can develop a "cosmic time" (the other two principles adopted by Swinburne as the basis of a cosmic time – isotropy and equivalent laws – are common enough in physics). We could then, again in theory, synchronize clocks in our basic frame with the clocks at distant fundamental particles. We would then know at what time a distant event occurred: at the instant shown by clocks in its basic frame. This principle of equivalent clocks cannot be held if we only consider the Special Theory of Relativity (as Swinburne realizes, p. 193). But modern cosmology based (among other things) upon the General Theory of Relativity, allows us to develop the notion of fundamental particles and basic frames of reference. This in turn leads to the idea of basic frames, in which simultaneity is genuine. The basic frames, then, are the frames in which we can make our simultaneity calculations, such that objects in distant regions are real now. Simultaneity-in-the-observer's-basic-frame satisfies Putnam's relation R in (10), without leading to incoherence. All frames of reference, then, are not created equal.

Some philosophers may ask, why adopt the convention of a fundamental particle, a basic frame, and a cosmic time? The answer to this question is, (*a*) the Newtonian concept of an absolute time is no longer viable, but (*b*) when we try to base an ontology for distant regions on the pure relativity of simultaneity found in the Special Theory of Relativity, it leads to incoherence with our fundamental intuitions about the world, and (*c*) the program suggested here also leads to laws and models for cosmology that are simple in form.

We have seen, then, that Putnam, Weingard and others who make similar arguments assume a particular view of simultaneity, and then equate this with *the* Special Theory of Relativity. In reality, they merely assume a particular interpretation of the STR. But there is no reason for philosophers to adopt the conclusion that future things are real, based on such an assumption. We are not forced by the Special Theory of Relativity to abandon (9), *pace* Putnam and Weingard. Much stronger arguments need to be given for us to give up this fundamental intuition. Furthermore, we have learned that any attempt to develop a theory of time (with a corresponding ontology) based solely on the Special Theory of Relativity is premature. Thus the "argument from science" for the stasis view of time should not be followed. But perhaps strong arguments can be given for the stasis theory – not supposedly "scientific" arguments, but philosophical ones.

PHILOSOPHICAL ARGUMENTS FOR THE STASIS THEORY

The Australian philosopher J.J.C. Smart has written, "I shall be advocating that we should think within a four-dimensional space-time framework. This has in fact been forced on physicists by the theory of relativity, but there are philosophical reasons for thinking in terms of space-time which are quite independent of relativity" (*Philosophy and Scientific Realism*, 130). The process theorist will have no objection to thinking and reflecting on reality from a four-dimensional perspective. But the fallacy of confusing the logical with the physical should give us some pause when moving from this reflective framework, to considering reality as it is in itself. Is this reflection upon reality from a four-dimensional perspective the only legitimate way of thinking about it? Is the world in itself a four-dimensional object, or is this just one helpful perspective, among other equally legitimate ones? Of course the utility and necessity of a stasis type of perspective on time, as a kind of "fourth dimension" for certain reflective activities, is not in question. What we want are reasons for adopting a stasis view of time as the only proper view of the physical universe as it is in itself. The reality of process strikes us forcefully as we act and react with the world. To quote Mellor, a stasis theorist: "Tense [i.e. process] is so striking an aspect of reality that only the most compelling argument justifies denying it" (*Real Time*, 5). Having already considered the argument from science, the philosophical reasons mentioned by Smart will now come under review. Only physical time will be considered, since proponents of the stasis view are generally speaking about this time. This excludes all problems with mental time, the specious present, and similar difficulties with the experience of time.[7]

There are eight arguments, other than those dealing with science, which philosophers have made in favor of the stasis theory of time: (*a*) The process view of time is contradictory; (*b*) all process facts can be reported as process-free facts; (*c*) true sentences containing process indexicals have process-free truth conditions; (*d*) the use of process facts like "*E* is past" in truth conditions makes sentences both true and false; (*e*) the idea of the "flow of time" requires another "supertime" to measure the rate of flow; (*f*) the process view requires a reason, above and beyond the fact that event *e* occurred at time *t*, to explain why event *e* occurred at time *t*; (*g*) the argument from the timelessness of propositional truth and "facts," and (*h*) the argument from the timelessness of the temporal relations "earlier" and "later". Let us consider each in turn.

Contradiction

I consider first the argument that the process theory of time is contradictory. The most famous advocate of this approach is John McTaggart Ellis McTaggart. In recent times, D. Hugh Mellor has revived this argument in his excellent work, *Real Time*.

In arguing that process is self-contradictory, no philosopher would deny that process is a universal aspect of human experience. In this sense, process is certainly "real." McTaggart raises a more fundamental issue: Is process a part of the real physical universe apart from human experience? His argument is, in brief, that process is not a part of reality because it is contradictory. Nothing contradictory can be real. Mellor (p. 92) tells us that the result of McTaggart's "proof" is: "Tense [i.e. process], it will turn out, is not being banished altogether, merely replaced where it belongs – in our heads."

The first step in this argument is to recognize, correctly, that past, present and future (abbreviated as *P*, *N*, and *F*) are mutually incompatible. It is analytically true that if an event is *N* then it is neither *P* nor *F*; if *F* then neither *N* nor *P*; and if *P* then neither *N* nor *F*. Thus if a state of an object is *P*, it cannot be *N* or *F*. If it is *N*, then it cannot be *P* or *F*, and so forth (McTaggart, *The Nature of Existence*, II, 20). The ordering of events in a *P–N–F* series McTaggart called the "*A* series". On the other hand, states or events can be ordered as earlier and later than one another, and this series McTaggart called the

"*B* series" (p. 10). The *B* series is unchanging. If World War I is before World War II it will always be so. The "flow" of time then consists in events of the *B* series having been F, then "becoming" *N*, and then becoming *P* for all time thereafter (pp. 13–15). In fact, every event in the *B* series must be *F* and *N* and *P*:

> If *M* is past, it has been present and future. If it is future, it will be present and past. If it is present, it has been future and will be past. Thus all three characteristics belong to each event (p. 20).

But this is contradictory, since *F*, *N*, and *P* are incompatible predicates. It is contradictory to suppose that any thing or event is both *F*, and *N* and *P*. Since nothing that is real can be contradictory, no event can really have A series predicates like *P*, *N* and *F*. The flow of time is contradictory, and for that reason unreal.

The obvious first response the process theorist will make is that no event in the *B* series is *P* and *N* and *F* *at the same time*. All events must be *P*, or *F*, or *N*, but none can be any two of these. McTaggart realizes this, and his rejoinder is that this explanation is itself dependent upon the *A* series. "When we say that *X* has been *Y*, we are asserting *X* to be *Y* at a moment of past time" (p. 21) He then continues:

> Thus our first statement about M – that it is present, will be past and has been future – means that M is present at a moment of present time, past at some moment of future time, and future at some moment of past time. But every moment, like every event, is both past, present, and future. And so a similar difficulty arises.

So to the response that at no moment of the past, for example, was a moment both *P* and *N* or *F*, McTaggart's response is that this does not banish the contradiction. It simply pushes it up into a "second-order" level of tenses (Dummett, "A Defense of McTaggart's Proof.") Instead of *P*, *N*, and *F* for any moment, we have nine tenses which every moment will possess: *PP*, *PN*, *PF*, *FF*, *FN*, *FP*, *NN*, *NP*, *NF* (where *PP* = past at a moment of past time, *NP* = present at a moment of past time, etc.) Now the new set of nine tenses, which each moment will possess, is just as contradictory as the first-order series of three tenses. Therefore, there is a contradiction in the first set of three tenses, and there is a contradiction in the second set of nine as well (Le Poidevin and Mellor, "Time, Change and the 'Indexical Fallacy'"). No matter how many levels of tense one adds, the contradiction does not go away, or at least so the argument goes.

One must be careful in such an argument not to commit an indexical fallacy (see Lowe, "Indexical Fallacy"). If a moment is past, it is wrong-headed to think that is "present in the past" or some such thing. For only present moments are present. A similar mistake would be made if, arriving at the end-point of our journey (which we referred to as "there" during the journey) one of our fellow-travelers remarked, "The 'there' has become 'here'." Once we are "here," then "there" becomes someplace else! What our friend should say is, the place we referred to as "there" on the journey is now "here." Likewise, once an episode earns the property of being past, whatever is present is at some other time. So McTaggart was somewhat confused when he wrote that "*M* is present" is logically equivalent to "future at some moment of past time" (p. 21). A better way to state such an idea is this: at some moment of past time, it was true to say, "*M* is future." The same is true of other process properties; for some past episode, *D*, it was true to say that "*D* is present." But this is not equivalent to *D* being present in the past, which is a confused and confusing phrase.

In order to shorten things, when a sentence of the form "X is present" was true in the past, I will say that *X was present-able*. Likewise, the same convention will apply to other process predicates. So when it is true to say that *D* is past, I will say that *D is past-able*. If something is future-able, in my convention, then it is true to say, "it is future." Using this convention, since *M* is present in McTaggart's example, M was future-able, is present-able, and will be past-able. In my convention, then, an iteration of verbs (was present-able, will be past-able, etc.) replaces the iteration of adverbial phrases in McTaggart (present in the past, past in the future, etc.) My convention is preferable because it avoids indexical mistakes.

Avoiding indexical mistakes, can one still generate a contradiction in the *A* series? Say some past event, *D*, occurred. Now *D was* present-able on the process view, but this is compatible with the fact that *D* is not present-able. Likewise, the sentence "the radio is on" *was* true, but today it is false. So only an event which is now both past-able and present-able will generate a contradiction in the *A* series, or process as I call it. Thus no contradiction results in *A* series, when indexical mistakes are avoided.

But what of the response that this avoidance itself depends upon the *A* series, and thus a vicious infinite regress is established (as Le Poidevin and Mellor claim)? An infinite regress can indeed be established, but it is not vicious. For no contradiction is ever generated at any of the levels. If an event is past, an infinite number of logically equivalent process properties could also be truly predicated of that event. As long as one remembers that no event can possess any two of the first level tenses, nor any two of the higher level tenses logically equivalent to any two of the first level tenses, no contradiction will ever result. So *D* is past, and this is logically equivalent to the fact that D was present-able, and at an earlier time *D* was future-able (to use second level tenses).

Further, one can go on without contradiction to a third level of tense, e.g., *it will be true to say that D* was present-able, which in McTaggart's terms is, *"D* is present in the past in the future." An infinite set of higher level tenses, logically equivalent to *"D* is past," can truly be predicated of *D*. However, at no level will a contradiction result in this example, as long as care is taken not to predicate of *D* tense which is logically equivalent to the first level tenses *N* or *F*. Surely Le Poidevin and Mellor are mistaken when they state (p. 535) that the process view implies all the infinite set of possible tenses are predicated of each event. On the contrary, such a position is true only if on the first level of tenses, the process view implies that each event is past, present and future. We have seen that this view, which goes back to McTaggart, is based upon an indexical mistake. No event, according to the process view, is ever any two of the first level of tenses. But if no event ever possesses all the first level tenses, then *a fortiori*, no event ever possesses all of the infinite higher level tenses.

A similar mistake often made is to think of process predicates as being "timelessly" predicated of some event (say, *M* is present) when in fact they are qualities which can truly be asserted of things at some times, but not at others. *M*'s being present is not something that is always true of *M*, even when we try to make an "eternal sentence" out of this fact (e.g. *"D* is present at 02–02–1989"). For example, Paul Horwich recently wrote:

> Suppose that at *t*1 I truthfully say "*E* is now", and at *t*2 I say "*E* is not now". Each of these utterances expresses facts, and each of these facts obtains throughout all time (*Asymmetries in Time*, 20).

Horwich errs in this quotation, if he thinks that *E*-is-now-at-*t*1 is ever true at any time *other than* *t*1. At *t*2, for example, one can only say that *E*-occurred-at-*t*1, and it is false to state that *E*-is-*now*-at-*t*1 for the simple reason that *t*1 is not *now*! If Horwich were correct, and process predicates could be understood to obtain throughout time, it is easy to see how a contradiction could be generated in the *A* series. But

Horwich is mistaken, and contradictions appear in the *A* series only when these or similar mistakes are made.

Yet another difficulty with positions such as McTaggart's is that they import the stasis theory of time into the argument, unfairly packing the bench against the process theory. On such views one gets the picture that all moments of time are somehow "there" no matter what time is "now." And this "thereness" is what allows all moments to be the subject of predicates like "future at a moment of past time." Levison ("Events and Time's Flow," 349) correctly notes that:

> McTaggart's argument against the reality of time's flow presupposes that events are atemporal or perhaps sempiternal entities which have various 'temporal properties' (McTaggart called them '*A*-series' properties), such as being past, present, or future.

It is this picture which generates the force of the paradox, and it is this picture which the process view of time denies in the first place. For all of these reasons, then, the argument that the process theory of time is contradictory fails.

Tenseless Facts

A more recent criticism of the process theory of time is this one: all process facts can be reported as process-free or "tenseless" facts, and in this way process facts reduce to process-free facts. In other words, for every true sentence containing process indexicals, there is another process-free true sentence reporting the same fact or event. Since the facts define what reality is, the argument runs, and process facts are not a necessary part of a complete description of reality, process should not be held a genuine part of reality. The question before us is, can every process fact be reported as a process-free fact?

Before we can further consider this question, I will need to clarify some terms, in particular, "fact" and "proposition." Just what is a fact? Some people see facts as states of affairs, others as true statements. I will follow Mellor, just for the sake of the argument, in understanding a fact to be whatever satisfies truth conditions, or in other words, whatever "makes" sentences true when they are true (*Real Time*, 42). It follows from this that there can be necessary facts, since there are necessary true sentences which have necessary truth conditions satisfied by necessary facts. It is a fact in this sense, therefore, that $2 + 2 = 4$. If a rational person knows a fact, it follows from this concept of "fact" that she will also know the truth value of any proposition she understands which asserts or denies that fact. So much, then, for the facts.

Following E. J. Lemmon, I also distinguish between statements and propositions.[8] A *proposition* I understand to be a state of affairs under a particular description. It thus turns out that what two synonymous sentences (which can bear a truth value) have in common is a proposition. So *"Der Schnee ist weiss"* and "Snow is white" express the same proposition. However, sentences which predicate the same properties to the same thing(s) at the same time and place, I will say, make the same *statement*. In these terms, if I say "My wife is intelligent and charming," and "Sally Padgett is charming and intelligent," I make the same statement even though I express two different propositions. Further, two different utterances of "It is raining," spoken a week apart, express the same proposition but make different statements.

With these clarifications in mind, we return to our question at hand. Let us say we have a specific dating system, by which we can specify any and every moment in our Measured Time. Further, let [D] stand for the true date of whatever moment happens to be present in this system, in any sentence in which [D] occurs. For convenience, I use the standard American dating system. Now the value of [D] changes over time, as different dates become present-able. That the present moment is [D], then, is a process fact. Process facts are what make sentences containing process indexicals true.

Can such a process fact be reported as a process-free or "tenseless" fact? Can the event of it now being a certain date be reported with a process-free sentence? Say that today is 02–02–1989 in our system. We can say that,

(20)   It is presently 02–02–1989.

This is clearly a process fact. Let's see if it can be reported as a process-free fact or event. Now a sentence like (20) is only true on at particular date; (20), then, is just one instance of a process type of fact. What we want is a process-free sentence that reports the same fact or event as (20). We might try:

(21)   It is 02–02–1989 on 02–02–1989.

If two facts are the same, surely propositions which report them will be true when uttered at the same time and place, by the same speaker. Note that (21) is always true, but (20) is only true on 02–02–1989. So

(21) and (20) do not report the same fact, in other words, the same fact does not make both (20) and (21) true. The fact that satisfies truth conditions for (20) is only a fact on a particular day, while the fact that makes (21) true is always a fact. In support of this conclusion, consider this: if a rational person knew only (21), she would not necessarily know the truth value of a sentence like "Today is 02–02–1989." She would need to know another fact, namely, what the date is today. Only a process sort of fact will tell us which date is present-able, while (21) will not. As Michelle Beer, a stasis theorist, correctly noted: "although we can know *a priori* that it is t_7 at t_7, we cannot know *a priori* that it is t_7 now" ("Temporal Indexicals", 160). Since knowledge of facts also gives us knowledge of the truth value of sentences asserting or denying them, (21) is not the same fact as (20).

Beer's own view is that (20) and (21) report the same event. For stasis theorists like Beer, the term "now" simply denotes some date, simultaneous with its utterance in a sentence. The event of today's date being present-able, then, is not an event over and above the tautology that today is today, or a certain date, say $T7$, is simultaneous with itself. As Beer wrote, "since 'now' denotes a time, 't_7's being now' . . . and 't_7's being simultaneous with t_7' are co-referential" (p. 162). Beer's claim is not the false one that "$T2$ is now," is the same proposition as "$T7$ is simultaneous with $T7$", but rather that they report the same event.

Surely there is something wrong with this view. As Beer herself noted, the second sentence is an analytic truth, while the first sentence is not. Furthermore, some date being simultaneous with itself is not an event, but a tautology true throughout time in every possible world. So however we understand event identity, (20) and (21) cannot report the same event. Consider further that a particular date is present-able, (i.e. that a process type fact is true), only when the date in question is present. "$T7$ is now" predicates a quality of the moment picked out by $T7$, viz. that it is the present date. Of course this quality only is true of $T7$ when $T7$ is present, and at other times such a predication would be false. "$T7$ is simultaneous with $T7$" does not predicate a quality of that moment which only obtains at certain times; rather $T7$ being simultaneous with itself is always true. The two sentences, then, do not even make the same statement. How can these two different statements report the same event? The first sentence reports an "event" (if it is an event at all) only true during $T7$; the other sentence is an analytic truth, which does not report any temporally located event. So Beer's theory cannot be accepted.

But perhaps I can suggest an improvement. Returning to the "same fact" approach, we could try,

(22) For any date, [D], if "Today is [D]" were uttered by a knowledgeable speaker of English at that date, it would express a true statement.

Yet (22) is not that same fact as some process fact. If one knows (22) in a "tenseless" or "eternal" sense only, then one does not know the present value of [D] in (22). For (22) must, because it is "tenseless" or process-free, apply equally to all dates, and therefore [D] cannot have a specific value for a "tenseless" fact like (22). Knowledge of (22) alone, then, will not give us knowledge of the truth value of (20). So (22) is no substitute for a process fact like what today's date is. One can only give [D] in (22) a specific value *if one knows the present date.* One has to know another fact, besides (22), to know the truth value of sentences like (20). So knowledge of what date becomes present-able, on different days, is knowledge of a process sort of fact, not knowledge of an "eternal" fact like (22).

Further consideration of what it means to understand and use a dating system makes the whole project of replacing process facts with process-free facts unlikely to succeed. Stasis theorists like Beer or Mellor rely upon a dating system, or a before-after structure such as the *B* series, to make their arguments. They fail to notice, however, that in order to understand and meaningfully use a system of dates, one must know what the date is today. To know that Alan Padgett is (tenselessly) born in 1955 does not tell you *how old* I am, unless you understand our dating system, *and know today's date.*[9] Knowledge of today's date, as we have seen, is a process fact which cannot be expressed in eternal or tenseless sentences; in other words, it is not a "tenseless fact." If all we knew were tenseless facts, which tell us nothing about the present (unless we know the present date!) we will be ignorant of important facts. If a rational person knew all and only process-free facts, she would still not know the truth value of sentences like "Today is Monday" or "Padgett is 35." Process facts, therefore, are different from proposed tenseless facts which are supposed to be the same. We couldn't fully grasp what the tenseless facts were, unless we understood the dating system – and we don't fully understand a dating system if we don't know what today's date is. Our knowledge of the world, then, includes process facts such as which date is present-able. There is no reason to think that reality is only made up of "tenseless" facts (see also Woltersdorff, "Can Ontology Do without Events?").

Tenseless Truth Conditions

At this point, the argument turns from "facts" to truths, or true sentences. As Mellor wrote concerning his project, "I argue in *Real Time* that reality is tenseless because all tensed truths have tenseless truth conditions" ("Tense's Tenseless Truth Conditions," 167). His position is that every true sentence containing process indexicals has process-free or "tenseless" truth conditions. This claim needs to be examined closely.

Making the standard distinction between a type and a token, if M is a past event, the sentence-token "M is happening now" if uttered now is false now (i.e. in the present).[10] A token of that type will also be false if uttered in the future. A token of that type was present-able, however, if uttered at the past moment when M took place. This example shows that the truth value of the statement made by a given sentence-token depends upon a relation between the statement and its truth condition at the moment that the token is uttered. In other words, the truth of the sentence when uttered depends upon the *Sitz im Leben* or truth-context. As Davidson realizes ("The Method of Truth in Metaphysics," 213):

> In adjusting to the presence of demonstratives, and of demonstrative elements like tense, in a natural language, a theory of truth must treat truth as an attribute of utterances that depends (perhaps among other things) on the sentence uttered, the speaker and the time.

Mellor's claim, to repeat, is that all sentence-tokens have process-free truth conditions. Take, for example, a particular token spoken on 4 April 1944:

(23)   Today is the 4th of April, 1944.

The normal, Tarski truth condition for this sentence is:

(24)   "Today is the 4th of April, 1944" is true iff today is the 4th of April, 1944.

Mellor wishes to transform (24) in order to give it a process-free truth condition. On his program, this would be:

(25) "Today is the 4th of April, 1944" is true iff the utterance of that token is simultaneous with 4 April 1944.

For any token sentence containing a process indexical, then, Mellor can give a process-free truth condition of the (25) sort.

Mellor's program, and others like it, raises the question of the equivalence of truth conditions for the same sentence-token. According to one theory of equivalence, two different truth conditions are equivalent if they have the same truth value in every possible world. Is this criterion an adequate one? Take the following sentence as an example:

(26) This square is rectangular.

The normal, Tarski sort of truth condition for this sentence would be:

(27) "This square is rectangular" is true iff this square is rectangular.

But consider this possible truth condition for (26):

(28) "This square is rectangular" is true iff a circle is round.

Like (24) and (25) above, both (27) and (28) will yield the same truth values for the token they are truth conditions for, in every possible world. Furthermore, whenever (26) is true, the truth conditions given by either (27) or (28) will be satisfied, and whenever it is false, they will not be satisfied. So why shouldn't (28) be a proper truth condition for (26), at least on the first criterion we are considering? Yet clearly (28) is not a proper truth condition for (26). Why not? In some sense, we want to say, the truth condition in (28) is *about a different fact* (or some similar expression) than the truth conditions in (27). Rectangularity in a square is a different fact from roundness in a circle. "Fact" however is a very slippery word. But it suggests a better criterion for truth condition equivalence.

A second criterion of equivalence for truth conditions could be: two different truth conditions are equivalent if and only if they make the same statement. Here "they make the same statement" is my technical way of saying "they state the same fact." Two sentences, remember, make the same statement if they attribute the same properties to the same thing(s) at the same time and place. On this second criterion, the truth conditions of (27) are not equivalent to the truth conditions of (28), since they do not make the same statement. Because it weeds out truth conditions of the (28) sort, the second criterion of equivalence for truth conditions is to be preferred.

Given this second, superior criterion for truth condition equivalence, can Mellor still legitimately carry out his program? Return to the example (23) given above. Mellor's sort of truth condition, (25), does not make the same statement as the truth condition for (23) given in (24). For the truth condition in (25) attributes simultaneity with 4 April 1944 to an utterance. This is a different object and a different property altogether from the truth condition in (24), viz. today being 4 April 1944 (the latter, I would say, is a process sort of fact – the former is not). Because (24) does contain proper truth conditions for (23), we ought not to accept (25) as stating proper truth conditions for (23), since (24) and (25) are not equivalent. Even though (25) yields the same truth values as (24), it does not make the same statement. In other words, the truth conditions suggested by Mellor are not about the same fact as the normal truth conditions which contain process indexicals. Given a more adequate criterion of equivalence for truth conditions, Mellor's program cannot legitimately be carried out: sentence-tokens containing process indexicals cannot all be given proper truth conditions which are process-free.

A stasis theorist like Mellor might claim, in response to my argument, that the first criterion is only meant to apply to contingent sentences, and not to necessary ones. Such a counter argument is *ad hoc*, adopted merely to save the appearances. Just what different criterion should we then apply to necessary sentences, if we adopt the first criterion for contingent ones? Why use two criteria when one will work? The second criterion has greater scope (viz. it applies to both necessary and contingent sentences) and greater simplicity; for these reasons it is a better one. In addition the criterion of sameness of statement satisfies our intuition about sameness of "fact" for truth conditions, while Mellor's criterion (i.e., the truth-conditions merely both being true) does not.

Perhaps a criterion of co-reference to the same fact or event might be proposed by the stasis theorist. Michelle Beer has in fact suggested something like it: however, I have already argued under the heading *Tenseless Facts* (above) that this criterion will not help the stasis theorist, any more than the first criterion did. Some process facts cannot be expressed in process-free sentences. Therefore, truth conditions will not be equivalent on this proposed criterion, when process-free truth conditions are given to sentences which express such process facts, e.g., "$T7$ is now." A sentence, "$T7$ is now," being simultaneous with *T*7 is not the same fact or event as the moment picked out by "*T*7" having the property of presentness.

Finally, a criterion on the basis of "believed by a rational person" might be proposed; two different truth conditions are equivalent if and only if any rational person who believed one would believe the other. However, even on this (rather dubious) criterion, Mellor's program fails. For one can easily believe that John is dead (our first truth condition) without also believing something about the temporal relations between a token of "John is dead" and the death of John (our other supposed truth condition). Some rational person may not know when the token was spoken, and thus have no belief about its temporal relations with the death of John, yet nevertheless believe that John is dead. It seems unlikely, then, that a stasis theorist would adopt such a criterion, for it does not save Mellor's program.

I conclude that no workable criterion for truth condition equivalence will save Mellor's program. For this reason, some sentences containing process indexicals cannot be given proper truth conditions that do not contain process indexicals. Reality does contain some process facts.

Process Truth Conditions

Mellor makes a slightly different claim against the process theory when he argues that using process indexicals like "past" in truth conditions will lead to absurd results. In particular, process indexicals in truth conditions will cause sentences to be both true and false (*Real Time*, 99; Le Poidevin and Mellor, 535). Mellor argues that a truth condition like *e is past* for tokens of "*e* is past" will either (i) generate again the McTaggart paradox, or (ii) have the contradictory truth values of true and false.

To take up the first objection: he would argue that the copula "is" in the truth condition must be either tensed or tenseless. If it is tensed (viz. the present tense) then the McTaggart paradox is generated all over again. If it is tenseless, then there must be some process-free or tenseless truth condition for the statement (*Real Time*, 92–101). Mellor argues that anyone who thinks the "is" in a sentence like "e is past" is tensed,

> will have to say what tense 'is' then has in 'e is now past'. It is clearly either tenseless or present tense – and if tenseless, McTaggart's

contradiction reappears at once, because '*e* is now past' is not always true . . . But if the 'is' in '*e* is now past' is tensed, as in '*e* is past', the same vicious regress appears in the form of the verb itself. For '*e* is past' meaning '*e* is now past' must now also mean '*e* is now now past' . . . the regress continues with '*e* is now now now past', '*e* is now now now now past', and so on *ad infinitum* (p. 97f.).

But as I have shown, even if we allow this proliferation of tenses, no contradiction results. Contradictions of the sort Mellor claims to find are based upon confusions already clarified through our discussion of McTaggart.

Yet in the above quotation, Mellor has a further problem with the tense of "is" in the truth condition we have suggested for "*e* is past." Let us allow, then, that some sentences can contain "omnitensed" verbs. An omnitensed verb is one which indicates a past, present or future tense as needed in the context. So one can say "Two plus two is equal (omnitensely) to four," and by this mean that two plus two was, is and will be equal to four. Likewise, "Ronald Reagan is (omnitensely) President," spoken today, expresses the proposition that Reagan was, is or will be President. If the predication of the omnitensed verb is understood to apply throughout time, then the verb should be understood as a conjunction (e.g. "is, was, and will be"); otherwise it will not, and the verb should be understood as a disjunction. Given such omnitensed verbs, the truth condition for tokens of "*e* is past" is, "*e* is (omnitensely) past [at the date when the token is spoken]." This convention solves Mellor's first problem.

To turn to another objection by Mellor, he holds that sentence-tokens like "*e* is past" will be both true and false in a tenseless perspective, when process indexicals are contained in their truth conditions.

> Since the truth-value of tensed tokens is never independent of their *A* series position, giving them now all the same truth-value will inevitably make some past or future tokens true and false. This, in token-reflexive terms, is McTaggart's contradiction . . . The alleged fact [viz., pastness] would by definition have to make all tokens of the type true, regardless of their *A* series positions, whereas in fact some are always true and others always false. Hence the contradiction. (p. 100f.)

I am not at all sure what Mellor means by "giving them now all the same truth-value," which in turn "makes some past or future tokens true and false." Tokens of many sentence-types will be true if uttered at some times, and false if uttered at others. Mellor admits as much (p. 40f.) So what is wrong with stating that tokens of the sentence-type "*e* is past" will be true if *e* is past at the date when the token is spoken? At the date for some tokens, *e* shall be past. But at the date for other tokens, *e* shall not be past. No contradiction results from the application of this truth condition for "*e* is past," nor does it yield both true and false as a truth value for any token of that type.

The central problem, for Mellor, has to do with his sentence: "The alleged fact would by definition have to make all tokens of the type true, regardless of their *A* positions, whereas some are always true and others are always false." For Mellor, a proper truth condition will apply to all statements made by tokens of that type, whether such statements were made in the past, present or future. He claims, however, that process facts cannot be made part of truth conditions without generating a contradiction: "the truth conditions of tensed sentences are either tenseless or self-contradictory" (p. 101) Can this be correct?

Consider the sentence-type,

(S)   John is dead.

Concerning this sentence, Mellor claims,

> TENSED sentence types cannot be made true by TENSED facts, like the fact that John's death is PAST. For suppose this alleged fact makes *S* true. Until John dies it is *not* a fact, so until then *S* is false, i.e. all its tokens are false. And afterwards, when it *is* a fact, *S* is true, i.e. all its tokens are true ("Tense's Tenseless Truth Conditions," 171).

If Mellor is right in this claim, then making process facts part of the truth condition for sentence-type will cause such sentences to be both true and false, which is absurd. But Mellor makes a mistake when he thinks that because John is not dead, then the sentence-*type* (S) is false! Sentence-*types* are not false simply because some tokens are false, nor are types true simply because some tokens are true. As Mellor himself wrote: "The truth and falsity of tensed sentences, therefore, are properties of their tokens rather than their types" (*Real Time*, 40). Now the truth condition of (S) is surely: "John is dead" is true iff John's death is (omnitensely) past [at the time the token is uttered]. So against Mellor, "all" tokens of (S) are not false "until John dies," since some tokens of (S) may well be uttered after John dies. And these future, true tokens are just as much tokens of the sentence-type (S) as those spoken before John dies. What Mellor surely means is that some tokens of (S) are false, namely those spoken before John is dead, while other tokens are true, namely those spoken after he is dead. But this fact, properly stated, is not absurd. For consider the sentence-type,

(R) The radio is on.

(R) expresses a proposition, but it does not make a statement, as a type. For in order to make a statement, (R) must refer to a particular radio at a particular time. But such reference will only take place when particular tokens of (R) are uttered. In its truth-context, a particular token of (R) will refer to a particular radio at a particular time. Therefore, (R) as a sentence-type does not make a statement. And (R) as a sentence-type is neither true nor false – truth or falsity can only be attached to particular utterances of (R), that is, to tokens of that type.

The same is true of (S). As a type, it is neither true nor false *per se*. Mellor is confused to assert that either, (*i*) *all* of the tokens of (S) are false, or (*ii*) this makes the sentence-type (S) false. Sentence-types like (R) or (S) are neither false nor true *as types*, but only particular tokens of them. The statements made by such tokens can, as Mellor insists, have permanent truth values. But the (permanent) falsity of some token of (S) does not cause (S) itself to be false. Tokens of (S) uttered before John dies make false statements, and such a statement is never true. Likewise, tokens of (S) spoken after John is dead are true, and such statements are always true. The truth conditions I have suggested for (S), then, do contain process indexicals (viz. "past"). *Pace* Mellor, however, no absurdity results, nor does this truth condition make tokens both true and false.

Does Time "Flow"?

Another argument raised by stasis theorists against the process view of time is, the idea of the "flow of time" requires another "supertime" to measure the flow. This argument is often associated with D. C. Williams ("The Myth of Passage"), though others have made it, too (e.g. Black, "The 'Direction' of Time," 185; Smart, 136). Williams writes:

> as soon as we say that time or the present or we move in the odd extra way which the doctrine of passage requires, we have no

recourse but to suppose that this movement in turn takes time of a special sort (p. 463).

Black puts the argument this way:

> if the claim that time always flows had a literal sense, we ought to be entitled to ask how fast time is flowing. And if so there would have to be a supertime for measuring the rate of flow of ordinary time (p. 185).

This argument is confused, as Zwart has shown (*About Time*, 69–71). To speak of the rate, tempo, or velocity of any process is to compare either the number of events with a given unit of time, (e.g., revolutions per minute) or the rate of change with a given unit of time (e.g., the GNP rose 7 per cent per annum). But the given unit of Measured Time, as argued in chapter one, is defined by measurement against a standard physical process or change, which we can call a "standard clock." The choice of standard clock and of units of time is an open one, as long as the clock chosen is accurate and regular (and people will want to find the most accurate such possible), and the unit of time has a publicly defined measurement against the standard clock. What Williams and Black are speaking of is a "supertime" which could measure the rate of the flow of time, or in which time itself would move. But having been confused by the grammar of questions like, "how fast does *x* go?," they believe that one can put "time" into the question as the "*x*," and so ask how fast time goes. But this is a question that makes no sense. In reality, they are asking to compare the standard clock with itself.

If we have a unit of time (say, a second) and we want to know how fast time goes, we can only compare our unit of time with the standard clock, which measures intervals of time for us. And of course time (viz., the standard clock) moves at a rate of one second per second, (or whatever standard unit of Measured Time one chooses). It is not the answer which is absurd so much as the question itself. There is no need for a "supertime" to measure the flow of time, any more than the movement of time takes "time of a special sort."

If we change the metaphor on Williams, and talk of objects "moving through time," then his entire position collapses. Williams and Black have both been fooled by the grammar of metaphor. Time does not *literally* move, and the process theory is not committed to the proposition that it does. It is we and our natural world with us that "move," (or more correctly, change) and Measured Time is generated by comparing any process of change in our world to a standard process ("standard clock").

The Problem of "Now"

There is a sixth objection raised by the stasis theorist against the process theory of time. Like the others, it is based upon a misunderstanding of the latter perspective. The process view (they argue) requires a reason, above and beyond a reason for the fact that event *e* occurred at time *t*, to explain why event *e* occurred "now", when "now" is time *t*. This objection is made by Smart (p. 135), and Grünbaum ("Temporal Becoming," 344) points to this as an "important perplexity" for the process view. Smart's argument reads as follows:

> If past, present and future were real properties of events, then it would require explanation that an event which becomes present in 1965 becomes present at that date and not at some other (and this would have to be an explanation over and above the explanation of why an event of this sort *occurred* [tenselessly] in 1965). Indeed, every event is 'now' at some time or another, and so the notion of 'now' cannot be that of an objective property in nature which singles out some events from others.

The substance of Smart's argument contains two objections against the process view. One has to do with the idea of an event "becoming present" at a specific time, and the other with the ontological "cash value" of the idea of presentness.

Consider the first of these two objections. To ask the question of why an event "becomes present" at a certain date is to have in mind already the B series of events spread out in the fourth dimension. Now the process theorist does not deny that it can be helpful in some cases to think in this manner. But the *B* series of events is ontologically dependent upon the *A* series events of "now" in the following manner. An event can occur (tenselessly) in the *B* series *only if* it was, is, or will be "now." Therefore, once one assumes the *B* series perspective, as Smart does, no further reasons can be given for why an event occurs (tenselessly) in 1965. For these same reasons are exactly the ones which must be given to explain why the event occurred "now," when the date in question was the present. Smart's first objection simply misunderstands the ontological basis of the *B* series, as the process theorist views things.

As for the second objection, Smart believes that since every event is *N* at some time or other, then *N* cannot be "an objective property in nature which singles out some events from others." Now we saw with Putnam's principle (9) that "is present" and "exists" are co-referential terms.[11] While these terms are not synonymous, they do pick out the same set of objects. So we might ask Smart, what "objective property in nature" does existence predicate of a (possible) object? In what sense does existence single out some possible events from others? When he answers this question, he will have answered the question of what subset "is present" selects out of the set of all possible events. We shall have to leave that matter at that. To develop a satisfactory account of the way in which existence is a property would take us too far afield from the subject of this chapter.[12]

Smart might reply to this that he can use the word "exists" tenselessly, as indeed he uses the word "occurred" in the quotation above. All the events in space-time exist (tenselessly): what subset does the "now" pick-out of this class? Up to this point, we have been employing the convention of allowing a "tenseless" use of a word in the same manner as Smart. But now this convention must be carefully examined. From a process perspective, Smart's use of words in a tenseless sense is not properly called "tense*less*" but "*omni*tensed." When Smart uses the word "occurred" in a so-called tenseless way, he means to include all things that occurred *P*, *N* and *F*. In other words, he means to include *all tenses*. Since any object which ever exists either existed (*P*), exists (*N*) or will exist (*F*), tense is caught up with reference to things which ever exist. If Smart were really speaking *apart from any tense at all* ("tenselessly"), then the word "occurred" *could not refer to any event in time*. What Smart clearly wants to include is all events in time. So he must speak omnitensely.

Two objections have been given to the idea of omnitensed rather than tenseless predication for propositions. First, Sellars objects that it does not do justice to mathematical propositions ("Time and the World Order," 529f.) But just what is the force of this objection? Take Sellars' example:

(29)   Two plus two is (omnitensely) equal to four.

Clearly from (29) a speaker could choose a particular tense, and say "Two plus two *was* equal to four." Sellars is right to point to the oddity of this sentence. To someone who expressed (29) this way, we would want to say, "Yes, but that is not enough. You have spoken the truth, but not all of it." We would, in fact, want to insist that two plus two was, *is and will be* equal to four. But this last idea is what (29) is supposed to signify! To limit (29) to just one tense is to misunderstand the convention of omnitensed predication.

A second objection comes from Zimmerman. She argues ("God and Time," 133f.) that a timeless world, with no past, present or future, is logically possible. Yet our concern is with propositions expressed in the actual world, which surely is temporal in the sense under consideration. Further, and decisively, one can understand omnitensed predication in necessary propositions to refer to the tense of any and all worlds in which the proposition would be expressed. This would include worlds which have no time as we know it; for even such timeless worlds, like God in the traditional view, have a present-like timeless instant which could serve as the "tense" for propositions timelessly believed in that world. Finally, the concept of omnitensed predication serves as a better model of predication in all types of propositions than the timeless predication Sellars and Zimmerman argue for. As argued against Smart, contingent propositions about the real world are not normally thought of as "tenseless" in the sense of excluding all tenses (*P, N* and *F*). This means that omnitensed predication is a simpler theory than dividing all propositions/sentences into "tensed" and "timeless." What is more, sometimes we argue about whether a proposition is a necessary one or not. Does this mean that if one changes one's mind about whether "a cat is an animal" is a necessary proposition, one must also change one's mind about whether it contains tensed or timeless predication? I certainly am not aware of any such change, when I contemplate changing my mind. For these reasons, omnitensed predication is preferable to some notion of "tenseless" predication.

With this digression's lessons in mind, the answer to Smart is clear. What subset does "now" (or "is present") pick out from the set of all existing (omnitensely) events? Clearly, it picks out *N* events, and excludes *P* and *F* events. Smart's objection that all times (and thus events at those times) are "now" is incorrect. Only present events are now. Similar indexical errors have already been corrected in other stasis theorists, and this need not detain us again. The word "exists," when not used omnitensely, picks out all events which exist, and excludes events which used to exist as well as events which will exist. The process view simply is that present episodes of real objects are alone real: future episodes and past episodes alike are not real in the fullest sense (the past used to be real, but this is a different matter altogether).

Smart might reply that N is only a temporal instant, and therefore can only select from the set of all existing (omnitensely) episodes those episodes which take place in an instant. A. C. Ewing, for example, specifically makes this point (*Value and Reality*, 181f.,281f.), Now things have no temporal parts, as Mellor correctly points out (p. 104f.). Any time-slice of a thing contains the whole of that thing. A time-slice out of the world-line of a proton, for example, contains the whole of that proton. So N can be used to select existing things from the set of all existing (omnitensely) things. Things are wholly present at each instant of time throughout their lifetimes. The problem is that all episodes and many events must have duration in order to occur. Say we are at a wedding, and that the wedding lasts one hour. The wedding then has a duration of one hour. But N does not have a duration of one hour (the objection could run), but only of a durationless instant. So does the wedding exist when we are 30 minutes into it? The obvious answer is yes, but how does the process view justify this answer?

The process defender could respond to this objection in the following manner. Let NOW stand for the instant that separates past from future. Let E be any episode of a thing or any event, and $E(x)$ be any durationless time-slice of that same event or episode. We can then say that for any E and for any x, E is N if and only if there is an $E(x)$ which is NOW. To return to the wedding example, the wedding exists because the instant of NOW occurs within it (30 minutes within it, to be exact).

The same holds for episodes, as well as events. Any episode of a physical object has some duration (Prior, *Time and Tense*, 4). Can one of these episodes, then, be N if NOW is durationless? Yes, because NOW only points to those episodes which are real within the history of all objects. It does not tell us how long those episodes last. Since episodes of various objects come and go at various rates, NOW must be durationless if it is going to pick out all and only those episodes that are real, without selecting two disjunct episodes of a quickly changing object, both of which cannot coexist. But this does not mean that NOW reduces all episodes to a durationless instant. Each episode in the history of an object has its own duration, depending upon what sort of object it is, and the kinds of changes it undergoes. NOW simply points out which episode is real. Of course other non-present episodes were real, or will be real – but this means they have no plain and simple reality without qualification.

We can now see more clearly the validity of our answer to Smart's first objection, concerning why an event "became present" in 1965. An event "became present" (to use Smart's question-begging terms) in 1965 because it existed ("occurred", "was real," or "happened") in 1965. Smart's quest for a reason over and above this reason rests on the fallacious idea that, for any event E, there is an event of "E becoming present" over and above the event of E existing or occurring at all (Gale, 242f.; Loizou, *The Reality of Time*, 5f.) And again we find underneath this notion the picture of all events spread out in space-time, and the "now" moving over these unchanging events like a spotlight sweeping over a dark landscape. Other stasis theorists make the same error in characterizing the process view (e.g., Sellars, p. 554). As Williams puts this same point (p. 461),

> over and above the sheer spread of events, with their several qualities, along the time axis, which is analogous enough to the spread of space, there is [according to the process view] something extra, something active and dynamic, which is often and perhaps best described as "passage."

The reason that Williams finds this passage a "myth" is that he has already contradicted it by assuming from the beginning a stasis theory of time. Smart, Sellars and Williams might reply that our understanding of "is present" assumes the reality of becoming, or of process, which they deny. This is correct, but then Smart's objection is suppose to raise an "important perplexity" against the process view of time. Of course it is necessary to assume the process view in order to expound and defend it against misunderstanding. Thus the important perplexity is only perplexing if one assumes the stasis view from the beginning.

Timeless Truth

Yet another argument in favor of the stasis view of time is more positive. Rather than criticizing the process view of time, this argument is based on the timelessness of propositional truth and "facts." It is generally but not universally held that if a statement is true, it is always true. Now the argument over whether true statements are always true falls within the sphere of the philosophical logic, not the philosophy of time (Butterfield, "Prior's Conception of Time.") Since this essay does not propose to solve every problem in philosophy, we shall accept – for the sake of the argument – the idea that true statements are always true, and false ones are always false. Does this idea of the omnitemporal nature of truth lead to the stasis theory of time?

Some analysis of statements is called for at this point. Recall our previous argument that only sentence-tokens always make statements. Two further reasons can be given for this view. First, take as an example the sentence-type:

(30) "It is raining."

Whenever this sentence-type is expressed in a particular token, the truth of the statement made will depend upon a its truth-context. The truth-context always includes the time of utterance. At some places and times, a token of (30) will make a false statement; at other times and places it will make a true statement. But if the sentence-type (30) made a statement as type, then it would be both false and true. For the sentence as type must apply to all of its tokens, whatever the time and place of utterance. Thus (30) when understood as a type, cannot make a statement, since no statement can be both true and false. This analysis could apply to many, many sentence-types. It is best, therefore, to hold that the sentence-type does not as type make a statement (whether sentence-types express a proposition will depend upon whether one holds that all propositions must be either true or false).

We are now in a better position to consider the argument for the stasis view from the timeless truth of statements and "facts." Sellars put the problem this way (p. 535):

> Unless, therefore, we are going to abandon the idea that statements about the future are ever true, we must find some explanation of how there can be the fact that S will be Φ_3 in 1959 although the episode of S's being Φ_3 does not exist.

And Schuster puts the same point in a slightly different way ("On the Denial of Past and Future Existence," 453):

> The point here at issue is whether one can agree that, at a certain time, there is a fact at that time, without also agreeing, simply, that there is a fact at that time.

Oaklander, Mellor and others have similar positions. The argument seems to run that, since something is a fact at time $T3$, and it is thus always a fact and can be expressed by a true statement that is always true, then in some way the fact of "the fact at $T3$" must always exist.

Here it will be helpful to make a distinction similar to our earlier distinction between (concrete) episodes and (propositional) states. There is a distinction between a "fact" from a logical point of view, and a "physical" fact. A "fact" from a logical point of view is the truth expressed by a true statement. Thus it is a "fact" that $2 + 2 = 4$, or that "London is south of Cambridge." A "physical" fact, on the other hand, is an event or some state of affairs in the world. I will call such things "physical states of affairs" (not to be confused with a "state" as I use this term). Examples of a physical state of affairs would then be: my having the thought I am having now, the hotness of the sun, and the liquidity of the water in my cup. Now physical states of affairs can only be real or existing events. Thus the difference between the stasis and the process views of time can be put this way: is it now a physical state of affairs that the sun rises (tenselessly!) on 4 July 1776? The process theorist says "No," and the stasis theorist says, "Yes." For the stasis view insists that, in some way or other, the event of the sun's rising exists (tenselessly) on 4 July 1776.

It is clear, given this important distinction, what the process theorist will think about Sellars' problem regarding the timelessness of true statements or "facts." The contingent facts about the world which are "always" true, because they are always a "fact," are facts from a logical point of view, i.e. truths. They are not physical states of affairs. The major problem with the stasis theory, then, is that it confuses physical "fact" (physical states of affairs) with "fact" from a logical point of view (truths).

This is another example of a philosophical fallacy which I have already considered to some extent, namely, *confusing the logical with the physical*. The two perspectives – concrete or physical *vs.* logical or mathematical – must be kept carefully distinguished if confusion and error are to be avoided. And it is not only stasis theorists who commit this fallacy. A. N. Prior once wrote, "there were no facts about me before I existed . . . so there will be no facts about me after my existence" ("Thank Goodness That's Over," 83). Here Prior was clearly thinking about physical states of affairs. But it does not follow that because there are no physical "facts" about Prior now that he is dead, there are no "facts" *from a logical point of view* about him after his death. Even Prior admits that "there is indeed a sort of 'being' that Napoleon has even after having ceased to 'exist'; he is at least a subject of predicates still" (*ibid.*) The statement made by me yesterday, "It is raining," is a "fact" in a certain sense; it is a truth. But it was only a physical state of affairs or physical fact at the time and place in question. It is no longer a physical fact. The statement is true, but it does not refer to an existing episode. Given that such a "fact" (that is, true statement) is always true, it does not follow that the rain on that day always exists, or "tenselessly" exists, or any of a number of confused expressions and ways of thinking (see Levison, 347–348). A statement which is always true can be made with sentences that use different grammatical tenses. Assuming it rained yesterday, this fact can be expressed two days ago as, "It will rain tomorrow," yesterday as "It is raining," and today by "It was raining yesterday." I will say of such statements that they are *omnitensely true*, since the same true statement can be made using different tenses. Yet there is no clear path from the omnitensed truth of "facts" from a logical point of view to the stasis theory of time. As I have already argued at length, some facts (i.e. some truths) cannot be expressed with process-free sentences.

Timeless Temporal Relations

A final argument for the stasis view of time is based upon the timelessness of the temporal relations "earlier" and "later". This argument is associated with Bertrand Russell ("On the Experience of Time.") His view has been extensively defended in a recent book by Oaklander (*Temporal Relations and Temporal Becoming*). The fundamental insight of this argument for the stasis view of time is, the temporal relations "earlier than" and "later than" are not themselves in time. For Russell, at least in 1915, P, N and F are relations between subject and object, while earlier and later are relations between object and object. Of course in this Russell simply assumes the stasis theory of time. But the point made is a strong one. For any physical object there will be some episodes which are before others. But this temporal relation is not itself in time. Indeed, I cannot think of any relation, *qua* relation, that is "in time" in this sense. Considered in itself, "earlier" is a possible relation events can have to each other: it is a universal, and as such does not occur at any time. Universals are *instantiated* at a time, however. Think of three states which refer to episodes of an object in Measured Time, and call the episodes which these states refer to $S1$, $S2$ and $S3$. Say that $S1$ is at time $T1$, $S2$ is at $T2$, and $S3$ is at $T3$. The temporal relation $S1$-earlier-than-$S2$ does not change, and is not itself in temporal relationship with anything. This fact, $S1$-earlier-than-$S2$, "neither stands in temporal relation to anything nor obtains at certain times nor obtains at every time" (Oaklander, 17.) Now this statement of Oaklander's is ambiguous between:

(31)   *S*1-earlier-than-*S*2 is true and asserting so at any time is true;

and

(32)   *S*1-earlier-than-*S*2 is "timelessly" true.

Now we can accept (31), but have argued above that (32) is an infelicitous way of understanding truths. Schuster has called the complex set of facts that is a temporal relation "occasions of precedence" ("On the Denial . . ."). Now like all true statements, or "facts" from a logical point of view, such occasions of precedence do not come into being, nor pass out of being. They exist, in Oaklander's badly chosen phrase, "eternally" (*ibid.*) since they are omnitensely true. The claim of the stasis theorist, then, is that the process theory cannot account for these "eternal" temporal relations.

In light of the answer to the problems considered above, it is clear what the answer will be to this Russellian conundrum. Temporal relations like *S*1-earlier-than-*S*2, or *S*3-later-than-*S*2 are "facts" from a logical point of view. Such relations are instantiated at a time, viz. over the whole period of time they cover. The relation *S*1-earlier-than-*S*2 is instantiated in the period of time *T*1 to *T*2, inclusive. I cannot see how Oaklander claims that such relations do not obtain at a time; surely they obtain over the time during which they are instantiated. Take an analogy: it has always been true that I am (omnitensely) born before my brother Carl. The relation of "born before" is a universal, and as a universal does not occur at any time. However, the relation Alan-born-before-Carl *was instantiated* at a particular time, viz. the time of and between our birthdays. The process theorist can agree, if need be, that "facts" like *S*1-earlier-than-*S*2 or Alan-born-before-Carl are "eternal" in that they are omnitensely true. Tensed sentence-tokens affirming their existence all make statements which are true, always were, and always will be. From this is does not follow, however, that the episodes referred to by *S*1, *S*2 and *S*3 exist eternally, anymore than it follows that Carl and I are "eternally" born, or exist "eternally." Oaklander and others who follow this argument have committed the fallacy of confusing the logical with the physical.

Having considered both the scientific and the philosophical arguments in favor of the stasis theory of time, I find no reason to believe this theory is true. Universal human experience leads to something like the process view. The process view is not contradictory, and it does allow for the omnitensed nature of true "facts" (better, truths) and temporal relations. Neither science in general, nor the Special Theory of Relativity in particular, force us to abandon the process theory. On the other hand, the stasis view rests upon a logical mistake: confusing the logical with the physical. In the argument from science to the stasis view, some philosophers made a similar mistake: they confused the mathematical (for example the Minkowski diagram) with the physical. Because of this mistake at the heart of the stasis theory of time, and because the process theory is not incoherent, I reject the stasis view in favor of a process theory of some kind.

Developing a full-blown, adequate theory of time would take us too far from the subject of divine eternity. Still, having learned about time from the debate with the stasis theory, it might be well to summarize what has been learned.

1. Only presently existing episodes of objects have reality in an unqualified sense. Past and future episodes can be thought or spoken of, but are not real. They will be real, or have been real, but this is simply to admit that they are not real *simpliciter*.

2. Some truths or facts cannot be expressed with process-free sentences, even though tensed sentences expressing such truths make statements which are always true.

3. The NOW is a durationless instant which picks out those episodes of objects which are real. This does not mean that the present episode of any given physical object is a durationless instant.

4. In order to avoid error and incoherence, care should be taken not to confuse the logical with the physical, and not to assume the stasis view in explaining the process view of time.

5. It is confusing to think of an event E "becoming present" as itself a "metaevent." This operates out of the picture of all events as already existing in some way or another, and then "becoming" present by entering the stage of history. If the event in question is understood as a state (a truth or "fact" from a logical point of view) it does not "become" at all! If, on the other hand, the event in question is seen as a physical state of affairs (a "physical fact"), it does not "become present" so much as become *simpliciter*: it comes into existence.

I have rejected the stasis theory of time. But this means that the coherent theory of divine timelessness developed in the previous chapter must also be rejected. Where does this leave us theologically?

6   A New Doctrine of Eternity

The relationship between God and time has formed the epicenter of our entire discussion. Since God changes, there is some sense in which he is temporal. It follows from this that God is in time. God really changes, as opposed to mere relational change, because of his real relations with the world. Remember principle (D2) from chapter one? It states that,

(D2)   Necessarily, if a change occurs then a duration occurs.

Since God really changes in relationship with the world, God must in some way be temporal. For whenever a change occurs the subject of the change goes through some interval of time. Therefore, God is not absolutely timeless, and the traditional doctrine of eternity must be abandoned.

Yet this answer does not fully satisfy us at some deeper theological level. As the infinite Creator of all things, including time itself, God should in some way transcend time. Transcendence, of course, is a metaphor like so much of our talk about God. In this chapter I will unpack the idea of God "transcending" time more fully. I hope to show three aspects of this transcendence: God's life is the ground of time; God is the Lord of time, who is unchanged by time and lives forever and ever; and God is relatively timeless.

GOD AS THE GROUND OF TIME

A timeless world is not an impossible world. This much, at least, has been argued well and at length by defenders of the traditional doctrine of divine eternity. Duns Scotus and his modern followers have shown us the ways in which something could be "alive" in an absolutely timeless world. Since an absolutely timeless world is possible, and God could live in such a world, it follows that the actual world could have been timeless. This means, further, that God has chosen eternally to live the kind of life he does, and has chosen eternally to have a temporal universe in which to live. This choice is an eternal one, in that it must have always been made. There is no time before which this choice was made.

God's choice, then, to live a certain kind of life – to be dynamic, active, changing – is the ground of the temporality of the universe. I have suggested that we understand time to be the dimension of the possibility of change. This dimension, like space, is a creation of God's. The world could have been different. God's choice (eternally) to live a certain kind of life, a temporal and changing life, is the ground of time. Time need not have been in God's creation. This is one way in which God transcends time.

GOD IS THE LORD OF TIME

To speak of God as the "Lord" of time is just another sort of metaphor, of course. What are the implications of this metaphor? First of all, it signifies that God has a design or plan which he is enacting in history. God is the Lord of heaven and earth, of time and eternity. Any changes that happen on earth do so because of the will and power of God, which sustain all changing things in their being. Even free and random events take place within the parameters established by God, and the things which undergo these random or free changes exist only because God causes their continued existence. Thus nothing happens outside the will of God, even though God does not will every event which takes place to happen in exactly the way it does. God sets the parameters within which all events take place, even those free events whose exact outcomes are not willed by God (i.e. are undetermined).

To say that God is the Lord of time would include the fact that he is not limited by any amount of time, either in the actions he can perform or the length of his life. While humans can fear the passage of time, because it brings them closer to the end of their life, God is everliving. He cannot die, and has nothing to fear from the future. Moreover, for God time does not press. Because of his infinite wisdom and power God is not limited in the amount of things he can accomplish, or problems he can work through, in a limited period of time. Nothing happens outside of his will, knowledge and power. In this way God's relationship to time is radically different from our human experience of time as a limitation upon us. John Lucas wrote in this regard (*Treatise on Time and Space*, 306):

To understand eternity therefore we should not think of it as timeless or changeless, but as free from all those imperfections that make the passage of time for us a matter of regret. God is the master of events, not their prisoner; time passes, but does not press.

For the Lord of time and eternity, time is a servant and not a master.

Related to the idea that God is Lord of time is the fact that he is a necessary being, unchanged by time, who lives forever and ever. In traditional language, God is *a se*, necessary and immutable. God cannot die, and does not change in his fundamental nature. The aseity of God, as I understand it, means that God does not owe his existence to any other being(s) or states of affairs outside himself. God's existence does not have a causal explanation outside of himself, nor does it depend upon anything or anyone else.[1]

As well as being *a se*, I understand God to be "metaphysically necessary." By this I mean that he is the or a cause of every logically contingent "fact," or state of affairs, at any time and at any place (cf. Penelhum, "Divine Necessity"). If any state of affairs obtains, then God must exist either at that time, or earlier, in order to cause it. Finally, I understand God to be immutable, in that he cannot change in his nature, character, or perfections.

The fact that something was not changed by time, for Aristotle, was an important part of its being "timeless." The understanding of divine eternity developed in this book implies the falsity of the old, absolute notion of the immutability of God which has always been associated with his eternity. But this does not mean that God is not immutable, when the latter doctrine is properly understood. God is immutable in his character, nature and perfections. Such is the way that I. A. Dorner understood the doctrine of immutability, in what is arguably the single most important discussion of this doctrine in modern times.[2] We are fortunate that such excellent work on the doctrine of immutability has gone before us, and further that this modern understanding of immutability dovetails well with the doctrine of eternity I am developing here.

On this view, God changes, indeed, but only in relationship to a changing reality of which he is the creator and Lord. God does not change in his basic nature, in his character, or in his perfections. The necessary existence of God, on the one hand, is immutable and eternal, since it is not affected or effected by anything else. But with respect to his power, for example, God's activity changes in relation to the changing world he sustains: but the fact that God is omnipotent does not change. God is immutable, therefore, but he is not absolutely immutable in the Augustinian–Thomistic sense. Paul Helm (*Eternal God*, 86) helpfully distinguishes between accidental and necessary immutability, and between immutability of all predicates and immutability of a particular set of predicates. In my view, then, God is necessarily or essentially immutable with respect to a limited set of predicates, which are his character and perfections.

From the properties of aseity, metaphysical necessity and immutability, it follows that God exists forever. As Lord of time, God cannot cease to exist, since he is immutable and his being is not caused by any other beings or states of affairs. Since God exists, he can never fail to exist, being immutable and *a se*. Thus God will always exist, and always has existed. This is a further aspect of his being the Lord of time.

The fact the God is the Lord of time I have understood to mean that he has a plan or design for human history, and nothing takes place outside of his will; that he is not limited or changed in any fundamental way by the passage of time; and that he is a necessary being (*a se* and metaphysically necessary) who lives forever and ever. These are further aspects of his transcendence of time.

GOD AS RELATIVELY TIMELESS

Is the "Lord of time" in time? Is he timeless or not? These are questions that need careful attention. Is some duration in God's life ever simultaneous, before or after some duration of our time? If so, it will follow that God is in our time, since we have defined a time as the sum of related moments.

Now it is hard to see how two temporal things, even if they are in different spaces, can lack temporal relations if they are causally connected. Consider the following logical necessity:

(33)   When both cause and effect are temporal, a cause must be temporally related to its effect.

Consider the case where V causes W, and both are in time. V will normally (or always) be before W in time. Perhaps, if one holds to simultaneous causation, V and W may be simultaneous. If one holds to retrocausation, then W may be before V. These different positions exhaust the logical possibilities. The gravamen is the same in any case: if V causes W, and both are temporal, then some temporal relation must (logically must) hold between *V* and *W*. If, as I have argued is the case with God, no duration occurs between direct divine act and immediate effect, then the divine cause will be Zero Time Related to the created effect. Since God is temporal in himself, and he sustains the world which is a causal relationship, there must be some temporal relationship between eternity and time.[3]

I have spoken previously of God being in our time. Yet the gravamen of this chapter will be to argue that, in fact, God transcends our time. Since this is the case, it is far more appropriate to say that we are in God's time, than that God is in our time. Since God is the ground of time, this is another reason to speak of us being in God's time, rather than God being in our time. The latter expression, though philosophically acceptable, is theologically backwards. It is not the Creator that is bound by and included in the creation; rather, the creation is bounded by the Creator. It is the Infinite that bounds the finite, not *vice versa*. Therefore it is best to speak of creation being "in" God's time or eternity.

God is in himself temporal in some ways: does this mean he cannot be timeless? This depends upon what one means by "timeless." Aristotle thought that something was timeless if (*i*) it was not measured by time, and (*ii*) it was not affected by time or "contained" by time. In a similar way, I have suggested that God is in fact both temporal and "relatively" timeless.

This revised doctrine of eternity is fully in harmony with the Biblical witness about God and his eternity, as well as some of the early Greek philosophers. In fact, Scripture declares that "a thousand years in Your eyes are like yesterday when it passes, or a watch in the night" (Ps. 90:4); and "with the Lord one day is like a thousand years, and a thousand years like one day" (2 Pet. 3:8). Does this not appear to be something like our notion of God's relative timelessness? Some traditional foundation, then, can be given to the revised doctrine of eternity I am developing.

It is my purpose to argue, then, that God is "timeless" in the sense that his time is immeasurable, meaning that he is not in any Measured Time. Measured Time Words, therefore, would not truly apply in eternity. It could be possible, of course, for God to simply decree that a certain Measured Time would apply to his eternity. Perhaps he might do this to ease communication with his creatures. But this would be a wholly arbitrary convention, and would apply to the whole of eternity only because of the power of the divine decree, and not by anything in the nature of God's time.

The laws of nature, or better the law-like regularities of nature, are essential to the measurement of time. It is the laws of nature, among other things, that allow for the periodic processes that underlie isochronic clocks. Is God in any Measured Time? If not, does our Measured Time measure the eternity of God? I will argue that God is not in any Measured Time, and is not measured by our time, based on two considerations: (*i*) God is not subject to the laws of nature, as anything in Measured Time must be; and (*ii*) any Measured Time is relative to a particular frame of reference, which need not apply to God's time.

God is not subject to any of the law-like regularities of the natural order. As the Creator of all things including the natural order itself, God is of course not subject to any laws of nature. While the actions of God are not arbitrary, and thus not "random" in one sense, from the point of view of a Measured Time God's acts are "random." He does not conform to any order of nature that would cause him to repeat the same process over and over again in a uniform manner, as an isochronic clock is supposed to do. Further, any laws of nature that may obtain are contingent, and can be altered by God. How, then, can God be limited or contained by them, or by any Measured Time dependent upon them? Since any Measured Time must depend upon the natural order, of which God is creator and Lord, God is not in and of himself in any Measured Time. There is nothing in eternity that could act as a kind of "intrinsic metric" for the time of God.[4] It would seem, then, that God is not in any Measured Time.

In and of himself, God cannot be subject to the laws of nature, as anything in Measured Time must be. Therefore he is not in any Measured Time. I also rejected, earlier, the notion of a Newtonian, "absolute time" against which God's life might be measured. There is no absolute "flow" of temporal measure which would act as an absolute guide by which any time, including God's, would correctly be measured.

But, an objector might urge, cannot the cosmic time of our universe itself act as a kind of "clock" in order to measure the duration of God's time?[5] After all, clocks can measure things that are fairly random and chaotic in themselves. It would thus seem that even if God is not subject to the order of nature, the universe might act as a kind of clock to measure some duration in eternity.

To develop this objection, suppose that God sustains two episodes of some object, *E*1 and *E*2. Say further that there is exactly one "Stund" between *E*1 and *E*2, a Stund being a measure of cosmic time based upon the flow of fundamental particles. God changes in his power-to-act at moments of eternity Zero Time Related to the times of $E1$ and $E2$. Doesn't this mean that the term "one Stund" has meaning for God as he is in himself? The fact that God acts in our time, and his life is sometimes simultaneous with our time, the objection will go, means that the universe itself could act as a sort of clock to measure the duration of God's being. Since God must exist in order for $E1$ and $E2$ to exist, and since they are one Stund apart, doesn't it follow that God lived for one Stund? But if this is so, then God cannot be timeless, even in a relative sense.

The problem with this argument is, assumptions are made about how God is in himself based upon how God seems from a limited temporal perspective (i.e. a particular frame of reference). For while the temporal measure between $E1$ and $E2$ in the cosmic time of our universe is one Stund, it does not follow that $E1$-to-$E2$ is one Stund in some absolute sense which would apply outside our universe and its Measured Time system. $E1$-to-$E2$ does not have to be one Stund in God's time. In fact I would argue that the word "one Stund" does not have any meaning in a language which refers to things outside our universe, such as God, or angles, or some other universe God may have created. From the fact that $E1$ is before $E2$ we can only infer that the act which sustained $E1$ came before the act which sustained $E2$, in God's time. But it does not follow that $E1$-to-$E2$ is one Stund in God's time.

In fact, it does not even follow for some other created observers, moving non-linearly with us at velocities near the speed of light relative to their basic frames, that $E1$-to-$E2$ is one Stund long. The fact that $E1$ is one Stund before $E2$ is a contingent fact. Indeed, even cosmic time is a contingent matter, which holds for any actual, but not every possible, proper frame of reference. We know that $E1$ is in the light cone of $E2$: since they are episodes of the same object, there is a causal link between them which established a conical order. But because of the well known fact of time dilation, an observer moving at a velocity near c relative to her basic frame *will not* measure the duration between $E1$ and $E2$ as one Stund. If, then, for different observers in our own space-time the difference between $E1$ and $E2$ is not always one Stund, how can we insist (as the argument above does) that the duration between $E1$ and $E2$ will be one Stund *in God's time*? Such a conclusion absolutizes our cosmos, as though God could not create a thousand such universes, all with different times. A "cosmic time" is not the same thing as an absolute, Newtonian time. Cosmic time is contingent, and applies to our universe alone, and to a limited and particular frame of reference. We cannot conclude that it applies to anything beyond or outside our universe, unless some method of synchronization is set up (as it might be between different spaces in the same Measured Time). Since God is not of himself limited by any law-like regularity of nature (there is no intrinsic metric in eternity), no synchronization can be established. Thus the argument above fails, and we can conclude that, indeed, God transcends any Measured Time, and is thus relatively timeless.

If God is indeed relatively timeless, does this mean that any language about God using Measured Time Words is false or meaningless? Not at all. Dates, for example, are our way of pointing to certain moments. So the sentence "God created the world in 4004 BC" is true if God created the world during the time picked out by our dating system as 4004 BC. Likewise, "God has been sustaining the world for one hour" is true if God has been sustaining the world for the duration picked out by our Measured Time as one hour. We must insist, however, that such a convention is simply our human way of thinking and it does not mean that hours, seconds and minutes have any application to eternity apart from this convention. It is also true to say that God has always existed in eternity. But what we cannot give is a definite measure to how long that is. For that would be to give a measure to the divine Being, which is immeasurable and infinite. Thus God is not in any Measured Time, and therefore not in the same Measured Time as we are. In this sense, God is timeless.

In arguing that God is relatively timeless, I have stressed the fact that he is "outside" of our universe. Let's explore this idea further. What does it mean to say that God is "outside" our universe? Doesn't he act all the time "in" our history, and "on" our world? While God does act in our history and in our universe, he is not contained within it. God is spaceless, that is, he does not have any spatial location or extension. This is what I understand by God being "outside" our space-time universe. He is free, in himself, to ground our universe, without entering into it as a member of it.

Granted that God does transcend space and time, must God, of logical necessity, transcend both space and time? Another way to ask this is, couldn't God have a body? A body gives an agent some particular spatial and temporal location. A body is a limited mode of action and knowledge acquisition, through a particular lump of matter. Agents normally and regularly act and know through their body, if they have one. Couldn't God have a "body" in this sense?

Here I think we must trade on our fundamental intuitions about God. Would such a limited being really be God? We must ask ourselves the question, is the being we call God essentially (*de re*) omniscient and omnipotent? Are these properties incompatible with having a body? I frankly find nothing logically impossible in the person we call God having a body, being measured by our time, and having a particular spatial location as opposed to some other. I do not find this incompatible with the properties of omnipotence or omniscience. However, as Swinburne has persuasively argued, the universe as a whole does not function as God's body. And I do not think that, as a matter of fact, in the actual world God does have a body in this technical sense. The Christian doctrine of incarnation, to be sure, does not teach that God as a whole is fully embodied. So God does in fact transcend time and space – but he does not have to. Further discussion of this point would take us beyond the scope of our present topic.[6]

God, then, can enter into our space or Measured Time at will, but is not contained within it of necessity. And this is as one might expect, since God is the Creator of space and time. It is he that calls the universe into existence, and thus he cannot be limited by that which is wholly dependent upon him. God transcends both time and space. I have argued that he transcends time in that his life is the ground of time, he is the Lord of time, and he is relatively timeless.

OBJECTIONS CONSIDERED

Having developed a new concept of eternity, it seems right to consider objections to it, since they will no doubt be raised in any case! It might be objected, first of all, that this revised understanding of eternity is not really a doctrine of time-*less* eternity, since it allows that God is in our time. If God is in some way temporal, how can we then assert that he is "timeless"? Against this objection, consider what the word "time" means in ordinary language. Expressions like "what time is it?" or "a long time ago" or "how time flies!" are examples of ordinary usage of the word in English. Some reflection upon the use of "time" in normal, everyday discourse indicates that in normal usage "time" refers to Measured Time, to our history, and to physical processes. In the loose and popular sense, "time" does not mean an ontological category but the specifically human time of our history and our universe: the time of seconds, days, and centuries; the time of our space-time. When "time" is used in this popular sense, then, *God is timeless*. Although we are in

God's time (and thus God is in our time, too) God transcends our time. I have tried to capture these insights by saying that God is (relatively) timeless. It is only when "time" is used in a very strict and narrow sense – when it refers to any sort of temporality – that the revised doctrine of eternity affirms that God is temporal. Several objections could and no doubt will come from the perspective of traditional Christian theology. Even if it is allowed that this new doctrine indeed teaches that God is "timeless" in one sense of the word, the fact that God changes makes this view of God unacceptable to traditionalists. These modern followers of Patristic and Medieval theologians will argue that God is simple, immutable and perfect. Therefore God is not just timeless in a relative sense, but in the absolute sense as well. There are basically four objections of this type to the revised doctrine of divine eternity. First, the traditionalist will argue, a changing God cannot be immutable. Second, since God changes in some ways, this undermines the divine perfection. Third, a changing God cannot be the ultimate explanation of the universe. Fourth, this revised doctrine undermines the simplicity of God. I will consider these before moving on to modern objectors.

Our basic question concerns divine eternity, not immutability, simplicity and perfection. But our partners in dialogue make some discussion of these last three divine attributes necessary. Thus each objection will be considered in turn, briefly looking at these three attributes as well. This will help to flesh out the revised doctrine of eternity which we are advocating. But a full and complete discussion of all these divine attributes would take us too far from our main subject.

I have already discussed the divine immutability. I understand God to be immutable, in the sense that his fundamental attributes, perfections and character – those attributes which he has eternally – cannot change or pass away. This, of course, is different from the traditional view of immutability, which states that God does not change in any way whatsoever. While acknowledging this difference, I deny that the traditional view is the only proper one.

The second objection arising from traditional theology concerns the divine perfection. If we allow that in eternity, God lives his life in stages, then God cannot be a perfect being as traditionally understood. As Aquinas wrote,

anything in change acquires something through its change, attaining something previously not attained. Now God, being limitless and embracing within himself the whole fullness of perfection of all existence, cannot acquire anything, nor can he move out towards something previously not attained. So one cannot in any way associate him with change (ST, Ia, q.9, a.1).

According to the revised doctrine of eternity, God does change. It would thus seem that he cannot be perfect. If anything changes, it either diminishes in perfection or it grows in perfection, "attaining something previously not attained." Since God changes, one of these two options must be true. But if God diminishes in perfection, then he is no longer a perfect being. On the other hand, if God grows in perfection, he was not a perfect being in the past. Either way, God is not essentially perfect.

Granted that this is a valid argument, is it a sound one? Just because something changes, it need not diminish or grow in perfection. This is the point in the above argument that we can and should call into question. A thing can change in response to a variety of changing circumstances, without itself growing better or worse. And changes in God, remember, are a result of his decision to create a changing world and to be really related to it. Therefore God can change in some ways, and still be immutable and perfect. An example can clarify this point.

Say that "Milton" is the name of an essentially perfect poet. After writing a perfect poem on the beauty of nature, Milton then writes another poem on the pathos of human life. It too is a perfect poem. Let us stipulate that in writing these poems, the character of Milton does not change. He is the same in writing each poem, in this sense. Yet clearly Milton has changed in one sense, in writing the two poems. He changed from writing about and considering beauty, to writing about and considering human fate, suffering and death. And surely this is a real change in Milton – but it is not a change for the better or the worse. In both cases, Milton is still the perfect poet, and his poems are the perfect poems about their subjects. But the subjects of the poems are different. Now this example (which is not about the historical Milton!) is coherent. And since it is coherent, something can change without either growing or diminishing in perfection. Thus it follows that the argument above is valid, but the conclusion is false: God can be perfect, and yet change in some ways. God can change in what he does, without changing who he is. God can be a perfect, immutable and timeless being, as I define these terms, even though he changes in relation to a changing world.

Traditional theologians will argue that God, as the source of all movement in other things, is himself unmoved. Nothing can affect, move or change God, since in order to affect God it would have to be stronger than God: which is impossible. What such an argument fails to consider is the idea that God might want to change himself, in order to be in relationship with a changing world (see further Ware, "Reexamination.") Now it was a principle of Aristotelian philosophy that nothing can move or change itself: but I see no reason to accept this principle, especially in the case of an omnipotent being. The ultimate explanation for why God changes can be found in himself alone, and in his will to be in relationship with his creatures. This fact is not true of created things. The answer to the third objection lies in this difference.

Traditional theologians will argue that a changing God cannot be the explanation of the world. For a changing thing requires an explanation of why it changes; the inference is, only an unchanging thing can be the ultimate explanation of all changes. Now on our understanding of his aseity and immutability, God is the ultimate explanation of change, including changes in himself. God is the ultimate origin of all changes, including changes that he himself undergoes in order to be really related to the world. The will of God, therefore, is the ultimate explanation of all change, including changes in God. Thus God does not require any explanation outside of himself, and this is certainly not true of changing things as we know of them in our world. The aseity of God means that he owes his existence to no other thing. Because of his aseity, God is not in the class of things that owe their existence or changes, ultimately, to things outside of themselves.

One might agree that things in the class of objects that owe their existence and changes to something outside of themselves, do as a class need some explanation. Let us agree, for the sake of the argument, that an infinite regress of causes in this class is inadequate as a complete explanation of the reality of the class as a whole. But this will only mean that God is not an element of the class of every changing thing which owes its changes to something outside of itself. It does not follow that God cannot change in some ways, namely in relation to a changing world. Further, since God is not a member of this class, he can be the ultimate explanation for the existence of the elements of this class, and the changes they undergo, without violating the insights of the traditionalist regarding the problems of an infinite regress of causes. Even given the point about an infinite causal regress being impossible (which could be questioned) God's will could still be the ultimate explanation for every event.

Anselm (*Monologion*, ch. 22) objected further to the idea that God changed himself, since a cause must precede its effect. This would mean that, if God changes, there was some aspect of the life of God that precedes another aspect; and further, that the prior aspect no longer exists, since it is replaced by the next stage in the life of God. Now on the doctrine of eternity we are developing it does follow that there will be stages in the life of God. Thus some stages in the life of God have ceased to exist in eternity. But Anselm objected to the idea that some stage in the life of God no longer exists, since this undermines the divine simplicity. So we now turn to this objection.

Traditionally, the divine simplicity has been defined as God being identical to all of his properties. This was made clear in my analysis of Aquinas, for example. None of God's actions can cease to exist, since the actions of God are identical with the essence of God, which necessarily exists. As Stump and Kretzmann put this Thomistic point, "the one thing that is God and is atemporally actual has a variety of effects in time . . . [These effects] are to be understood as various temporal effects of the single eternal act indentical [*sic*] with God" ("Absolute Simplicity," 356). If we follow the revised doctrine of divine timelessness, and the doctrine of immutability in the tradition of Dorner which it implies, this conception of divine simplicity must be abandoned. But this doctrine seems more at home in a Neoplatonic theology, such a Plotinus's, than in the Biblical theology of a dynamic God passionately involved in history.

I have responded to the four arguments which arise from traditional theology, with its emphasis on God as the ultimate origin of all things, and on his simplicity, immutability and perfection. One other traditional attribute of God is usually linked to his eternity, and that is his foreknowledge. We owe the emphasis on this link to Boethius. But space does not permit further discussion of this divine attribute, since it is so involved with a number of other philosophical and theological difficulties. The doctrine of divine timelessness is theologically distinct from the discussion of divine foreknowledge. One may first examine the problem of what eternity is, and then turn to the problems associated with foreknowledge. This, at least, is the order I have followed.

Having dealt with problems arising from traditional theology, other possible objections to the revised doctrine of eternity come from two recent books: David Braine, *The Reality of Time and the Existence of God* and Paul Helm, *Eternal God*. Braine's stimulating and interesting work takes up the task of proving the existence of God from the reality of temporal order. Most of what Braine discusses will not concern us here. But Braine's concept of God as "incomposite" is at odds with the revised doctrine of eternity. And like the present work, Braine bases his conclusions about God on the fact that God sustains the world of changing things. Thus some response is in order, if only because of the similarity of topics.

With Braine I agree that God is "intrinsically underivative," or as I have expressed it, God has the properties of metaphysical necessity and aseity. God is not the effect of anything or anyone else. But Braine also insists that God is "incomposite," by which he means to contrast temporal things, which are "composite." Braine explains the term "composite":

> Temporal things, and anything whose existence is caused or contingent, are (we may say) 'composite,' defining compositeness in these rather abstract terms: a thing (or, we shall equivalently say, a thing's existence) is composite if and only if the distinction between a thing and its existence is positively pertinent to the efficient causal explanation of the thing's existence (p. 148).

What this seems to mean is, that every "substance" in an Aristotelian sense has a "nature" and an "existence." The "nature" of a thing,

> as a quasi-abstract object in the case of what has a cause is part of the formal specification of the causal background to the thing *qua* external or prior ground of its possibility, and in this way has its quasi-abstract existence prior to the actual existence of the thing (p. 166).

Thus the "nature" of an effected substance is the set of properties of a substance which it must have in virtue of those causes which bring it into being. God on the other hand, is "incomposite," in that he has no prior "nature" which is in any way different from his active existence. Since anything which is temporal must be composite, argues Braine, God is timeless.

Braine explains that "if the central indispensable realization of God's life and existence is not successive, then despite the tensedness of our statements about God, it will be false to describe the reality or nature they indicate as in itself temporal" (p. 132). Here we have to disagree with Braine. God may not change on his account, and may not have any succession. But this does not affect the judgment that God is in our time (or as I prefer to say, we are in God's time). As long as God's life can be measured by our Measured Time, or is temporally related to our time, then God is in our time. And Braine explicitly rejects the idea that God is "in eternity" and only God's effects are "in time."

> [I]t is vital to maintain the dependence of the tensing of existential statements about substances on the tensing of predications of their actions – and vital that the time of God's actions is the time of its 'effects' (p. 131).

It seems then, from this quotation, that Braine ought to think that God himself is in our time, since his effects are in our time. Now the principle just cited, upon which Braine makes this conclusion, is wrong in our view. God can be in eternity, and his effects can indeed be in our time, without God himself being in our time. But if one accepts Braine's point, then one ought to maintain that God is everlasting in our time, and not timeless. On our own understanding of what it means to be in Measured Time, Braine's view of God ought to be that he is in our Measured Time, and not timeless even in a relative sense. This ought to be, since for him God's "substance" is certainly datable by the date of its effects, and thus God should be in Measured Time.

One further point should be made. While I am willing to grant that God is not "composite" in Braine's sense I cannot conclude from this fact alone that God is simple in the Thomistic sense, as Braine does (e.g. pp. 161, 223). In fact, Braine sets up a false dichotomy between temporal, mundane things as "composite," and God as the "incomposite" as he interprets it (viz. simple in the Thomistic sense). In his own terminology, I question the timelessness of the incomposite. In fact, I have demonstrated above that if God does sustain the world of time, then he must change in some ways, and cannot be incomposite as Braine has it.

In his recent book, *Eternal God*, Paul Helm objects to arguments for God's temporality, on the grounds that, *mutatis mutandis*, such arguments lead to the conclusion that God must be located in space (ch. 3). Since I affirm both that God is not necessarily embodied, and that he is not absolutely timeless, Helm's indirect proof could have force against the position I am developing. So consider in brief the following argument for God's being temporal.

(34) God directly causes different effects at different times.
(35) Agents can only directly cause different effects at different times if they change their action.

(36) God changes his action.
(37) Anything that undergoes real change is temporal.
(38) Changing one's action is a real change.
(39) God is temporal.

If Helm's criticism is correct, then the above argument should lead to the conclusion that God must be in space, if terms for time are replaced by terms for space. These changes yield the following revised argument:

(34′) God directly causes different effects at different places.
(35′) Agents can only directly cause different effects at different places if they change their action.
(36) God changes his action.
(37′) Anything that undergoes real change is spatial.
(38) Changing one's action is a real change.
(39′) God is spatial.

While the first argument is sound, the second Helmian modified argument is not. (37) in the first argument is true, for example, while (37′) is not. The difference between time and space ensures the absurdity of the second argument. God can spacelessly act directly upon two different places simultaneously, because two different places can coexist at the same time. But God cannot timelessly act directly upon things at two different *instants*, because two different instants cannot coexist (that is, cannot be simultaneous) at the same place. So Helm's criticism fails, and one can coherently hold that God is both not essentially embodied and not absolutely timeless.

I have considered objections to the revised doctrine of divine eternity, and found none of them convincing. Further criticisms may be forthcoming, but for now we can conclude that the concept is internally coherent, and congruent with other Christian doctrines (which the traditional view is not). In its essence, the revised doctrine of eternity rests upon the basic intuition that God transcends time, as its infinite Creator. God, then, exists in a "timeless time" which we call eternity. In order to deepen our understanding of this new doctrine of eternity, I will compare it to the doctrine of eternity in two major modern thinkers: Karl Barth and Alfred North Whitehead. By comparing and contrasting these three different views, we will get a better insight into the revised doctrine I am proposing.

ETERNITY IN WHITEHEAD AND BARTH

Having developed a revised doctrine of divine eternity in dialogue with classical Christian theology, I will now examine more recent writing on this doctrine, in order to compare and contrast these views with my own. For this purpose, I have chosen Karl Barth and Alfred North Whitehead as major representatives of modern theology. Both men have had great influence on modern Christian thought, and both of them had significant things to say about the eternity of God.

Both men could be considered advocates of a "third view" of divine eternity. It is sometimes asserted that there is a third concept of eternity, other than everlastingness and timelessness. J. S. Mackenzie, for example, wrote of this third notion "as that which includes time, but somehow also transcends it."[7] My own doctrine of relative timelessness could be understood as such a "third view." In the same vein, John Macquarrie has written,

> There is no doubt a sense in which God transcends history, yet history is also the region or medium in which he realizes his purposes, and surely this is important to him and makes some difference to him. God is not simply above history, unaffected and unchanged by it, nor is he simply within history as a kind of evolving God in the way that some empiricists have visualized him. He is both above and within, however difficult it may be for us to conceive this (*Thinking about God*, 113).

As we shall discover, Barth and Whitehead could also be considered advocates of this "third view," since for both of them God is timeless and yet in some way takes time into himself.[8] Thus they make fitting partners in dialogue, as we locate the new doctrine of eternity in the context of modern theology.

I begin with the philosopher A. N. Whitehead. Whitehead's thought has has a tremendous impact upon modern theology, through the growth of "process theology." This movement has deep roots in Whitehead's thinking. Whitehead's philosophy of process centers on the "actual entity" or "actual occasion." These are the fundamental real things, and all objects in our lived world are made up of them: "there is no going behind actual entities to find anything more real" (PR, 18). Actual occasions are not material entities, like Democritus' atoms. Instead, they are like "monads" in the cosmology of Leibniz. Actual occasions are mental, and can be divided or analyzed into their constituent "prehensions": a term which, Whitehead tells us, is "a generalization from Descartes' mental 'cogitations,' and from Locke's 'ideas'."(PR, 19). Because they are constituted by their prehensions, "these actual entities are drops of experience, complex and interdependent" (PR, 18). God is a "dipolar" actual entity. For Whitehead, "the nature of God is dipolar" (PR, 345). The two basic natures or aspects of God he called the "primordial nature" and the "consequent nature." The primordial nature of God, especially the "eternal objects" which occur in it, plays the role of the Platonic Forms in Whitehead's philosophy (PR, 44, 291). Each actual occasion must choose, in its own process of becoming, between various forms of definiteness given to it by these "eternal objects." And these eternal objects are not allowed to exist apart from some actual entity.

> Everything must be somewhere . . . Accordingly the general potentiality of the universe must be somewhere; since it retains its proximate relevance to actual entities for which it is unrealized . . . This 'somewhere' is the non-temporal actual entity. Thus 'proximate relevance' means 'relevance as in the primordial mind of God.' (PR, 46).

In his primordial nature God is timeless, the "non-temporal actual entity" (PR, 7, 16, 40, 46, 346). The primordial Mind of God, the "somewhere" of eternal objects, is related to every actual occasion as the initial aim towards a particular definiteness: the structuring or ordered principle upon which anything must draw in order to exist at all.

The primordial nature of God is active; the consequent nature is passive. In his consequent nature God receives the world back into himself, in order to give it back again to the world as the datum for further process (PR, 350f.)

> Each actuality in the temporal world has its reception into God's nature. The corresponding element in God's nature is no temporal actuality, but it is the transmutation of that temporal actuality into a living, ever-present fact (PR, 350).

In his consequent nature, God receives the best of the world into himself. The consequent nature is conscious, while the primordial nature is unconscious; in his consequent nature, God realizes the actual world according to his conceptual experience of it. For this reason the consequent nature is, in a sense, God's judgment upon the world.

The consequent nature of God is his judgement on the world. He saves the world as it passes into the immediacy of his own life. It is the judgement of a tenderness which loses nothing that can be saved (PR, 346).

Because the consequent nature of God is his reception and synthesis of the world, it cannot be timeless. Instead, Whitehead thought that this aspect of God was everlasting (PR, 345–351). Whitehead's "dipolar theism" is his understanding of God as having two aspects or natures: one timeless and the other everlasting in time. This dipolar theism is perhaps best summed up by Whitehead in his lectures on *Religion in the Making* (p. 93):

> Since God is actual, He must include in himself a synthesis of the total universe. There is, therefore, in God's nature the aspect of the realm of forms as qualified by the world, and the aspect of the world as qualified by the forms.

For Whitehead, therefore, God has both a timeless and a temporal aspect to his being.

The revised doctrine of eternity argued for in this essay is quite a different conception of God. For one thing, the revised doctrine does not insist that God is both timeless (in the absolute sense of the word) and everlasting in time. It is hard to see how one "actual entity" can exist in two antithetical modes of being, without destroying the unity of that entity. Since timelessness as Whitehead and most thinkers have understood it is the antithesis of time, no one being can be both timeless (in this sense) and temporal. Even if we allow God's timeless primordial nature to be purely mental, how can the "mind" of a single actual entity be timeless when its "body" is temporal? Instead of this apparent incoherent conception, the revised doctrine *redefines the meaning of "timeless."* By pointing out the differences between a popular sense of "time" which refers to Measured Time (or to the time of our space-time universe) and the strict ontological sense of "time" used in philosophy, we assert that God is timeless in the former but not in the latter sense. Thus God can be both timeless, in a relative sense, and temporal – something which on Whitehead's understanding of these terms is impossible, since one term is the contradiction of the other.

Further, the revised doctrine of divine timeless eternity is consistent with the traditional doctrine of God's miraculous intervention in human time. On Whitehead's view, however, God cannot so act. The primordial nature of God is unconscious, and "acts" by being prehended by actual occasions as the forms or structures of possibility. The consequent nature "acts" by being the concrete datum for the next phase of universal history.[9] In no case does God perform a specific, direct action at one particular spatio-temporal point that is not similarly performed for every actual occasion at every other spatio-temporal point.

What Whitehead's view and the revised doctrine of eternity have in common is a concern that God will be timeless in some sense, and yet also temporal and really related to the world of changing things. But while Whitehead retains the Platonic insistence that the mind of God is timeless in the absolute sense, I advocate that "God is timeless" must be redefined in order to be coherent with some changes in God, viz. changes he undergoes due to his real relations with a changing world.

In contrast to Whitehead's metaphysical bent, Karl Barth is passionately involved with theology. In a way that is typical of his "dialectical theology," Barth wants to say two things at the same time about divine eternity. On the one hand, Barth wrote: "Time has nothing to do with God" (CD, II/1, p. 608). On the other hand, he also wrote: "Even the eternal God does not live without time. He is supremely temporal" (III/2, p. 437). Making sense out of these seemingly contradictory statements will lead us into Barth's doctrine of eternity.

According to Barth, humans cannot know about time apart from revelation. Barth points to three great philosophical difficulties with the common sense view of time: (*i*) what is the present?, (*ii*) does time have a beginning?, and (*iii*) what is the relationship between time and eternity? (CD I/2, p. 48). Rather than deal with these philosophical problems as philosophy, Barth rejects the ability of philosophers like Augustine and Heidegger to come up with a true conception of time (I/2, p. 46). Rather, in a way typical of Barth, he asserts that true time can only be known by revelation, that is, through Jesus Christ the Word of God (I/2, p. 45).

The Word of God is the act of God. With respect to revelation and time, "God's word is God's act means first its contingent contemporaneousness" (CD, I/1, p. 164). The Word of God is contemporary with every human time. Barth speaks in this section of three types of time. The first type, originative time, is the time of Jesus Christ. This is not to be identified with 4 BC to AD 30, but instead signifies "the time of the direct, original utterance of God Himself in His revelation" (*ibid.*)

Originative time, then, is the time of the procession of the Son from the Father. The second type of time is the time of testimony, the time of the Bible. The third type of time is our time, the time of the church. The act of the Word of God in revelation means that "without the removal of the difference the time of Christ is made contemporary with the time of the prophets and apostles by the free act of God" (I/1, p. 168). By this same act, the time of the Biblical witnesses becomes contemporaneous with our time. Thus revelation bridges the gap of history between the time of God, the time of the Biblical revelation, and our time when we hear – here and now – the Word of God spoken to us. Revelation as God's act in something that is both past, present and future. And this act is the Being of God (CD, II/1, p. 263).

When he comes to speak of our time, Barth tells us "the time we think we know and possess, 'our' time, is by no means the time God created" (CD, I/2, p. 47). According to Barth, our time is lost, fallen time. But because the time of Jesus Christ is the time of a human being, Jesus raises human time up into his divine time, or eternity. The time of Jesus Christ is the time of the Lord of time.

> Here the dilemma does not arise, between a present that disappears midway between past and future, and a past and future that dissolve for their part into a present. Here there is a genuine present . . .The Word of God is. It is never "not yet" nor "no longer" . . . The Word spoken from eternity raises the time into which it is uttered (without dissolving it as time), up into His own eternity, as now His own time (I/2, p. 52).

Barth feels that our time is deficient in some ways. In this passage he raises again the philosophical problem of the present. Again we see that this philosophical problem is resolved by a theological reality: Jesus Christ and his time which is eternity.

In the section of "The Eternity and Glory of God" (CD, sec. 31.3) Barth brings into focus his discussion of time and eternity. God's time, or eternity, does not have the characteristics of past, present and future. "[T]he being is eternal in whose duration beginning, succession and end are not three but one . . . one simultaneous occasion as beginning, middle and end" (CD, II/1, p. 608). It is in this context that Barth asserts that "time can have nothing to do with God." Here Barth is considering God as he is in himself. And as he is in himself, God is non-temporal.

Nevertheless, Barth also asserts that "The theological concept of eternity must be set free from the Babylonian captivity of an abstract opposite to the concept of time" (CD, II/1, p. 611). God includes and has time in His eternity: time for us, the time of revelation. Because God became man in Jesus Christ, eternity became time.

> The fact that the Word became flesh undoubtedly means that, without ceasing to be eternity, in its very power as eternity, eternity became time. Yes it became time . . . If this is so, from this standpoint too we cannot understand God's eternity as pure timelessness (II/1, p. 616f.)

Because of his emphasis on incarnation and Jesus Christ the God-man, Barth cannot accept the definition of eternity as the opposite of time. Instead, Barth insists that God's time or eternity contains the past, present and the future. God's own time is "simultaneous with all our times" (II/1, p. 612). In order to explain himself better, Barth uses the image of the ocean (eternity) surrounding the land (time) on all sides. "So the eternal God coexists with the time created by Him . . . God's eternity in its eternal Now embraces and contains all parts of time and all things in itself simultaneously and at one moment" (II/1, p. 614). God's eternity, then, is a simultaneous moment that includes and embraces all of time in an eternal Now.

Because God's time embraces all of time in an eternal Now, it is possible for God to become time without destroying either the nature of time or the nature of eternity. Barth refuses to define eternity as the antithesis of time, but instead argues that eternity is *the fullness of time without the defects of succession.* What is missing from eternity as God's time is the past-present-future distinction, which I have called process.

What Barth's doctrine does in effect is to call into question the reality of process. The time that we know of, with its past, present and future, is fallen and lost time. God's time does not have this defect. Since our time of process is not time as God originally created it, it is not "real time." Only God's time is real time (CD, I/2, p. 49). Real and genuine time, time as God intended it to be, God's time and the time of Jesus as the Lord of time: all these exclude succession and process. Barth insists that his doctrine of God entering time and lifting time up into eternity does not destroy or "dissolve" the character of time. But here we must ask: just what is the character of time that is preserved in the non-successive time of Jesus Christ and the Father? Time as duration is clearly preserved, since eternity is a duration: but time as process must be left behind in the human, fallen, lost time. As Roberts correctly concludes in his excellent essay on "Barth's Doctrine of Time":

> The contrast between the 'duration' of the simultaneity of the past, present, and future and the "succession and division of past, present and future' is the *only* logical or conceptual distinction between eternity and time. In 'healing' time, eternity implants its durational simultaneity into the succession and division of time. This is the distinction that arises in every context in which temporal categories are employed . . . in the *Church Dogmatics* (p. 134; italics and quote marks as in original).

Real time, time as it was meant to be, excludes process. Thus just as we saw with Aquinas, Barth's doctrine of eternity and time implies the stasis theory of time, at least for "real time."

Barth's insistence that the time of Jesus Christ is simultaneous with all times only makes sense given the stasis theory of time. His concept of eternity as that which embraces time, and contains past, present and future in one simultaneous Now, also points in the direction of the stasis view. What is more, Barth's teaching that the Incarnation means that the time of Jesus, as a portion of world history, is taken up into eternity and becomes God's time also makes sense only in the context of the stasis theory of time. For the time of Jesus would still exist (tenselessly) in order to be part of eternity. If the stasis theory of time were true, then all of these various human times still exist (tenselessly), and thus can be related to the ultimate Reality of God. But we have seen that there is no reason to accept the stasis theory. In fact, some adherents to the stasis theory of time commit a philosophical mistake (viz. confusing the logical with the physical). Therefore, as much as I feel that Barth's doctrine of time is an improvement over Aquinas', I cannot accept Barth's view any more than I could accept the Thomistic doctrine.

Given the process view of time, it is simply contradictory to assert that all of the past, present and future can be one simultaneous Now to God. Those events that existed in the past, or will exist in the future, are not real and cannot be in "eternity" any more than they exist (tenselessly) here on earth. It is incoherent, therefore, to assert that the time of Jesus Christ can be simultaneous with all other times.

Yet much of Barth's teaching on time and eternity rings true. With Barth, I too believe that the timeless God "became time" in the life of Jesus Christ. With Barth I want to say that God is both timeless and temporal. Unfortunately, Barth simply accepted most of the concept of timeless eternity as he found it in the tradition. His only correction is to insist that eternity is not the opposite of time. Barth still accepted the idea that God's eternal Now includes all other human times: past, present and future. And this is what leads Barth's doctrine into contradiction.

The movement from past to present to future is not a "fallen" or lost defect in human time: it is a function of any changing thing. Anything that becomes different goes through episodes, and changes from one state to another. Barth has no problems with asserting the becoming of God: "What is real in God must, precisely because it is real in G o d . . . constantly be b e c o m i n g real again" (CD, I/1, p. 489; spacing as in original). If God becomes, then of logical necessity succession also applies to him. God's time cannot be non-successive, if God's Being goes through becoming. Barth's notion of eternity is, then, inconsistent even within the terms of his own system. Though a more sympathetic interpreter than Roberts, Colin Gunton comes to basically this same conclusion (*Becoming and Being*, 177–185). He writes of Barth's view of time and eternity, that:

> despite Barth's attempt to see God's eternity as a kind of eminent temporality, the tendency to define eternity in opposition to time, and therefore as a *negation of the historical orientation of the understanding of revelation, is very marked* (p. 183, his emphasis).

Barth's doctrine of time and eternity, then, is inconsistent at the very point where he accepts the traditional doctrine of divine non-temporality.

This examination of two important thinkers has helped to delineate the new doctrine of divine timelessness being developed, and set it in the context of modern doctrine. With both Whitehead and Barth, we want to say that God is timeless and yet still includes time within himself. The problem with both men is that they did not re-examine the notion of "timeless" they inherited from Christian tradition. As a result, their conception of God is in conflict with itself, and in Barth's case, with the process theory of time. As long as eternity is defined as either the negation of time, or the "fullness of time" when that is understood as a simultaneous Present that includes all times within itself, a doctrine of God who changes with time or enters into real relations with temporal reality will be incoherent. It is only when "timeless" is redefined in its application to God that one can assert without contradiction that God is timeless and also that God is temporal, sustaining the world and entering into relationships with his temporal creation.

SUMMARY AND CONCLUSIONS

The time has come to draw this inquiry to a close. We have discovered that the ancient doctrine of divine timelessness is true and coherent with the doctrine that God sustains the universe only if the stasis theory of time is true. I have shown, further, that arguments for the stasis theory of time from a philosophical or scientific basis are not compelling, and in some cases rest upon a philosophical mistake. Since the doctrine that God sustains the world is central to theism I have rejected the traditional doctrine of divine timelessness. But I have not abandoned the idea that God is timeless. Instead, I have redefined "God is timeless" to mean that God is relatively timeless, i.e. he is not measured by time nor is he affected by the negative aspects of temporal passage. God is the ground of time, and the Lord of time. This new doctrine of eternity leads to a non-traditional conception of divine immutability and perfection. But properly understood, these doctrines can still be held in the light of the new doctrine of divine eternity.

The Lord God is Master of heaven and earth, time and eternity, and transcends our created time. But God does change in relationship with his created world of time, and thus he is eminently temporal. This new doctrine of eternity I am proposing, unlike the old one, is coherent with the idea that God's power sustains the world in process. Thus we can assert that "God is timeless" yet still consistently proclaim that "He is before all things, and in him all things hold together" (Col. 1:17).

Notes and References

1   Establishing the Parameters

1. Pike, *God and Timelessness*, ix.
2. Two recent exceptions are Laura Zimmerman [now Garcia] and Delmas Lewis.
3. If one holds to the "hard fact/soft fact" distinction, then a state will only includes "hard facts" about an object at a particular time. Hard facts are, on this view, those true statements about an object at the time referred to whose truth conditions are fulfilled by the object at that time, and not at some other. Soft facts about an object at some time, however, are true at that time, at least in part, in virtue of what happens at some different time than the one in question. For example, the statement "Eighty years ago, Paul mowed his lawn" is a hard fact about Paul 80 years ago. But the proposition, "Eighty years ago, Paul knew that he would mow his lawn today" is a soft fact about Paul 80 years ago. For the latter can only be true if in fact Paul mows his lawn today, i.e. if in fact he both believed 80 years ago that he would mow his lawn in the future and it is true that he mows his lawn in the future (i.e. today). But whether or not Paul mows his lawn today can only be satisfied in the present (i.e. at a time different from 80 years ago). Therefore, Paul's knowledge 80 years ago that he would mow his lawn today is a soft fact about Paul 80 years ago. For more on the hard/soft fact distinction, see Hoffman and Rosenkranz, "Hard and Soft Facts."
4. As I hope to show below, any real change takes time to occur. Coming into existence or ceasing to exist are real changes. So no object can come into existence and pass out of existence at the same instant, since an instant is a durationless "point" of time, and real change requires duration.
5. See further, Grünbaum, *Philosophical Problems of Space and Time*, ch. 1.
6. See Grünbaum, *ibid.*; Whitrow, 33–36.
7. Geach called merely relative changes, "Cambridge changes" in *God and the Soul*, 71f.
8. Following T. P. Smith, "On the Applicability of a Criterion of Change," 328.
9. This entire section is in debt to David Lewis's work on the logic of conditionals, *Counterfactuals*. I translate the operator $\Box\!\rightarrow$ as "if . . . then it would have to be the case that . . ." My terms "if . . . then it might be the case that . . ." are a translation of his operator $\Diamond\!\rightarrow$. See his pp. 1–4. For clarity, I here give my argument in symbolic logic. Let d stand for "a duration occurs," and let c stand for "a change occurs at that time.".

   1. $\Box\,(\sim d \rightarrow \sim c)$ [premise = (D1)]
   2. $\Box\,(c \rightarrow d)$ [from (1)]

147

3.	$d \ \Box \mapsto \sim c$	[assumption, I.P.(Indirect Proof)]
4.	c	[assumption]
5.	d	[from (2) & (4)]
6.	$\sim d$	[from (3) & (4)]
7.	$d \ \& \ \sim d$	[from (5) & (6)]
8.	$\sim (d \Box \mapsto \sim c)$	[from (7), I.P.]
9.	$d \Diamond \rightarrow c$	[from (8), dfn. $\Diamond \rightarrow$]

10. This section has been strengthened by criticisms from Professor Keith Ward, for which I am grateful.
11. This assumes that it is possible for there to be more than one space. For a defense of this idea, see Swinburne, *Space and Time*, 28–41.
12. Following A. C. Danto, "Basic Actions."
13. This view appears to be compatible with the position Ehring argues for: see his "Non-simultaneous Causation," p.31f.

2 The Witness of Scripture

1. Jenni, "Das Wort $^c\hat{o}l\bar{a}m$ im Alten Testament," and his "$^c\hat{o}l\bar{a}m$.". See also Barr, *Biblical Words for Time*, 123f.; Long, "Notes on the Biblical Use of ^{c}ad $^c\hat{o}l\bar{a}m$." The recent study by Gerelman, "*Die sperrende Grenze*" who argues that the basic meaning is "border, limit" (Germ. *Sperren*) is more ingenious than convincing. Even so, for our purposes in this essay, can his suggested meaning, "horizon (of time)" be that different from the definition "remote time" Jenni gives? Long's suggestion (p.83), that the word has no "time aspect" is equally dubious.
2. "Furthermore, the word $^c\hat{o}l\bar{a}m$ cannot be burdened with so much theological and philosophical baggage" (Jenni, 25).
3. "We do not derive the concept of eternity from that of time, but only in opposition to time . . . Everything which the concept of time signifies is by the concept of eternity negated."
4. "A synthesis of all this OT thinking about the beginninglessness and endlessness of God is discovered in Ps. 90:2."
5. *Op. cit.*, p. 30: "What Isaiah wants to emphasize through this text is, (i) Yahweh's absolute timelessness."
6. See Barton, *Book of Ecclesiastes*, 105; a full discussion of the options is found in Ellermeier, *Qohelet*, I/1, 309–322.
7. See Eccl. 1:13, 2:26, 3:10f.,5:18f., 6:2, 8:15, 9:9, 12:7,11.
8. See Jenni, "Time," 645; and Barr, *Biblical Words for Time*, 128.
9. 2 Enoch 65:6f. See also 33:1f. Charlesworth, 2:96f. dates the original version (in Greek) to the late first century AD (this dating should not be attributed to F. I. Andersen, who himself refuses to date 2 Enoch with any specificity). Strictly speaking, one would have to argue that these verses in 2 Enoch could be translated into Greek or Hebrew without going outside the lexical stock of the Bible, since the text is Slavonic.
10. I owe my understanding of metaphor, expressed here, to J. M. Soskice, *Metaphor and Religious Language*.
11. "God's eternity and human time are in the last analysis incommensurable: that is the intention of this expansive rhetoric": *Psalmen*, II, 630.

12. "Who is God? He is the Eternal, whose time is a different one from the time of man": p. 632.
13. See *Genesis Rabbah* 8:2, and *Leviticus Rabbah* 19:1. Both texts are collected and translated in *Midrash Rabbah*, eds. Freedman and Simon.
14. See Jubilees 4:30, 2 Enoch 33:1, Epistle of Barnabas 15:4.
15. De Vries, *Yesterday, Today, and Tomorrow*, 343 n.3.
16. Bauckham, *Jude, 2 Peter*, 306–310 provides an excellent discussion.

3 The Doctrine of Divine Timelessness: An Historical Sketch

1. For an introductory overview of the history of the idea of eternity, see Brabant, *Time and Eternity in Christian Thought*. Borges, *Historia de la Eternidad* makes interesting reading, but is not "scholarly." Brabant should be supplemented by Sorabji, *Time, Creation and the Continuum* for ancient thought in general, and Parmenides, Plato and Boethius in particular. My exposition is in debt to both Sorabji and Brabant. On other specific themes in the history of the idea of eternity, see: Assmann, *Zeit und Ewigkeit im Alten Ägypten*; Whittaker, "The 'Eternity' of the Platonic Forms," his "Ammonius on the Delphic E," and his *God, Being, Time*; Plass, "Timeless Time in Neoplatonism" and his "The Concept of Eternity in Patristic Theology"; Beierwaltes, *Plotin über Ewigkeit und Zeit*; Meijering, *Augustin über Schöpfung, Ewigkeit und Zeit*; Pike, *Timelessness*, 130–188 [on Anselm and Schleiermacher]; Broussard, "Eternity in Greek and Scholastic Philosophy"; Langston, *God's Willing Knowledge*, [on Scotus, Molina and Leibniz]; Hallett, *Aeternitas: A Spinozistic Study*; Lauer, *Hegel's Concept of God*; Schmidt, *Zeit und Ewigkeit* [on Dialectical Theology]; and Cairns, "The Concept of Eternity" [on Idealism].
2. For the traditional view that Parmenides' thought that Being was timeless, see Guthrie, *History of Greek Philosophy*, II, 29; G.E.L. Owen, "Plato and Parmenides on the Timeless Present"; Sorabji, *Time*, 98–108, 128–130; Coxon, *Fragments of Parmenides*, 196f.; for the opposing view, cf. Schofield, "Did Parmenides Discover Eternity?"; and Whittaker, *God, Being, Time*, 16–32.
3. Ordinatio, d. 38 and 39 = 1963 Vatican ed., appendix A. The authenticity of this section is doubtful; see pp. 26*–30* of the Vatican ed. However, the ideas may go back to Scotus, since similar points are made in the *Lectura*.
4. "*cum tempus non sit circumferentia stans sed fluens, cuius circumferentiae nihil est nisi instans actu, – nihil etiam eius erit praesens aeternitati (quae est quasi centrum) nisi illud instans quod est quasi praesens; et tamen si per impossibile poneretur quod totum tempus esset simul stans, totum esset simul praesens aeternitai ut centro*" (*Ordinatio*, I, d. 39, q. 5, sec. 35 = Vatican ed., appendix A, p.442).
5. A. Kenny, ed., *Descartes Philosophical Letters*, 232; Spinoza, *Ethics*, I, def. 8; Malbranche, *Dialogues on Metaphysics*, 7.9; Leibniz' Fifth Paper, sec. 44,49 and Clarke's Fifth Reply, sec. 42–45 in H. Alexander, ed., *The Leibniz–Clarke Correspondence*.

6. Bacon, *Novum Organum*, I, aph. 48; Hobbes, *Leviathan*, 4.46; C. B. Brush, tr., *The Selected Works of Pierre Gassendi*, 396; Locke, *Essays Concerning Human Understanding*, II, 29.15.
7. Leibniz' Fifth Paper, sec. 44,49; Clarke's Fifth Reply, sec. 42–45.

4 A Coherent Model of Absolute Timelessness

1. Note that I am assuming that it is possible for there to be a timeless world, and for some object to exist in that world. It is hard to see how the notion of timeless causation could be defended without these assumptions.
2. See, i.a., Augustine, *Confessions*, 7.17, 11.6–10; Aquinas, ST Ia, q.10, a.5; q.18, a.4; SCG I.13 & 15; Mascall, *He Who Is*, 99f.; Pike, 39–44; Zimmerman, "God and Time," 94–97, 126–129.
3. For example, Mascall, *He Who Is*; Davies, *Thinking About God*.
4. This assumes that the agent's power-to-act is a necessary cause of the effect's continuance, as it will be in cases where God is the agent.
5. The idea of ET-simultaneity has been criticized by others but not thoroughly enough, nor along the lines I follow with respect to the Special Theory of Relativity. See Davis, *Logic*, 16–24; Lewis, "Eternity Again"; Fitzgerald, "Stump and Kretzmann on Time and Eternity"; and Nelson, "Time(s), Eternity and Duration."
6. This point was made by Walker, "Time, Eternity and God" as early as 1919; and in more recent times, by Kellett, "Time and Eternity," Hebblethwaite, "Some Remarks," 434–436, Craig, "Was Thomas Aquinas a B-Theorist of Time?", Mellor, "History Without the Flow of Time," and Lewis, "God and Time." Note that Hebblethwaite and Lewis reject the stasis theory.
7. The analogy between time and space is sometimes used to argue that a spaceless God can act on objects at every point of space; so also an absolutely timeless God can act on every point of time from outside of it, even given the process view of time (e.g. Hasker, "Concerning the Intelligibiligy of 'God is Timeless'"). But this simply misunderstands the analogy between time and space. God can act on the here-now; God can act on the now at different places; and God can act on the here at different times. None of this implies that God can "timelessly" act on the here at all dates "at once." This is true of both space and time. As Here-Now exists, so There-Now exists over there; but it is absurd to say that There-Now exists *here*. Likewise, as Here-Now exists, Here-Then existed back then; but it is absurd to think that Here-Then exists *now*! Careful analysis of the analogy between space and time undermines the conclusions that Hasker wishes to draw.
8. Assuming, that is, that the arguments of Kretzmann, "Omniscience and Immutabililty," and Gale, "Omniscience–Immutability Arguments," are valid against the criticism of Castañeda, "Omniscience and Indexical Reference," and Helm, *Eternal God*, 74–84.
9. See Oaklander, *Temporal Relations and Temporal Becoming*, 195–222, who rightly criticizes Cahn's argument in *Fate, Logic and Time*, 126–137, that the stasis theory of time implies determinism.

5 The Stasis Theory of Time: A Critique

1. E.g., Fitzgerald, "The Truth about Tomorrow's Sea Flight," or Your-grau, "On the Logic of Indeterminist Time."
2. See Baker, "Temporal Becoming," or Davies, *The Physics of Time Asymmetry*, 2f., 21.
3. Grünbaum might respond that the world U is impossible, because process itself is incoherent. I will consider such arguments in the second section of this chapter.
4. Brent Mundy has shown that such a signal is not forbidden in principle by the Special Theory of Relativity. See his "The Physical Content of Minkowski Geometry"; "Optical Axiometrization of Minkowski Space-Time Geometry"; and "Special Relativity and Quantum Measurement." He writes that "The standard theories forbid spacelike (superluminal) causation only insofar as we have *independent reasons* to believe (a) that all causation is mediated by particles and fields propagating in the standard manner, and (b) that all states of inertial motion are determined from prior states of timelike motion by continuous finite acceleration" ("Special Relativity," 208, my italics).
5. See Reichenbach, *Philosophy of Space and Time*, 123–135; Grünbaum, *Philosophical Problems*, 342–368; Stein, *art. cit.*; and Janis, "Simultaneity and Conventionality."
6. Whitrow, *Natural Philosophy of Time*, 283–313; Swinburne, *Space and Time*, 184–204.
7. On these difficult problems, Loizou, *The Reality of Time* is particularly helpful.
8. See Lemmon, "Sentences, Statements and Propositions," and also R. G. Swinburne, "Tensed Facts" who develops and uses a similar distinction.
9. Swinburne, "Tensed Facts," makes this point well.
10. A sentence-token is any sample of a given sentence-type. It can be written, spoken, or otherwise expressed. A sentence-type consists of a series of marks on paper, or a series of phonemes in a natural language. It is the model or type which all given tokens have in common. Sentence-types cannot be uttered as types, for if they were they would only be a given token of that type. For example, "Snow is white" can be expressed in many times and places, and in various media (speech, writing, etc.). But the type itself can only be referred to, not uttered. What these tokens of the sentence-type "Snow is white" have in common is the type itself. This distinction is made in Bar-Hillel, "Indexical Expressions."
11. Putnam used the two-place predicates, "is real to" and "is simultaneous with," but the point is the same.
12. For a helpful discussion of this vexing problem, see A. N. Prior, *Logic and Ethics*, 109–121, and David Braine, *The Reality of Time and the Existence of God*, pp.84–174.

6 A New Doctrine of Eternity

1. I exclude from this, of course, "states of affairs" which are themselves entailed by "God exits" (see Swinburne, *Coherence*, 250, 266).

2. Dorner, "*Unveränderlichkeit Gottes.*" Ware, "Evangelical Reexamination of the Doctrine of the Immutability of God" is a significant thesis which develops Dorner's view in dialogue with process theology. My understanding of immutability is in debt to Dorner and Ware.

3. This consideration answers the problem raised by H. J. Nelson, "Time(s), Eternity, and Duration," 9. He argues that "God's time" cannot contain a trans-universal present which contains in one "now" the quite different presents of two different universes which by definition do not have the temporal relations of simultaneity, before or after. But since God must create both universes in order for them to exist at all, and since creating and sustaining are causal processes, from God's perspective at least there will be temporal relations between the two universes, given principle (33) above. Either God will create one and then the other after that one; or else the histories of the two will overlap and some instants will be simultaneous with some instant in God's time. Since simultaneity is a transitive relation, the two worlds will either sometimes be simultaneous, or one will be wholly before the other. In both cases temporal relations will exist between the two worlds. Therefore, Nelson was wrong in the beginning to stipulate that two universes, both created by God, cannot have any temporal relations between them.

4. I argue this in my article, "Can History Measure Eternity?" which is a reply to William Lane Craig, "God and Real Time."

5. This is the main point of W. L. Craig, "God and Real Time," a reply to an earlier article of mine, "God and Time."

6. For further discussion, see Grace M. Jantzen, *God's World, God's Body*, and T. F. Tracy, *God, Action and Embodiment*. Cf. R. G. Swinburne, Coherence, 99–125.

7. "Eternity," 401. See also Ramige, *Contemporary Concepts of Time and the Idea of God*, 98–103.

8. I have not included this "third view" in my definition of eternity in chapter one, since we must still ask of that which is "both above and within" time, whether it is everlasting or timeless. There is, therefore, no real alternative to these two definitions.

9. See D. D. Williams, "How Does God Act?"; Shubert Ogden, *The Reality of God*, 164–187; and John Cobb, *God and the World*, 46–90.

Bibliography

Abbreviations

AJP = *Australasian Journal of Philosophy [and Psychology]*
APQ = *American Philosophical Quarterly*
BK = Biblischer Kommentar
CUP = Cambridge University Press, Cambridge
FC = Fathers of the Church
F & P = *Faith and Philosophy*
HAT = Handbuch zum Alten Testament
ICC = International Critical Commentary
IDB = *Interpreters Dictionary of the Bible*, ed. G. Buttrick, 4 vols. (Nashville: Abingdon, 1962)
IJPR = *International Journal for Philosophy of Religion*
IPQ = *International Philosophical Quarterly*
ISBE = *International Standard Bible Encyclopedia*, 4 vols., ed. G. W. Bromiley (Rev. ed., Grand Rapids: Eerdmans, 1979–1988)
JAAR = *Journal of the American Academy of Religion*
JPhil. = *Journal of Philosophy*
ModSch = *The Modern Schoolman*
NewSch = *New Scholasticism*
NIDNTT = *New International Dictionary of New Testament Theology*, 3 vols., trans. ed. C. Brown (Grand Rapids: Zondervan, 1975–1978).
NZST = *Neue Zeitschrift für systematische Theologie und Religionsphilosophie.*
OTL = Old Testament Library
OUP = Oxford University Press, Oxford and London
PAS = *Proceedings of the Aristotelian Society*
PPR = *Philosophy and Phenomenological Research*
PhilRev = *Philosophical Review*
PhilStud = *Philosophical Studies*
PhSc = Philosophy of Science
PQ = *Philosophical Quarterly*
PS = *Process Studies*
RKP = Routledge and Kegan Paul, London
RS = *Religious Studies*
RevMeta = *Review of Metaphysics*
SBT = Studies in Biblical Theology
SG = *Studium Generale*
TDNT = *Theological Dictionary of the New Testament*, 10 vols., eds. G. Kittle and G. Fredrich (Trans. ed. G. W. Bromiley, Grand Rapids: Eerdmans, 1964–1976)
THAT = *Theologisches Handwörterbuch zum Alten Testament*, 2 vols., eds. E. Jenni and C. Westermann (Munich: Kaiser, 1971–1972)
WBC = Word Biblical Commentary

WTJ = *Westminster Theological Journal*
ZAW = *Zeitschrift für die alttestamentliche Wissenschaft*
ZTK = *Zeitschrift für Theologie und Kirche*

Aquinas, Thomas. 1924–1929. *Summa contra Gentiles.* 4 vols. Trans. English Dominican Fathers. London: Burnes and Oates.
—— 1962. *Aristotle: On Interpretation.* Trans. J. T. Oesterle. Milwaukee: Marquette University Press.
—— 1964–1981. *Summa Theologiae.* 61 vols. Eds. T. Gilby, *et al.* London: Eyre and Spottiswoode.
Alexander, H. A. 1956. Ed., *The Leibniz–Clarke Correspondence.* Manchester: Manchester University Press. First pub., 1717.
Alexander, Samuel. 1927. *Space, Time and Deity.* 2 vols.London: Macmillan.
Anscombe, G. E. M. 1957. *Intention.* OUP.
Anselm, St. 1903. *Proslogium, Monologium, An Appendix on Behalf of the Fool by Gaunilon, and Cur Deus Homo.* Trans. S. N. Deane. Chicago: Open Court.
—— 1965. *Proslogion.* Trans. M. J. Charlesworth. OUP.
Aristotle. 1929. *The Physics*, vol. 1. Loeb. Trans. P. H. Wicksteed and F. M. Cornford. London: Heinemann.
—— 1939. *On the Heavens.* Loeb. Trans. W. K. C. Guthrie. London: Heinemann.
Assmann, Jan. 1975. *Zeit und Ewigkeit im Alten Ägypten.* Abhandlungen der Heidelberger Akademie der Wissenschaften, Philosophisch-historische Klasse. Heidelberg: C. Winter.
Augustine, St. 1950–1954. *City of God.* 3 vols. FC. Trans. L. B. Zema, *et al.* Washington, D.C.: Catholic University of America Press.
—— 1961. *Confessions.* Trans. R. S. Pine-Coffin. Harmondsworth: Penguin.
Ayer, A. J. 1954. *Philosophical Essays.* London: Macmillan.
—— 1956. *The Problem of Knowledge.* London: Macmillan.
Bacon, Francis. 1859. *Novum Organum.* Trans. A. Johnson. London: Bell and Daldly. First pub., 1620.
Baier, A. C. 1971. "The Search for Basic Actions." *APQ.* 8: 161–170.
Baker, Lynne Rudder. 1975. "Temporal Becoming: The Argument from Physics." *Philosophical Forum* 6: 218–236.
—— 1979. "On the Mind-dependence of Temporal Becoming." *PPR* 39: 341–357.
Bar-Hillel, Y. 1954. "Indexical Expressions." *Mind.* 63: 359–369.
Barnes, J. 1979. *The Presocratic Philosophers*, vol 1. RKP.
Barr, James. 1961. *The Semantics of Biblical Language.* OUP.
—— 1969. *Biblical Words for Time.* 2nd. ed. SBT. London: SCM.
Barth, Karl. 1936–1974. *Church Dogmatics.* 12 part-vols. Trans. ed. G. W. Bromiley, *et al.* Edinburgh: Clark.
Barton, G. A. 1908. *The Book of Ecclesiastes.* ICC. Edinburgh: Clark.
Bauckham, Richard. 1983. *Jude, 2 Peter.* WBC. Waco: Word Books.
Bauer, W. 1979. *A Greek-English Lexicon of the New Testament.* 2nd Eng. ed. Trans. and eds. W. F. Arndt, F. W. Gingrich and F. W. Danker. Chicago: University of Chicago Press.

Baumer, Michael. 1984. "Whitehead and Aquinas on the Eternity of God." *ModSch*. 62: 27–42.

Beer, Michelle. 1988. "Temporal Indexicals and the Passage of Time." *PQ*. 38: 158–164.

Beierwaltes, Werner. 1967. *Plotin über Ewigkeit und Zeit (Enneade III,7)*. Frankfurt: Klostermann.

Benz, Ernst. 1978. "Zeit, Endzeit, Ewigkeit." *Eranos*. 47: 1–39.

Black, Max. 1959. "The 'Direction' of Time." Reprinted in Black, 1962: 182–193.

—— 1962. *Models and Metaphors*. Ithaca: Cornell University Press.

Boethius, Anicius. 1973. *The Theological Tractates and the Consolation of Philosophy*. Loeb. Trans. S. J. Tester, *et al*. London: Heinemann.

Borges, Jorge L. 1953. *Historia de la Eternidad*. Buenos Aires: Emece Editores.

Brabant, F. H. 1937. *Time and Eternity in Christian Thought*. London: Longman, Green.

Braine, David. 1988. *The Reality of Time and the Existence of God*. OUP.

Brambaugh, R. S. 1984. *Unreality and Time*. Albany: SUNY Press.

Brandon, E. P. 1986. "What's Become of Becoming?" *Philosophia*. 16: 71–77.

Braithwaite, R. B. and C. D. Broad and J. Macmurray. 1928. "Symposium: Time and Change." *Aristotelian Society, Supplement*. 8: 143–188.

Briggs, C. A. 1907. *The Book of Psalms*, vol. II. ICC. Edinburgh: Clark.

Broad, C. D. 1938. *Examination of McTaggart's Philosophy*, vol. II, Part I. CUP.

Broussard, Joseph. 1963. "Eternity in Greek and Scholastic Philosophy." Ph.D. thesis. Catholic University of America.

Brown, David W. 1985. *The Divine Trinity*. London: Duckworth.

Brown, F., S. R. Driver and C. A. Briggs. 1906. *A Hebrew and English Lexicon*. OUP.

Brunner, Emil. 1954. *Eternal Hope*. Trans. H. Knight. London: Lutterworth.

Bultmann, R. 1964. "ginōskō". TDNT 1: 689–719. First pub., 1933.

Burell, David B. 1979. *Aquinas: God and Action*. RKP.

—— 1984. "God's Eternity." *F&P*. 4: 389–406.

Butterfield, Jeremy. 1984. "Prior's Conception of Time." *PAS* 84: 193–209.

Cahn, Stephen. 1967. *Fate, Logic and Time*. New Haven: Yale University Press.

Cairns, Grace Edith. 1942. "The Concept of Eternity." Ph.D. thesis. University of Chicago Press.

Čapek, Milic. 1961. *The Philosophical Impact of Contemporary Physics*. Princeton: Van Nostrum.

—— 1971. *Bergson and Modern Physics*. Dordrecht: Reidel.

—— 1976. Ed., *The Concepts of Space and Time*. Dordrecht: Reidel.

Carnap, Rudolf. 1966. *Philosophical Foundations of Physics*. New York: Basic Books.

Cassirer, Eva. 1971. "On the Reality of Becoming." *SG*.24: 1–9.

Castañeda, H. N. 1966. "'He': A Study in the Logic of Self-consciousness." *Ratio*. 8: 130–157.

—— 1967. "Indicators and Quasi-indicators." *APQ*. 4: 85–100.

—— 1967a. "Omniscience and Indexical Reference." *JPhil*.64: 203–210.

—— 1977. "Perception, Belief and the Structure of Physical Objects and Consciousness." *Synthese*. 35: 285–351.

Charlesworth, J. H. 1983–1985. Ed., *Old Testament Pseudepigrapha*. 2 vols. Garden City: Doubleday.

Christiansen, F. 1974. "McTaggart's Paradox and the Nature of Time." *PQ*. 24: 289–99.

—— 1976. "The Source of the River of Time." *Ratio*. 13: 131–144.

Clarke, B. L. 1980. "God and Time in Whitehead." *JAAR*.48: 563–579.

—— 1983. "Process, Time and God." *PS*. 13: 245–259.

Clarke, Samuel. 1738. *The Works of Samuel Clarke, D.D.* 4 vols. London: John and Paul Knapton.

Clarke, William N. 1909. *The Christian Doctrine of God*. Edinburgh: Clark.

Clément, Olivier. 1959. *Transfigurer Le Temps*. Neuchatel: Delachaux et Niestlé.

Cleugh, Mary F. 1937. *Time*. London: Methuen.

Cobb, John. 1969. *God and the World*. Philadelphia: Westminster.

Cobern, Robert. 1963. "Professor Malcom on God." *AJP*. 41: 143–162.

Collins, Robert E. 1970. "Eternity and Time as Predicated of God, Angels and Men." Ph.D. thesis. Marquette University Press.

Cook, Robert. 1987. "God, Time and Freedom." *RS*. 23: 81–94.

Costa de Beauregard, Olivier. 1963. *Le Second Principe de la Science du Temps*. Paris: Seuil.

—— 1966. "Time in Relativity Theory." Fraser, 1966: 417–433.

Coxon, A. H. 1986. *The Fragments of Parmenides*. Assen: Van Gorcum.

Craig, William Lane. 1978. "God, Time and Eternity." *RS*. 14: 497–503.

—— 1985. "Was Thomas Aquinas a B-Theorist of Time?" *NewSch*. 59: 475–483.

—— 1990. "God and Real Time." *RS*. 26: 335–347.

—— 1991. *Divine Foreknowledge and Human Freedom*. Leiden: Brill.

Creel, Richard. 1986. *Divine Impassibility*. CUP.

Crombie, I. M. 1987. "Eternity and Omnitemporality." *The Rationality of Religious Belief*, pp. 169–188. Eds. W. J. Abraham and S. W. Holtzer. OUP.

Cullmann, O. 1951. *Christ and Time*. Trans. F. V. Filson. London: SCM. Rev. ed., 1962.

Danto, A. C. 1965. "Basic Action." *APQ*. 2: 141–148.

Davidson, Herbert. 1987. *Proofs of Eternity, Creation, and the Existence of God in Medieval Islamic and Jewish Philosophy*. OUP.

Davidson, Donald. 1967. "Truth and Meaning." Reprinted in Davidson, 1984: 17–36.

—— 1977. "The Method of Truth in Metaphysics." Reprinted in Davidson, 1984: 199–214.

—— 1980. *Essays on Actions and Events*. OUP.

—— 1984. *Inquiries into Truth and Interpretation*. OUP.

Davies, Brian. 1982. *Introduction to the Philosophy of Religion*. OUP.

—— 1983. "A Timeless God?" *New Blackfriars*. 64: 215–224.

—— 1985. *Thinking About God*. London: Geoffrey Chapman.

Davies, P. C. W. 1977. *The Physics of Time Asymmetry*. 2nd ed. Berkeley: University of California Press.

Davis, Stephen T. 1983. *Logic and the Nature of God*. London: Macmillan.

Descartes, René. 1970. *Descartes Philosophical Letters*. Trans. and ed. A. Kenny. OUP.

De Vries, S. J. 1975. *Yesterday, Today, and Tomorrow: Time and History in the Old Testament.* London: SPCK.

Dingle, H. 1979. "Time in Philosophy and in Physics." *Philosophy.* 54: 99–104.

Dobbs, H. A. C. 1969. "The 'Present' in Physics." *BJPS.* 19: 317–324.

—— 1970. "Reply to Prof. Gruenbaum." *BJPS.* 21: 275–278.

Dorner, I.A. 1883. "Über die richtige Fassung des dogmatischen Unveränderlichkeit Gottes." *Gessamelte Schriften,* pp. 188–377. Berlin: W. Hertz. First pub., 1856. Partial Eng. trans. in Welch, 1965: 115–180.

Dummett, M. 1960. "A Defense of McTaggart's Proof of the Unreality of Time." Reprinted in Dummett, 1978: 351–357.

—— 1964. "Bringing About the Past." Reprinted in Dummett, 1978: 333–350.

—— 1969. "The Reality of the Past." Reprinted in Dummett, 1978: 358–374.

—— 1978. *Truth and Other Enigmas.* London: Duckworth.

Earman, John, Clark Glymour and John Stachel. 1977. Eds., *Foundations of Space-Time Theories.* Minnesota Studies in the Philosophy of Science, vol. 8. Minneapolis: University of Minnesota Press.

Ehring, D. 1987. "Non-Simultaneous Causation." *Analysis.* 47: 28–31.

Einstein, Albert. 1954. *Relativity: The Special and General Theories.* London: Methuen.

—— and H. Minkowski, *et al.* 1923. *The Principle of Relativity.* Trans. and ed. W. Perret and G. B. Jeffrey. London: Methuen.

Ellermeier, F. 1967. *Qohelet,* vol. I/1. Herzberg: E. Jungfer.

Ellis, Brian. 1971. "On Conventionality and Simultaneity." *AJP.* 49: 177–203.

Ewing, A. C. 1973. *Value and Reality.* London: Allen and Unwin.

Farnell, Lewis R. 1925. *The Attributes of God.* O. U. P.

Ferre, F. 1970. "Gruenbaum vs. Dobbs." *BJPS.* 21: 278–280.

—— 1972. "Grünbaum on Temporal Becoming." *IPQ.* 12: 426–445.

Findlay, J. N. 1978. "Time and Eternity." *RevMeta.* 32: 3–14.

Fitzgerald, Paul. 1968. "Is the Future Partly Unreal?" *RevMeta.* 21: 421–446.

—— 1969. "The Truth about Tomorrow's Sea Flight." *JPhil.* 66: 307–328.

—— 1980. "Is Temporality Mind Dependent?" *PSA 1980,* vol. 1, pp. 283–291. Eds. P. D. Asquith and R. N. Giere. East Lansing: PhSc Association.

—— 1985. "Stump and Kretzmann on Time and Eternity." *JPhil.* 82: 260–269.

Ford, Lewis S. 1968. "Boethius and Whitehead on Time and Eternity." *IPQ.* 8: 38–67.

Fraser, J. T. 1966. Ed., *Voices of Time.* New York: Braziller.

—— 1972–1981. Ed., *The Study of Time.* 4 vols. Vienna: Springer.

Freedman, H. and M. Simon, *et al.* 1939. Trans. and eds., *Midrash Rabbah.* 10 vols. London: Soncino.

Freundlich, Yehudah. 1973. "'Becoming' and the Asymmetries of Time." *PhSc.* 40: 496–517.

Friedman, Michael. 1983. *Foundations of Space-Time Theories.* Princeton: Princeton University Press.

Gale, R. M. 1967. Ed., *The Philosophy of Time.* Garden City: Doubleday.

—— 1968. *The Language of Time.* RKP.

—— 1986. "Omniscience-Immutability Arguments." *APQ.* 23: 319–335.

Galling, Kurt. 1961. "Das Rätsel der Zeit im Urteil Kohelets (Koh 3,1–15)". *ZTK.* 58: 1–15.

—— 1969. *Der Prediger Salomo.* HAT. Tübingen: Hinrichs.

Gassendi, Pierre. 1972. *The Selected Works of Pierre Gassendi*. Ed. and trans. C. B. Bruch. New York: Johnson Reprint.

Geach, Peter T. 1969. *God and the Soul*. RKP.

—— 1972. *Logic Matters*. Oxford: Blackwell.

—— 1977. *Providence and Evil*. CUP.

—— 1979. *Truth, Love and Immortality: An Introduction to McTaggart's Philosophy*. London: Hutchinson.

Gerelman, Gillis. 1979. "De sperrende Grenze. Die Wurzel ^{c}*lm*, im Hebräishen". *ZAW*. 91: 338–349.

Godfrey-Smith, William. 1979. "Special Relativity and the Present." *PhilStud*. 36: 233–244.

Goodman, Nelson. 1977. *The Structure of Appearance*. 3rd ed. Dordrecht: Reidel. First pub., 1951.

Gowen, Julie. 1987. "God and Timelessness: Everlasting or Eternal?" *Sophia*. 26/1 (March): 15–29.

Griffin, David. 1986. Ed., *Physics and the Ultimate Significance of Time*. Albany: SUNY Press.

Gunton, C. E. 1978. *Becoming and Being: The Doctrine of God in Charles Hartshorne and Karl Barth*. OUP.

Grünbaum, Adolf. 1967. "The Status of Temporal Becoming." Gale, 1967: 322–354.

—— 1968. *Modern Science and Zeno's Paradoxes*. London: Allen and Unwin.

—— 1968a. *Geometry and Chronometry in Philosophical Perspective*. Minneapolis: University of Minnesota Press.

—— 1969. "Are Physical Events Themselves Transiently Past, Present and Future?" *BJPS*. 20: 145–162.

—— 1973. *Philosophical Problems of Space and Time*. 2nd. ed. Dordrecht: D. Reidel. First ed., 1963.

Gurt, J. 1978. "Time". NIDNTT 3: 826–833.

Guthrie, W. K. C. 1965. *A History of Greek Philosophy*. Vol. 2. CUP.

Hahn, H. C. 1978. "Time". NIDNTT 3: 833–845.

Hallett, H. F. 1930. *Aeternitas: A Spinozistic Study*. OUP.

Hankey, W. J. 1987. *God in Himself*. OUP.

Harper, Charles L. 1988. "On the Nature of Time in Cosmological Perspective." D.Phil. thesis. Oxford University.

Harris, E. E. 1976. "Time and Eternity." *RevMeta*. 29: 464–482.

—— 1989. *The Reality of Time*. Albany: SUNY Press.

Harris, James. 1987. "An Empirical Understanding of Eternality." *IJPR* 22: 165–183.

Hasker, William. 1983. "Concerning the Intelligibility of 'God is Timeless'." *NewSch*. 58: 170–195.

—— 1989. *God, Time and Knowledge*. Ithaca: Cornell University Press.

Healey, Richard. 1981. Ed., *Reduction, Time and Reality*. CUP.

Hebblethwaite, Brian. 1979. "Some Reflections on Predestination, Providence and Divine Foreknowledge." *RS*. 15: 433–448.

—— 1979a. "Time and Eternity and Life 'After' Death." *Heythrop Journal*. 20: 57–62, 187–188.

Hegel, G. W. F. 1895. *Lectures on the Philosophy of Religion*. Trans. E. B. Spires and J. B. Sanderson. 3 vols. London: Kegan Paul. First pub., 1832.

—— 1970. *Hegel's Philosophy of Nature.* Trans. A. V. Miller. OUP. First pub., 1847.
—— 1977. *Phenomenology of Spirit.* Trans. A. V. Miller. OUP. First pub., 1807.
Heidegger, Martin. 1962. *Being and Time.* Trans. J. Macquarrie and E. Robinson. Oxford: Blackwell. First pub., 1927.
Heim, Karl. 1926. "Zeit und Ewigkeit." *ZTK.* 7: 403–429.
Helm, Paul. 1985. "Time and Place for God." *Sophia.* 24/3 (October): 53–55.
—— 1988. *Eternal God: A Study of God without Time.* OUP.
Hengstenberg, E. W. 1860. *Commentary on Ecclesiastes.* Trans. D. W. Simon. Edinburgh: Clark.
Hengenstenberg, Hans. 1969. "Überzeitlichkeit und Zeitlosigkeit als ontologische Katagorien." *Zeitschrift für philosophische Forschung.* 23: 516–537.
Henry, Carl. 1982. *God, Revelation and Authority,* vol. 5. Waco: Word Books.
Henry, D. P. 1955. "The *Proslogion* Proofs." *PQ.* 5: 147–152.
Heppe, H. 1950. *Reformed Dogmatics.* Trans. G. T. Thompson. London: Allen and Unwin. First pub., 1861.
Heron, A. I. C. 1986. "The Time of God." *Gottes Zukunft – Zukunft der Welt: Festschrift für Jürgen Moltmann,* pp. 231– 239. Ed. H. Deuser, *et al.* Munich: Kaiser.
Hinckfuss, Ian. 1975. *The Existence of Space and Time.* OUP.
Hobbes, Thomas. 1946. *Leviathan.* Ed. M. Oakeshott. Oxford: Blackwell. First pub., 1651.
Hoffman, Joshua and Gary Rosenkranz. 1984. "Hard and Soft Facts." *PhilRev.* 93: 419–434.
Holt, Dennis C. 1981. "Timelessness and the Metaphysics of Temporal Existence." *APQ.* 18: 149–156.
Horwich, Paul. 1987. *Asymmetries in Time.* Cambridge: MIT Press.
Jacobs, Louis. 1969. "Time and Eternity." *Judaism.* 18: 458–463.
Janis, Allen. 1983. "Simultaneity and Conventionality." *Physics, Philosophy and Psychoanalysis,* pp. 101–110. Eds. R. S. Cohen and L. Laudin. Dordrecht: D. Reidel.
Jantzen, Grace. 1984. *God's World, God's Body.* London: Darton, Longman and Todd.
Jenni, Ernst. 1952. "Das Wort ᶜolam im Alten Testament". *ZAW* 64: 197–248 and 65 (1953) 1–35.
—— 1962. "Time". IDB 4: 643–649.
—— 1972. "ᶜolam". THAT 2: 228–243.
Kähler, Martin. 1913. *Zeit und Ewigkeit. Dogmatischen Zeitfragen,* III Band. 2. Aufl. Leipzig: A. Deichert.
Kant, Immanuel. 1929. *Critique of Pure Reason.* Trans. N. K. Smith. London: Macmillan. First pub., 1781.
—— 1978. *Lectures on Philosophical Theology.* Trans. A. W. Wood and G. M. Clark. Ithaca: Cornell University Press First pub., 1817.
Kellett, B. H. 1971. "Time and Eternity." *Church Quarterly.* 3: 317–325.
Kenny, Anthony. 1979. *The God of the Philosophers.* OUP.
—— 1987. *Reason and Religion.* Oxford: Blackwell.
Khamara, E. J. 1974. "Eternity and Omniscience." *PQ.* 24: 204–219.

King-Farlow, John. 1963. "Could God be Temporal?" *Southern Journal of Philosophy*. 1: 21–28.
—— 1974. "The Positive McTaggart on Time." *Philosophy*. 49: 169–178.
Kneale, Martha. 1969. "Eternity and Sempiternity." *PAS*. 69: 223–238.
Kneale, W. C. 1961. "Time and Eternity in Theology." *PAS*. 61: 87–108.
Kraus, H. J. 1961. *Psalmen*, II Band. BK. 2. Aufl. Neukirken-Vluyn: Neukerchener.
Kretzmann, Norman. 1966. "Omniscience and Immutability." *JPhil*. 63: 409–421.
Lango, John W. 1969. "The Logic of Simultaneity." *JPhil*. 66: 340–350.
Langston, Douglas. 1986. *God's Willing Knowledge*. University Park: Pennsylvania State University Press.
Lauer, Quentin. 1982. *Hegel's Concept of God*. Albany: SUNY Press.
Lauha, A. 1978. *Kohelet*. BK. Neukierchen-Vluyn: Neukirchener.
Lavelle, L. 1945. *Du Temps et de l'éternité*. Paris: Aubier.
Leftow, Brian. 1984. "Simplicity and Eternity." Ph.D. thesis. Yale University
1988. "The Roots of Eternity." *RS*. 24: 189–212.
Lemmon, E. J. 1966. "Sentences, Statements, and Propositions." *British Analytic Philosophy*, pp. 87–107. Eds. B. Williams and A. Montefiore. RKP.
Le Poidevin, Robin and D. H. Mellor. 1987. "Time, Change and the 'Indexical Fallacy'." *Mind*. 96: 534–538.
Levison, Arnold. 1987. "Events and Time's Flow." *Mind*. 96: 341–353.
Lewis, David. 1973. *Counterfactuals*. Oxford: Blackwell.
Lewis, J. Delmas. 1984. "Eternity Again: A Reply to Stump and Kretzmann." *IJPR* 15: 73–79.
—— 1985. "God and Time." Ph.D. thesis. University of Wisconson- Madison.
—— 1987. "Timelessness and Divine Agency." *IJPR* 21: 143–159.
—— 1988. "Eternity, Time and Tenselessness." *F&P*. 5: 72–86.
Lindsay, James. 1930. "Eternity". *ISBE* (1st. ed.) 2: 1011–12.
Lloyd, G. 1977. "Tense and Predication." *Mind*. 86: 433–438.
—— 1978. "Time and Existence." *Philosophy*. 53: 215–228.
Locke, John. 1884. *Essays Concerning Human Understanding*. 2 vols. Ed. A. C. Fraser. OUP. First pub., 1689.
Long, Brian. 1978. "Notes on the Biblical Use of ᶜad ᶜolam". *WTJ*. 41: 68–83.
Long, E. T. 1987. "Temporality and Eternity." *IJPR* 22: 185–189.
Lowe, E. J. 1987. "The Indexical Fallacy in McTaggart's Proof of the Unreality of Time." *Mind*. 96: 62–70.
—— 1987. "Reply to Le Poidevin and Mellor." *Mind*. 96: 539–542.
Lucas, J. R. 1973. *A Treatise on Time and Space*. London: Methuen.
—— 1984. *Space, Time and Causality*. OUP.
—— 1989. *The Future*. Oxford: Blackwell.
Maas, Wilhelm. 1974. *Unveränderlichkeit Gottes*. Munich: Schoningh.
MacBeath, Murray. 1983. "God's Timelessness and Spacelessness." *Sophia*. 22/2 (July): 23–31.
—— 1988. "Dummett's Second-Order Indexicals." *Mind*. 97: 158–164.
—— 1989. "Omniscience and Eternity." *Aristotelian Society, Supplement*. 63: 55–73.
Mackenzie, J. S. 1912. "Eternity." *Encyclopedia of Religion and Ethics*, vol. 5, pp. 401–403. Ed. J. Hastings. Edinburgh: Clark.

Macquarrie, John. 1975. *Thinking About God*. London: SCM.

Malament, David. 1977. "Causal Theories of Time and the Conventionality of Simultaneity." *Nous*. 11: 293–300.

Malebranche, Nicholas. 1980. *Dialogues on Metaphysics*. Trans. W. Doney. New York: Abaris Books. First pub., 1688.

Mann, William. 1982. "Divine Simplicity." *RS*. 18: 451–471.

—— 1983. "Simplicity and Immutability in God." *IPQ*. 23: 267–276.

Marsh, John. 1947. "A Theological Examination of the Relationships of Time and Eternity." D.Phil. thesis. Oxford University.

—— 1952. *The Fulness of Time*. London: Nisbet.

Mascall, E. L. 1966. *He Who Is*. 2nd. ed. London: Darton, Longmans and Todd. First pub., 1943.

McCann, Hugh. 1974. "Volition and Basic Action." *PhilRev*. 83: 451–473.

McTaggart, John M. E. 1908. "The Unreality of Time." *Mind*. 18: 457–84.

—— 1909. "The Relation of Time and Eternity." *Mind*. 18: 343–362.

—— 1927. *The Nature of Existence*, vol. II. Ed. C. D. Broad. CUP.

Mehlberg, Henry. 1980. *Time, Causality and the Quantum Theory*. 2 vols. Dordrecht: Reidel.

Meijering, E. P. 1979. *Augustin über Schöpfung, Ewigkeit und Zeit*. Philosophia Patrum, 4. Leiden: Brill.

Mellor, D. H. 1974. "Special Relativity and Present Truth." *Analysis*. 34: 74–77.

—— 1981. *Real Time*. CUP.

—— 1981a. "McTaggart, Fixity and Coming True." In Healey, 1981: 79–97.

—— 1981b. "'Thank Goodness That's Over'." *Ratio*. 23: 20–30.

—— 1986. "History without the Flow of Time." *NZST*. 28: 68–76.

—— 1986a. "Tense's Tenseless Truth Conditions." *Analysis*. 46: 167–172.

Meyerson, E. 1930. *Identity and Reality*. Trans. K. Loewenberg. London: Allen and Unwin. First pub., 1908.

Michel, A. 1912. "Éternité." *Dictionnaire de Théologie Catholique*, tome 5, col. 912–921. Ed. A. Vacant, et al. Paris: Letouzey.

Moen, A. J. 1979. "God, Time and the Limits of Omniscience." D.Phil. thesis. Oxford University.

Moltmann, Jürgen. 1985. *God in Creation*. Trans. M. Kohl. London: SCM.

Mundy, Brent. 1986. "Optical Axiometrization of Minkowski Space-Time Geometry." *PhSc*. 53: 1–30.

—— 1986a. "The Physical Content of Minkowski Geometry." *BJPS*. 37: 25–54.

—— 1986b. "Special Relativity and Quantum Mechanics." *BJPS*. 37: 207–212.

Nash, Ronald. 1983. *The Concept of God*. Grand Rapids: Zondervan.

Nelson, Herbert J. 1987. "Time(s), Eternity, and Duration." *IJPR* 22: 3–19.

Neville, Robert C. 1968. *God the Creator*. Chicago: University of Chicago Press.

Newton, Issac. 1934. *Sir Issac Newton's Principles of Natural Philosophy*. 2 vols. Trans. A. Motle, ed. F.Cajori. Berkeley: University of California Press [1962]. First pub., 1687.

Newton-Smith, W. H. 1980. *The Structure of Time*. RKP.

Oaklander, L. N. 1984. *Temporal Relations and Temporal Becoming: A Defense of a Russelian Theory of Time.* Lanham: University Press of America.

Ockham, William. 1977. *Scriptum in librum primum Sententiarum (Ordinatio),* d. 4–18. *Opera Theologica,* vol. 3. Ed. G. I. Etzkorn. St. Bonaventure: Fransiscan Institute Press.

O'Donnell, John. 1983. *Trinity and Temporality.* OUP.

Ogden, Shubert. 1967. *The Reality of God and Other Essays.* London: SCM.

Orelli, Conrad von. 1871. *Die hebräischen Synonyma der Zeit und Ewigkeit.* Leipzig: Lorentz.

Origen. 1936. *On First Principles.* Trans. G. W. Butterworth. London: SPCK.

Owen, G. E. L. 1966. "Plato and Parmenides on the Timeless Present." *The Monist.* 50: 317–340.

Owen, H. P. 1971. *Concepts of Deity.* London: Macmillan.

Padgett, Alan. 1989. "God and Time." *RS.* 25: 209–215.

—— 1991. "Can History Measure Eternity? A Reply to William Craig." *RS.* 27 (Sept).

Pears, D. F. 1950. "Time, Truth and Inference." *PAS.* 51: 1–24.

Penelhum, Terrence. 1960. "Divine Necessity." *Mind.* 69: 175–186.

Perry, John. 1979. "The Problem of the Essential Indexical." *Nous.* 13: 3–21.

Philip, Robert. 1846. *The Eternal.* London: Ward and Co.

Philo. 1930. *On the Unchangeableness of God. Philo,* vol. 3, pp. 10–101. Loeb. Trans. F. H. Colson and G. H. Whitaker. London: Heinemann.

Pike, Nelson. 1970. *God and Timelessness.* RKP.

Plantinga, Alvin. 1980. *Does God Have a Nature?* Milwaukee: Marquette University Press.

Plass, Paul. 1980. "Timeless Time in Neoplatonism." *ModSch.* 55: 1–20.

—— 1982. "The Concept of Eternity in Patristic Theology." *Studia Theologica.* 36: 11–25.

Plato. 1953. *Timaeus. The Dialogues of Plato,* vol. 3, pp. 631–780. 4th ed. Trans. B. Jowett. OUP.

Plathow, M. 1984. "Zeit und Ewigkeit." *NZST.* 26: 95–115.

Plecha, James. 1984. "Tenselessness and the Absolute Present." *Philosophy.* 59: 529–534.

Plotinus. 1966–1984. *Enneads.* Loeb. 5 vols. Trans. A.H. Armstrong. London: Heinemann.

Plutarch. 1936. *On the E at Delphi. Plutarch's Moralia,* vol. 5, pp. 199–253. Loeb. Trans. F. C. Babbitt. London: Heinemann.

Priest, Graham. 1986. "Tense and Truth Conditions." *Analysis.* 46: 162–166.

—— 1987. "Tense, *tense,* and TENSE." *Analysis.* 47: 184–187.

Prigigone, Ilya. 1980. *From Being to Becoming: Time and Complexity in Science.* San Francisco: Freeman.

Prior, A. N. 1957. *Time and Modality.* OUP.

—— 1959. "Thank Goodness That's Over." Reprinted in Prior, 1976: 78–84.

—— 1962. "The Formalities of Omniscience." *Philosophy.* 37: 119–129. Also in Prior, 1968.

—— 1967. *Past, Present and Future.* OUP.

—— 1968. *Papers on Time and Tense.* OUP.

—— 1970. "The Notion of the Present." *SG.* 23: 245–248.

—— 1971. *Objects of Thought.* Eds. P. T. Geach and A. Kenny. OUP.

—— 1976. *Papers on Logic and Ethics.* Eds. P. T. Geach and A. Kenny. London: Duckworth.

Putnam, H. 1967. "Time and Physical Geometry." *JPhil.* 64: 240–247.

Quine, W. V. O. 1960. *Word and Object.* Cambridge: MIT Press.

Quinn, John M. 1960. "The Doctrine of Time in St. Thomas." Ph.D. thesis. Catholic University of America.

Rahner, Karl. 1983. "Eternity from Time." *Theological Investigations,* vol. 19, pp. 169–177. Trans. E. Quinn. London: Darton, Longman and Todd.

Ramige, E. A. 1935. *Contemporary Concepts of Time and the Idea of God.* Boston: Stratford Company.

Ramsey, Ian T. 1970. "The Concept of the Eternal." *The Christian Hope,* pp. 35–48. G. B. Caird, *et al.* SPCK Theological Collections 13. London: SPCK.

Ratschow, Carl H. 1954. "Anmerkungen zur theologischen Auffassung des Zeitproblems." *ZTK.* 51: 360–387.

Reese, W. L. 1964. Ed., *Process and Divinity: The Hartshorne Festschrift.* LaSalle: Open Court.

Reichenbach, H. 1958. *The Philosophy of Space and Time.* Trans. M. Reichenbach and J. Freund. New York: Dover. First pub., 1928.

Richard of St. Victor. 1958. *De Trinitate.* Ed. Jean Ribailler. Paris: Vrin.

Rietdijk, C. W. 1966. "A Rigorous Proof of Determinism Derived from the Special Theory of Relativity." *PhSc.* 33: 341–344.

Robb, A. A. 1913. *A Theory of Time and Space.* Cambridge: Heffer and Sons.

—— 1921. *The Absolute Relations of Time and Space.* CUP.

—— 1936. *The Geometry of Time and Space.* CUP.

Roberts, R. H. 1975. "Eternity and Time in the Theology of Karl Barth." Ph.D. thesis. University of Edinburgh.

—— 1979. "Karl Barth's Doctrine of Time." *Karl Barth: Studies in his Theological Method,* pp. 88–146. Ed. S. W. Sykes. OUP.

Ruben, David-Hillel. 1988. "A Puzzle about Posthumous Predication." *PhilRev.* 97: 211–236.

Russell, Bertrand. 1903. *The Principles of Mathematics.* CUP.

—— 1915. "On the Experience of Time." *The Monist.* 25: 212–233.

Russell, D. S. 1964. *The Method and Message of Jewish Apocalyptic.* OTL. London: SCM.

Sasse, H. 1964. "*aiōn*". TDNT 1: 197–209. First pub., 1933.

Schleiermacher, F. D. E. 1928. *The Christian Faith.* Trans. eds. H. R. Mackintosh and J. S. Stewart. Edinburgh: Clark. First pub., 1822.

Schmidt, Hans Wilhelm. 1927. *Zeit und Ewigkeit.* Gütersloh: Bertelsmann.

Schmidt, Johannes. 1940. *Der Ewigkeitsbegriff im alten Testament.* Alttestamentliche Abhandlung. Munich: Aschendorff.

Schneider, E. E. 1958. "Die Bedeutung der Begriffe Raum, Zeit und Ewigkeit in der christlichen Verkündigung und Lehre." *Kerygma und Dogma.* 4: 281–286.

Schofield, M. 1970. "Did Parmenides Discover Eternity?" *Archiv für Geschichte der Philosophie.* 52: 113–135.

Schoonhoven, C. R. 1982. "Eternity". ISBE 2: 162–164.

Schuster, M. M. 1961. "An Analysis of Relational Time." *RevMeta.* 15: 209–224.

—— 1968. "On the Denial of Past and Future Existence." *RevMeta.* 21: 447–467.

—— 1986. "Is the Flow of Time Subjective?" *RevMeta.* 39: 695–714.

Scotus, John Duns. 1963. *Ordinatio, d. 26–48. Opera Omnia*, vol. 6. Ed. P. C. Balic, *et al.* Vatican: Typis Polyglottis.

—— 1966. *Lectura. Opera Omnia*, vol. 17. Ed. P. C. Balic, *et al.* Vatican: Typis Polyglottis.

—— 1975. *God and Creatures: The Quodlibetal Questions.* Trans. F. Alluntis and A. B. Wolter. Princeton: Princeton University Press.

Seddon, Keith. 1987. *Time: A Philosophical Treatment.* London: Croom Helm.

Sellars, Wilfrid. 1962. "Time and the World Order." *Scientific Explanation, Space and Time.* Minnesota Studies in the Philosophy of Science, vol. 3, pp. 527–616. Eds. H. Feigl and G. Maxwell. Minneapolis: University of Minnesota Press.

Shapiro, Stewart. 1983. "Mathematics and Reality." *PhSc.* 50: 523–548.

Shields, George. 1987. "Davies, Eternity and the Cosmological Argument." *IJPR* 21: 21–37.

Shoemaker, Sydney. 1969. "Time without Change." *JPhil.* 66: 363–381.

Simons, John. 1989. "Eternity, Omniscience and Temporal Passage." *RevMeta.* 42: 547–568.

Sklar, L. 1974. *Space, Time and Spacetime.* Berkeley: University of California Press 1981. "Time, Reality and Relativity." Healey, 1981: 129–142; also in Sklar, 1985.

—— 1985. *Philosophy and Spacetime Physics.* Berkeley: University of California Press.

Smart, J. J. C. 1963. *Philosophy and Scientific Realism.* RKP.

—— 1980. "Time and Becoming." *Time and Cause*, pp. 3–15. Ed. P. van Inwagen. Dordrecht: Reidel.

Smith, Joseph W. 1984. "Towards Putting Real Tense Back into the World." *Kinesis.* 14: 3–12.

Smith, Quentin. 1987. "Sentences about Time." *PQ.* 37: 37–53.

Smith, T. P. 1973. "On the Applicability of a Criterion of Change." *Ratio.* 15: 326–333.

Sosa, Ernset. 1979. "The Status of Becoming: What is Happening Now?" *JPhil.* 76: 26–42.

Soskice, Janet M. 1985. *Metaphor and Religious Language.* OUP.

Sorabji, Richard. 1983. *Time, Creation and the Continuum.* London: Duckworth.

Stein, H. 1968. "On Einstein–Minkowski Space-Time." *JPhil.* 65: 5–63.

Stromseth, Walter. 1961. "The Time-Eternity Correlation in Western Theology." Ph.D. thesis. Yale University.

Stump, Eleanore and Norman Kretzmann. 1981. "Eternity." *JPhil.* 77: 429–458.

—— 1985. "Absolute Simplicity." *F & P.* 2: 353–382.

—— 1987. "Atemporal Duration: A Reply to Fitzgerald." *JPhil.* 84: 214–219.

Sturch, R. L. 1974. "The Problem of Divine Eternity." *RS.* 10: 487–493.

Sutherland, S. R. 1979. "God, Time and Eternity." *PAS.* 79: 103–121.

Swinburne, Richard. 1968. "The Timelessness of God." *Church Quarterly Review.* 116: 323–337, 472–486.

—— 1977. *The Coherence of Theism*. OUP.
—— 1981. *Space and Time*. 2nd. ed. London: Macmillan. First pub., 1968.
—— 1986. *The Evolution of the Soul*. OUP.
—— 1990. "Tensed Facts." *APQ*. 21: 117–130.
Talbott, T. B. 1986. "On Divine Foreknowledge and Bringing About the Past." *PPR* 46: 455–469.
Tennant, F. R. 1930. *Philosophical Theology*. 2 vols. CUP.
Tomkinson, J. 1982. "Divine Sempiternity and Atemporality." *RS*. 18: 177–189.
Torrance, T. F. 1969. *Space, Time and Incarnation*. OUP.
—— 1976. *Space, Time and Resurrection*. Edinburgh: Hansel Press.
Tracy, T. F. 1984. *God, Action and Embodiment*. Grand Rapids: Eerdmans.
Van Frassen, B. 1970. *Introduction to the Philosophy of Space and Time*. New York: Random House.
Vardy, P. C. 1984. "The Concept of Eternity." Ph.D. thesis. University of London.
Walker, Leslie. 1919. "Time, Eternity and God." *Hibbert Journal*. 18: 36–48.
Ward, Keith. 1982. *Rational Theology and the Creativity of God*. Oxford: Blackwell.
Ware, Bruce. 1984. "An Evangelical Reexamination of the Doctrine of the Immutability of God." Ph.D. thesis. Fuller Theological Seminary. Partial pub. as Ware, 1985, 1986.
—— 1985. "An Exposition and Critique of the Process Doctrines of Divine Mutability and Immutability." *WTJ*. 47: 175–196.
—— 1986. "An Evangelical Reformulation of the Doctrine of the Immutability of God." *Journal of the Evangelical Theological Society*. 29: 431–446.
Weingard, R. 1972. "Relativity and the Reality of Past and Future Events." *BJPS*. 23: 119–121.
—— 1977. "Space-Time and the Direction of Time." *Nous*. 11: 119–132.
Weiser, A. 1962. *The Psalms*. Trans. H. Hartwell. OTL. London: SCM.
Welch, Claude. 1965. *God and Incarnation in Mid-Ninteenth Century German Theology*. OUP.
Westermann, C. 1969. *Isaiah 40–66*. Trans. D. M. G. Stalker. OTL. London: SCM.
Weyl, H. 1950. *Space-Time-Matter*. Trans. H. L. Bose. New York: Dover. First pub., 1919.
Whitehead, A. N. 1929. *Religion in the Making*. New York: Macmillan.
—— 1978. *Process and Reality*. Corrected edition, ed. D. R. Griffin and D. W. Sherburne. New York: Free Press. First pub., 1929.
Whitrow, G. J. 1980. *The Natural Philosophy of Time*. 2nd. ed. OUP. First pub., 1961.
Whittaker, John. 1968. "The 'Eternity' of the Platonic Forms." *Phronesis*. 13: 131–144.
—— 1969. "Ammonius on the Delphic E." *Classical Quarterly*. 19: 185–192.
—— 1971. *God, Time, Being*. Symbolae Osloenses, Supp. 23. Oslo: Universitetsforl.
Wiehl, Reiner. 1975. "Time and Timelessness in the Philosophy of A. N. Whitehead." *PS*. 5: 3–30.
Wierenga, Ed. 1989. *The Nature of God*. Ithaca: Cornell University Press.

Wilch, J. R. 1975. *Time and Event*. Leiden: Brill.
Williams, C. E. 1974. "'Now,' Existential Interchangeability, and the Passage of Time." *Philosophical Forum*. 5: 405–423.
——— 1976. "Meaning, Reference and Tense." *Analysis*. 36: 132–136.
Williams, D. C. 1951. "The Myth of Passage." *JPhil*. 48: 457– 472.
Williams, S. G. 1986. "On the Logical Possibility of Time Without Change." *Analysis*. 46: 122–125.
Wisdom, John. 1929. "Time, Fact and Substance." *PAS*. 29: 67–94.
Woltersdorff, Nicholas. 1979. "Can Ontology Do without Events?" *Essays in the Philosophy of Roderick Chisholm*, pp. 177–201. Ed. E. Sosa. Amsterdam: Rodopi.
——— 1982. "God Everlasting." *Contemporary Philosophy of Religion*, pp. 77–98. Ed. S. M. Cahn and D. Shatz. OUP. First pub., 1975.
Yarnold, G. D. 1966. *The Moving Image: Science and Religion, Time and Eternity*. London: Allen and Unwin.
Yourgrau, Palle. 1985. "On the Logic of Indeterminist Time." *JPhil*. 82: 548–559.
——— 1986. "On Time and Actuality." *BJPS*. 37: 405–417.
Zeilicovici, David. 1986. "A (Dis)solution of McTaggart's Paradox." *Ratio*. 28: 175–195.
Zeis, John. 1984. "The Concept of Eternity." *IJPRESS* 16: 61–71.
Zimmerman, Laura. 1983. "God and Time." Ph.D. thesis. University of Notre Dame.
Zwart, P. J. 1976. *About Time*. Amsterdam: North-Holland.

Author Index

Scripture Index

Old Testament

Genesis
1:1 25

Exodus
3:14 33

Deuteronomy
32:7 24
15:17 24

1 Kings
9:3 24

Nehemiah
2:3 24

Psalms
78:66 24
83:5 31
89:2 24
90 26, 29
90:2 26, 29, 36, 148n.4

90:4 35, 36f., 126
110:4 32

Proverbs
8:22f. 25
8:30 37

Ecclesiastes 148n.7
1:4 24
3:11 27f.

Isaiah 26f., 29
40:28 26, 29
41:4 26f., 29
43:10 26f., 29
44:6 26f., 29
48:3 26f., 29
57:15 24

Malachi
3:6 33

New Testament

John 31f.
8:58 33
12:34 32
14:16 32

Romans
1:20 29

Ephesians
3:21 31

Colossians
1:17 146

Hebrews 31f.
6:20 32
7:17, 21, 24, 28 32
9:26 32
13:8 32

James
1:7 33

2 Peter
3:8 36f., 126

Revelation
2:21 30
10:6 30

170

Other Early Judeo-Christian Literature

Subject Index

Note: Page numbers in **bold** face indicate *definitions.*